After Love

After Love Queer Intimacy and Erotic Economies in Post-Soviet Cuba

NOELLE M. STOUT

Duke University Press   Durham and London   2014

Printed in the United States of America on acid-free paper ∞
Typeset in Chaparral Pro and Avenir by Graphic Composition, Inc.

Library of Congress Cataloging-in-Publication Data
Stout, Noelle M., 1976–
After love : queer intimacy and erotic economies in post-soviet
Cuba / Noelle M. Stout.
pages   cm
Includes bibliographical references and index.
ISBN 978-0-8223-5673-8 (cloth : alk. paper)
ISBN 978-0-8223-5685-1 (pbk. : alk. paper)
1. Gays—Cuba.   2. Homosexuality—Cuba—History—20th
century.   3. Gender identity—Cuba.   I. Title.
HQ75.6.C9S76 2014
306.76′6097291—dc23
2013042795

Duke University Press gratefully acknowledges the support of
the Humanities Initiative Grants-in-Aid, New York University,
which provided funds toward the publication of this book.

Contents

Acknowledgments

This book would not have been possible without the generosity and kind-heartedness of the friends, collaborators, and contacts I grew to know during my time in Havana. They shared their lives and their stories with me, introduced me to their families and friends, fed me, took care of me when I was sick, and showed me the power of lasting friendship. Cuban scholars generously offered their time and insights, in particular Alberto Roque Guerra, Jorge Pérez at the Pedro Kouri Tropical Medicine Institute, Victor Fowler at the International Film School, and film professor Gustavo Arcos. For endless conversations about all things queer and historical in Cuba, I am especially thankful to my colleague, friend, and partner in crime, historian Abel Sierra Madero.

At Harvard University, I would like to thank Mary Steedly who taught me, in the classroom and beyond, the power of ethnographic storytelling. Jorge Domínguez taught me nearly everything I knew about Cuba before I landed in Havana. His disciplined and thoughtful approach to Cuban studies is something to which I continually aspire. Lucien Taylor believed in my abilities when I had little to show for myself and taught me to see the world through a new and more fascinating lens. His encouragement, behind the camera and in life, has been an enduring gift. A number of individuals also provided their insights during various stages of my research: Arachu Castro, Byron Good, Susan Eckstein, Brad Epps, Michael Herzfeld, J. Lorand Matory, Anna Tsing, Kay Warren, and Kath Weston. Graduate students at Harvard engaged in ongoing discussions that contributed to this project especially: Angela Garcia, Joon Michael Choi, Akin Hubbard, Katrina Moore, Tim Smith, Michelle Tisdel, and Peter Benson (who encouraged me to pursue this research one fateful night over a beer, despite my protests that studying Cuba was a "leftist cliché"). The David Rockefeller Center for Latin American Studies at Harvard generously dealt with the endless paper trail that comes with travel to Cuba. In particular, Lorena Barberia and Yadira Rivera offered me guidance and critical contacts in Cuba. My former advisors from Stanford University, Sylvia Yanagisako and Jane Collier, continued to offer invaluable support. To this day, I continue to draw on the lessons—both personal and intellectual—that they have taught me.

I was fortunate to work on this book during my first years in the Department of Anthropology at New York University. For their tireless mentorship, friendship, and feedback I am grateful to Faye Ginsburg and Emily Martin. Cheryl Furjanic was a friend, co-teacher, and master storyteller who pushed me to keep my work relevant. Fred Myers offered daily advice and reassurance. The "junior league" writing group, Sonia Das, Tejaswini Ganti, Haidy Geismer, Nathalie Peutz, and Anne Rademacher, gave me critical feedback and commiseration. I am also grateful to the following individuals for comments on my research and writing: Ada Ferrar, Nadine Fernandez, Bruce Grant, Rayna Rapp, Renato Rosaldo, Michael Ralph, and Rafael Sánchez. A small but mighty nation of Natives at NYU, especially Max Liborion, Rick Chavolla, Anna Ortega Chavolla, and Desiree Barron, helped me to feel more at home and never gave me a hard time when I had to skip Fry Bread Fridays to write.

Funding for my work was generously provided by the National Science Foundation, the Department of Anthropology at Harvard University, the Graduate School of Arts and Sciences at Harvard, the Harvard Film Study Center, the David Rockefeller Center for Latin American Studies at Harvard, the Department of Anthropology at NYU, the Center for Caribbean and Latin American Studies at NYU, and assistance for publication costs was provided by the Humanities Initiative at NYU.

Editors and reviewers helped me strengthen my analysis and polish my writing in substantial ways. Susan Murko offered unrivaled editorial assistance in the final months of revisions. At Duke University Press, my editor Ken Wissoker offered patience and advice, as well as the reassuring sense that publication was a happy inevitability. I am especially thankful to Deborah Thomas and the three anonymous reviewers who strengthened the book with their careful attention and comments.

I am forever indebted to Alphonso Morgan who first introduced me to gay enclaves in Havana and since that night has traveled alongside me as a collaborator and brother. In countless ways, this book would not have been possible without him. I am also grateful to Dominique Fontenette who took a hiatus from medical school to suffer through nine months of blackouts by my side during fieldwork, and to friends who journeyed with me in Cuba: Farren Briggs, Sandra Dong, Sherri Taylor, and Omar Washington.

My deepest gratitude goes to my family. My mom, Dolores Gray, whose love and sense of adventure provided the confidence needed to undertake this book. I am thankful for the support of my aunts Michelle Comeau and Linda Kunsemiller and my dad, Ervin Stout, who taught me that sometimes being lucky is more important than being good. I am especially grateful to Matthew Lehman for eight years of unconditional love, support, and daily encouragement. His tireless proofreading was matched only by his willingness to pack and move my mountain of books from island to island and from state to state. He's shown me the profound benefits of having someone permanently on my team. And finally, to Damian who bravely, and often against his will, shared his infancy with this manuscript. I am forever grateful that he weathered my divided attention during his early years. I dedicate this book to him with the hope that by the time he's old enough to understand it, the concept of sexual inequality will be forgotten history.

Can't Be Bought or Sold?

LOVE AND INTIMACY IN THE AFTERMATH OF CRISIS

Love happens in the street, standing in the dust.
—José Martí, *Love in the City*

Ruso took long strides down the smooth cement slope of 23rd Street toward the sea. Inhaling on his Hollywood cigarette, which he preferred over the cheaper Cuban brand, he belted out the lyrics to La Charanga's latest hit. "Soy Cubano, soy natural. Y eso nadie me lo quita. Porque yo traigo la razón y te regalo la verdad, lo que tengo ni se compra ni se vende. (I'm Cuban, I'm real. No one can take that away from me. I bring you the reason and give you truth: What I have can't be bought or sold.)"

At the ocean, Ruso jumped on the Malecón, the thick cement wall that snaked around Havana. He shouted to a group of boys waiting to dive off the rocky shore, shivering despite the merciless August sun. Getting no response, Ruso focused on me. I had been tagging along with him for almost a month but had never asked him about his sexuality. I asked if he identified as gay.

"Look, we in Cuba have something that is called *bisexual*," said Ruso. "A *bisexual* is someone who sleeps with both men and women. I like to have sex with women, but I like men more. Because I like both, I am *bisexual*." He paused again and instructed me to write down the term in my notebook.

"It's the same word in the United States," I told him.

He looked skeptical.

"What is a *jinetero*?" I asked. The question hung in the air between us.

"It's a Cuban who goes with gays. They take them to a place and have sex with them for money or clothes, and rip them off by charging too much."

"Why are you a *jinetero*?"

"I'm not," he told me, taking a drag off his cigarette.

"Why did you come to Havana from the provinces then?"

He hesitated, gulped water from my bottle, and wiped his mouth with his T-shirt. "Because I needed things—money and clothes," he said. "I came to Havana to see if some gays could help me out, help me get stuff. But I'm not a *jinetero*." Before I could press the issue, he turned away and leapt down to join the boys on the rocks below.

Almost twenty-two years old, Ruso had come to Havana from Ciego de Ávila, a province known for cattle ranching and pineapple farms, to make hard currency working with gay tourists. Lithe and muscular, he had quickly become one of the higher paid hustlers on the Malecón. Ruso's dirty blond hair and gray eyes had inspired the nickname Ruso or "the Russian," a leftover from the previous three decades when Cuba had close ties with the Soviet Union. Ruso's mother, a heavy drinker, had abandoned him when he was a toddler, and his grandmother had taken him in. He had the irreverent confidence of a boy raised by a doting grandmother who had been too aged and kind to discipline him. He spent a good portion of his earnings on a collection of cotton nightgowns that he planned to take back for her.

I first met Ruso in the summer of 2002 outside the Yara cinema on a Friday night as he ran between clusters of men in tight flared jeans and fitted polyester shirts. He stood out with his spiked hair, a small gold hoop in each ear, and a cherry red T-shirt. Within a month, I had become Ruso's full-time sidekick. I accompanied him as he tracked down gay clients, met with foreign tourists for liaisons in rented apartments, and sold clients' used clothes on the black market. We spent afternoons eating garbanzo beans and rice on the couch that he rented for a dollar a day from a middle-aged Cuban mariachi singer called "el Mexicano." We loitered outside of the Yara as Ruso floated moneymaking schemes by hustlers and smoked their cigarettes. He told people that I was his half-sister *de parte de padre* from the United States to explain why we were together so much but not having sex.

Why would Ruso remain cagey about his relationships with foreign clients, even as I witnessed his work with foreigners? Ruso wanted to distance himself from the *jinetero* (hustler) identity because of rampant criticism that sex workers symbolized a lapse in socialist values. Ruso distinguished between having sex as a legitimate form of labor, thus keeping with the hard work ethic of socialism, and overcharging people or "ripping them off," which would reflect an embrace of the emergent capitalist economy associated with self-interest. After the dissolution of the socialist bloc in 1991, Cuba lost massive Soviet subsidies and entered a severe economic crisis that continued to impact life on the island. Daily conversations centered on the rise of relations *por interés* (motivated by status or money), as urban residents expressed anxiety over how rising poverty and inequality reshaped intimate relationships. These discussions were particularly pronounced around sex work because prostitution had largely been eradicated within Cuban socialism, and after four decades without formal prostitution, Havana witnessed a flood of sex work following the introduction of foreign tourism in the 1990s.

Criticism of the sex trade was especially acute among Havana's marginalized sexual niches, where young heterosexual men arrived to find gay clients. In our discussions, many urban gays, lesbians, and *travestis* forcefully distinguished between those who had sex for money and those who had sex for pleasure or love. The rise of material inequalities alongside unprecedented opportunities for individual, rather than collective, gain inspired important debates about the potential for "genuine" affection to survive in the new economic landscape. What happens to people who are forced to use someone they love? Do new modes of entrepreneurial self-interest leave people "empty" or without feelings? For men, women, and *travestis* born after the 1970s and raised under socialism, these questions shaped decisions from how to distribute food within a household to more complicated issues of sexual identity and desire.

In this book, I am interested in what these disagreements about intimacy in the context of rising inequality can teach us about how young Cubans made sense of their lives, their relationships, and their place in this post-Soviet nation. I explore how people on Havana's sexual margins marked boundaries between labor and love, affection and exploitation, and desire and decency. I do not arbitrate between who possessed genuine sentiments and who false affections.[1] Instead, I am interested in how these newly erected boundaries constantly blurred in practice. From openly homophobic hustlers having sex with urban gays for room and board to lesbians disparaging sex workers but initiating intimate relationships with foreign men for money to foreign tourists espousing socialist rhetoric while handing out Calvin Klein bikini briefs, the shifting economic terrain opened unexpected gaps between values and practices.

Unprecedented encounters between gay Cubans, foreign tourists, and sex workers reorganized life on Havana's sexual margins in a way that embodied the contradictions of the new Cuban society. While each group inhabited a distinct social network, they collided nightly in Havana's informal, public queer nightlife in parks, outside cinemas, and along the Malecón. Gays, sex workers, and tourists came to rely on one another in a way that led each to blame the other for rising materialism and social decline. Hence, rather than focus my analysis on one group, such as gay Cubans, I explore the multiple and shifting encounters between groups to better understand how divisions around intimacy and respectability were drawn. In doing so, I illuminate how, a decade after Cubans began their rocky transition from Soviet-style communism to late socialism, people whose sexual desires or practices failed to conform to mainstream standards struggled to redefine love in the aftermath of disaster.

In studying postcommunist transitions, analysts have often focused on macroeconomic questions, tracing the rise of black markets or predicting the instability of government regimes. Anthropologists have been especially adept at illuminating how massive economic restructuring influence how people make sense of their own desires, and how these desires foster new, often fraught, connections between people. Hence, I aim to show how intimacy and desire were not private, innate feelings but rather were fundamentally shaped by and in turn influenced the cultural meaning of the introduction of capitalism to Cuba.[2] As feminist and queer theorist M. Jacqui Alexander (2005) asserts, in the postcolonial Caribbean context public displays of nonnormative gender and sexuality, such as homosexuality and prostitution, continue to challenge aspirations to present the nation as developed and disciplined. In the post-Soviet Cuban context, sex served as both a powerful instance of boundary crossing between social groups and an opportunity for self-regeneration, influencing people's fundamental values and forcing them to question deeply held assumptions about themselves and others. At times, intimacy offered a refuge, a potential sanctuary, but it also emerged as a dangerous terrain in which the new inequalities inherent in capitalist markets could undercut loyalty and reframe the meaning of genuine affection.

FRAMING LOVE AND INTIMACY

At the start of the twenty-first century, a decade after the official transition to post-Soviet socialism, Cubans continued to experience an ontological crisis within which love and intimacy symbolized neoliberal incursions and national uncertainty. According to many in Havana, true love threatened to rot on the vine during the decades following the economic crisis of the 1990s. True love, however, is a tricky affair. While love and intimacy may appear to spring from the depth of an individual, untainted by cultural forces, instead they are always a product of never innocent social power.[3] A vast scholarship has traced the multiple forms of cultural ideas about love and intimacy in different historical moments (e.g., Ahearn 2001; Giddens 1992; Jankowiak 1995).[4] Particularly germane to understanding how the Cuban entry into global capitalist markets reshaped everyday ideas about love and intimacy, anthropologists have described the connections between changing regimes of markets and subsequent shifts in ideas about love, intimacy, marriage, and romance (Collier 1997; Constable 2003; Freeman 2007; Friedman 2005; Hirsh and Wardlow 2006; Lipset 2004; Rebhun 1999). Jane Collier (1997), for example, has shown how the entry of an Andalusian village into the global market in the 1980s shifted people's understanding of domestic arrangements. Marriage, which was previously seen as an important social obligation, was transformed into a product of individual desires.[5] In preindustrial Spanish society, notions of love existed, but romance and the promise of emotional self-fulfillment through marriage were not precursors to conjugal relationships as they are today.

In a related vein, anthropologists have recently attended to how aspects of seemingly private and intimate relations have been increasingly commodified within neoliberal globalization. Through ethnographic research on female caretakers, nannies, sex workers, hostesses, and mail order brides, anthropologists have uncovered the increasing demand for commodified affect as well as the gendered power dynamics of new global economic systems (e.g., Allison 1994; Bernstein 2007; Brennan 2004; Choy 2003; Constable 1997, 2003, 2005; Ehrenreich and Hochschild 2003; Parreñas 2001). In her study of contemporary sex work in the United States, Elizabeth Bernstein (2007) argues that global economic restructuring has fostered new erotic dispositions as male clients are looking for "bounded authenticity" or an experience in which a woman performs the emotional and sexual labor of a girlfriend without the ongoing obligations. The appearance of forms of intimacy in the postindustrial sexual transaction contrasts with industrial forms of sex work, which were seen as a form of sexual release devoid of emotion. Like the scholarship on marriage and modernity, the rich scholarship on the commodification of intimacy has focused largely on heterosexual encounters, with primarily female caregivers and male consumers.

When anthropologists have discussed homoerotic relationships in relation to contemporary globalization, they have often focused on identities, politics, migration, and sex work. Scholars have debated whether or not "gay globalization" or the spread of Western queer identities and values beyond their geographical borders would either liberate or homogenize non-Western same-sex communities (Altman 1997, 2001; Drucker 2000). As anthropologists studied these trends more closely, however, many began to question the idea that local sites would be either liberated or colonized by the introduction of gay tourists, gay-themed media, and gay rights politics from the West (e.g., Boellstorff 2003, 2007; Cruz-Malavé and Manalansan 2002; Donham 1998; Manalansan 2003; Parker 1999; Povinelli and Chauncy 1999; Rofel 1999, 2007).[6] Accounts within queer studies have similarly focused on the rise of modern homosexual identities and communities, which were enabled by capitalist industrialization and the liberation of people from the heteronormative expectations of family life (D'Emilio 1983).[7] These investigations of homosexuality, industrialization, and, later, recent forms of capitalist globalization tend to focus on how people define queer identities, practices, and liberation politics in relation to economic shifts.

The development of two distinct realms of scholarship addressing sexuality and contemporary transnational capitalism inadvertently associates practices of love, intimacy, and kinship with heterosexuality, while leaving identities and sex practices to queers. By analyzing the "political economy of love" (Padilla et al. 2007) I combine the scholarship on the commodification of love and intimacy with research on homoeroticism and globalization to provide a more accurate view of how people interpret, resist, and reproduce forms of global capital, sexual subjectivity, and intimacy in their daily lives. In doing so, I join with analysts who have explored what Ara Wilson (2004) describes as "intimate economies," or dynamic entanglements of markets and everyday intimacies that clarify how global capitalism is embodied and reproduced. As Elizabeth Povinelli (2006) highlights, analyzing "intimate events" promises to reveal the otherwise obscured connections between "micro-practices of love" and "macro-practices" of state governance and political economic systems (2006: 191).[8] Hence, I follow the domestic cycle of households to illuminate the lived realities of topics that were defining themes of the post-Soviet era such as family and kinship, gendered divisions of labor, racialization, economic inequities, and migration. Examining contestations over queer love and intimacy introduces themes of kinship and family because discourses of love continue to play such a fundamental role in crafting kin ties (Padilla et al. 2007). As Florence Babb (2006) notes, "queering" love and globalization requires reexamining deeply held assumptions about gender and the domestic sphere, in addition to sexuality.

THROUGH THE LENS OF TOURISM

I arrived in Cuba eager to investigate how state-sponsored initiatives to promote gay tolerance beginning in the 1990s had had an impact on the lives of gays and lesbians. After nearly half a century of institutionalized homophobia, a number of research studies and journalistic accounts had celebrated an opening up toward homosexuals in Cuba, as gay themes appeared in state-run media and arts industries. Yet when I asked gays, lesbians, and *travestis* about these new social gains, people redirected the conversation to criticize the changes brought about by rising inequalities and the sex trade. I came to recognize that important gains in official and everyday forms of gay tolerance were often overshadowed by the rise of poverty and the return of socioeconomic disparities. Most studies of Cuban homosexuality that I had read before my arrival in Havana had been conducted before or during the early years of the post-Soviet crisis, when the sex trade was just gaining prominence in Havana's queer nightlife.[9] By the beginning of the twenty-first century, however, the explosion of sexual labor in Havana had become a defining factor of queer social life. Following my respondents' cues, I investigated the impact of the most far-reaching capitalist reform in Havana—the introduction of the tourist industry and the rise of the sex trade—as a means to explore the dilemmas of new post–Cold War intimate economies that my interlocutors described.[10]

For my respondents, the rise of the tourist sector embodied how daily life had been reordered by the transition to post-Soviet socialism. When the Socialist Bloc disbanded, the Cuban economy was almost completely dependent on Soviet subsidies, making the loss of support catastrophic.[11] Cuba had imported two-thirds of its food, nearly all of its oil, and 88 percent of its machinery and spare parts from the Socialist Bloc (Hamilton

2002: 23). Making matters worse, the United States government tried to use the crisis to force a change in Cuban leadership by tightening sanctions in 1996 and penalizing any foreign company that traded with Cuba. Known as the "Special Period in Times of Peace" due to the destitute wartime conditions, Cubans suffered massive shortages of food, electricity, and fuel, and the return of nutritional deficiencies.[12] The government was forced to decrease food and eliminate "nonessentials," such as clothing and toiletries, from the rations. Cubans suffered extreme income polarization as approximately half of the population gained access to dollars either through family remittances or work incentives, and 15 percent of families came to control 70 percent of the wealth (Ferriol 1998).

Despite the extreme hardship, leaders rejected state decentralization and refused widespread foreign investment or privatization.[13] To buoy the failing economy, however, in 1992, the Cuban National Assembly amended the constitution to allow for controlled foreign investment in the tourist sector.[14] Within the first decade, the number of foreign visitors to the island increased from 370,000 in 1990 to 1.8 million by 2000 (Brundenius 2002: 383) and continued to rise to 2.53 million by 2010.[15] The Cuban tourist industry promoted values that orthodox communists had struggled to eliminate, including leisure, sexual indulgence, and privilege, while exacerbating inequalities of race and class, as white Cubans were hired preferentially within the tourist trade.

The tourist industry therefore exacerbated racial inequalities that were already resurfacing during the post-Soviet transition. For instance, white and black Cubans had unequal access to remittances, which were a mainstay of the post-1990s Cuban economy. White Cubans were more likely to be wealthy at the time of the 1959 revolution and left in far greater numbers than Afro-Cubans, who benefited from the revolutionary promises of economic redistribution and racial integration. Because white Cubans experienced higher rates of emigration, their kinship networks allowed increased access to hard currency from relatives abroad during the post-Soviet crisis. Constraining the roles that black Cubans could play in the tourist industry compounded the already limited access that darker-skinned Cubans had to hard currency and made informal black markets a primary option for survival.[16]

As the recipient of the majority of foreign tourists, people in Havana disproportionately felt the negative impacts of the tourist trade. Residents witnessed increased urban migration as rural dwellers sought opportunities in nascent black markets that sprang up around the tourist industry and new forms of conspicuous consumption became available in dollar stores geared to foreigners.[17] Perhaps the most troubling consequence was the psychological impact of tourist segregation. As the government opened the island to capitalist foreigners, officials prohibited Cubans from staying in tourist hotels and required using separate taxis, restaurants, hospitals, nightclubs, and shops that dealt in hard currency. After decades of egalitarian rhetoric, Cubans were suddenly second-class citizens.[18]

Rampant inequalities remerged in what Cuban sociologist Myra Espina Prieto (2001) has identified as the "restratification of Cuban society." Before the 1990s, wages had been relatively equal, with the highest salary theoretically not exceeding the lowest by more than five times (Espina Prieto 2001). During the 1990s, however, a salary earned in black markets or the tourist sector could easily exceed by ten times even the most prestigious career in state employment. In an environment in which a waiter's tips could surpass the six-month salary of a university professor, highly skilled labor migrated toward low-skilled jobs (Martínez et al. 1996; Urrutia 1997). The tourist sex trade exemplified this stark inversion of cultural and financial capital.[19] For example, in 2002, an income study of residents in Havana showed that a female prostitute working with foreigners typically earned between $240 and $1,400 a month, whereas a university professor made no more than $22 monthly, an engineer or a physician grossed between $12 and $25, and an officer in the armed forces or a cabinet minister received no more than $23 (Mesa-Lago and Pérez-López 2005: 75).

The development of the Cuban tourist industry in Havana also reintroduced forms of emotional and sexual labor that had been largely eradicated under socialism. Prerevolutionary Cuba had been known as the "brothel of the Caribbean" and, through employment and educational programs for female prostitutes, the revolutionary government had largely eradicated the sex trade. Following the loss of Soviet subsidies in 1991, sex work became pervasive even though the socialist government still prohibited prostitution, strip clubs, erotic massage parlors, and adult entertainment industries.[20] The elimination of prostitution had been a great source of pride among Cubans, so the dramatic return of the sex trade to Havana embodied the most troubling aspects of the transition to post-Soviet society (Whitfield 2009: 30).

For many Cubans, the young people who hustled foreign tourists for *visa y divisa* (a visa and hard currency) personified the devastation following the collapse of the Socialist Bloc. As a powerful emblem of the changes that capitalism would wreak—what Ariana Hernandez-Regaunt (2009) has called the wheeling, dealing, and gleaning that characterized daily life—the *jinetera* or female sex worker emerged in the works of Cuban social scientists, journalists, artists, writers, and musicians as an icon of post-Soviet demise.[21] Prostitutes were no longer viewed as the unwitting victims of capitalist exploitation but rather as strategic *jineteras* (literally horse-jockeys) or *pingueros* (literally dick-workers) who would ride foreign tourists for fast cash.[22] In her study of Cuban sex work, Amalia Cabezas usefully reframes incentivized relationships as "tactical sex" to highlight Cuban perspectives that distinguished the post-Soviet sex trade from earlier eras (Cabezas 2009: 118).[23]

Although many relationships were transformed by the rise of market relations in the post-Soviet era, the impact of liberalization on queer social life was especially concentrated and pronounced. Given the historically marginal status of homosexuals in Cuba, at the time of my research, there were only a handful of public places that gays publicly gathered in Havana—three public parks, two cinemas, and a block-long stretch along the Malecón sea wall. By the early twenty-first century these informal gatherings had been largely reoriented around commodified sex. As Lawrence La Fountain-Stokes (2002) describes, the introduction of foreign tourism split Havana's queer social worlds between "respectable" gays involved with the arts and those tied to *jineterismo* and the sex trade. Wherever urban gays were known to congregate, one would find young hustlers, fresh from the provinces, hoping to make a living from gay Cuban and foreign clients. In part, male and female sex workers' attraction to informal queer enclaves reflected the marginality of these spaces, which allowed sex workers to blend in with other social outcasts (Allen 2011). The overwhelming presence of sex workers also justified police crackdowns and often led authorities to disband the gatherings for days or weeks at a time, intensifying feelings of marginality. How individuals navigated these changes, often simultaneously embracing and criticizing nascent forms of commodified love and sex, shed light on how wide-scale political economic transitions were internalized, manifesting their effects in the most intimate practices of quotidian life.

Exploring the new forms of masculinity that emerged among male sex workers, ethnographers including Jafari Allen (2007, 2011), G. Derrick Hodge (2001), Gisela Fosado (2005), Amalia Cabezas (2009), and Abel Sierra Madero (2012) found that the economic crisis morphed traditional categories of same-sex practice among straight men into new identities tied to the market.[24] While gay men have often appeared in these studies as the clients of sex workers, less attention has been paid to their concerns over the rise of inequalities and materialism exemplified by the sex trade. By focusing on the Cuban consumers of commodified homoerotic relationships and the lesbians and *travestis* whose lives were also changed by the rise of commodified sex, we can discover even more about dilemmas regarding intimacy and belonging. Comparative perspectives on homoerotic labor in the Dominican Republic offer a fruitful comparative model (e.g., Cabezas 2009; Padilla 2007; Padilla et al. 2007).[25] For instance, in research on the Dominican homoerotic sex trade Mark Padilla (2007) has expanded the scope of analysis beyond the sex tourist-sex worker encounter to investigate the sex trade's impact on intimate relationships between Dominican male sex workers and their female partners.

Exploring the myriad of forms of queer intimacy that emerged in post-Soviet Cuba also provides an important comparative perspective on capitalist contexts throughout the Caribbean and Latin America. The impact of tourism's reintroduction in Cuba reflected broader global trends in which an explosion of sex tourism has perpetuated inequalities and neocolonial forms of domination throughout the region, even as it might offer new opportunities and identities to sex workers (see Altman 2001; Brennan 2004; Kempadoo and Doezema 1998; Sanchez Taylor 2001). In the Caribbean, where national economies have become increasingly reliant on tourism, the transformative impact of erotic-economic exchanges with foreign tourists has been particularly profound (Brennan 2004; Cabezas 1998; Castaneda et al. 1996; Kane 1993; Kempadoo 1999, 2004; Padilla 2007; Pruit and LaFont 1995). Citing the history of slavery and colonialism, many scholars have pointed out how sex tourism perpetuates racist ideas about the hypersexuality of the region as sexuality becomes a commodity on the global market in ways that national governments can capitalize on (Kempadoo 1999; Padilla 2007). While the parallels between Cuba and other Caribbean nations are striking, key differences demand consideration. Most significantly, Cuba's socialist history and the government's attempt to curb sex tourism radically differ from other contexts, where economic restructuring has included an embrace of neoliberal capitalism and wide-scale privatization.

QUEER CRITIQUES OF COMMODIFICATION

People on Havana's sexual margins forcefully criticized the sudden and seemingly omniscient reach of sexual and affective commodification. I interpreted nostalgia and melancholy for "authentic" love and intimacy to represent anxieties about broader socioeconomic changes. For many urban gays in their twenties and thirties, years of dedication to career tracks and educational goals were dramatically upended in the post-Soviet economy. Across the households, my white and lighter-skinned respondents had all been raised by parents who were staunch revolutionary communists. Like their Afro-Cuban counterparts whose families had remained in Cuba and had no access to remittances, the only way they could access hard currency was through work in the tourist industry or informal black markets. This uneven economic landscape meant that those who held cultural capital, such as educated urban gay professionals from patriotic families, often lacked access to dollars, while the incomes of uneducated young Cubans with inroads into informal economies, such as sex work, surpassed the earnings of gays. By criticizing rising materialism embodied by the sex trade, gays, lesbians, and *travestis* challenged these emergent post-Soviet hierarchies.[26]

Although people criticized the unequal class configurations of wealth and status resulting from the mixed market economy, many reinvested in the privileges of skin color, education, and urban origins through a discourse of "culture." Rather than perpetuate a moral panic over the promiscuity of prostitutes, gay men and women often criticized the *nivel cultural* (cultural level) of sex workers. Historically, notions of "cultural level" had provided a coded reference to race and class in an environment in which the state prohibited these discussions because socialism had supposedly eradicated inequalities (Fernandez 2010: 134). While the Cuban Revolution racially integrated workplaces and neighborhoods, lighter skin privilege continued to organize social hierarchies both institutionally and culturally. In post-Soviet Havana, lighter-skinned Cubans benefited from racial privileges in the hiring practices of the formal tourist industry as well as greater protection in informal markets, where they were less likely to be considered "criminal" because of their skin color. The idiom of "cultural level" indicated how cultural and symbolic capital and habitus—the habits of everyday life—could define one's social status just as much as wealth (Bourdieu 1984).[27]

Despite hostility toward the post-Soviet economic landscape, young Cubans with nonconforming gender and sexual identities were increasingly forced to participate in the new cultural-economic systems they disparaged. Many of the urban gay men and lesbians I knew participated in black markets—some even siphoned goods from state factories and sold them—but they described their efforts as hard work, whereas to sell sexual acts devoid of pleasure or, even worse, to commodify emotional bonds suggested the erosion of fundamental human values. Witnessing the lives of younger generations of white and lighter-skinned urban gays over a number of years also revealed interesting contradictions, as many who had harshly criticized strategic intimacies also engaged in relations *por interés*. For instance, lesbians met foreign boyfriends who would send them money, and gay male students or professionals would experiment with commodified sex with older tourists whom they found unattractive. Despite forays into commodified sex and affect, my gay friends and respondents would never describe their tactical sexual relationships with foreigners as "sex work." On the contrary, for many urban gays the growing gaps between values and daily realities intensified their criticism of sexual commodification. From my perspective, it seemed that skin color played a crucial role in protecting their activities from accusations of *jineterismo*, as blackness could often become synonymous with criminality in the post-Soviet context.

As the tourist industry commodified Cuban culture and bodies for foreigners, what counted as "hard work" versus "easy money" signaled value judgments about the legitimacy of certain types of labor and the appropriate spaces within which labor should occur.[28] Cubans involved in Havana's queer social networks explicitly rejected and refused the tenets of cultural capitalism despite their entrenchment in its new forms of labor, production, and consumption.[29] An ethnographic perspective illuminates how people made sense of their own involvement in the very systems that they denigrated and reveals how they strained to erect boundaries between decent desires and forms of intimacy in the new mixed-market context. The boundaries around commodification proved to be deeply cultural, and through close observation of daily practice, I began to ascertain how certain desires, sentiments, and relationships came to be viewed as outside of the market economy (Yanagisako 2002). My attention to how ideas about decent forms of love and intimacy related to forms of privilege, such as whiteness, offers a critical complementary perspective to studies on blackness and marginality in post-Soviet Cuba.[30]

SOCIALIST MORALITY AND DISCOURSES OF RESPECTABILITY

The everyday dramas that played out in Havana's queer nightlife and social networks were unique in the sense that they reflected a specific history of marginalization and stigmatization for those with noncon- forming genders and sexualities. Yet, at the same time, my respondents' anxieties, doubts, and hopes for the future embodied general trends in post-Soviet society. Questions about intimacy and instrumentality plagued relationships in Havana—straight and gay, foreign and local, kin and commodified—as new unstable economic imaginaries blurred the boundaries between these distinctions. While my respondents' sto- ries can be read as an important chapter in the history of gays in Cuba, it more accurately elucidates widespread social trends in post-Soviet Cuba told through the lens of a group of people poised to articulate the impact of these new social and economic realities.

Prompted by the post-Soviet crisis, people lamented the rise of rela- tions *por interés*, but it was not the first time strategic intimacies existed on the island. Before the crisis, people had utilized sex to gain access to power and the comforts reserved for party officials, but these strategic intimacies did not dominate people's perceptions of love. Yet gay and straight critics alike ignored how relationships frequently involved ma- terial considerations and incentives, such as decisions about livelihood, housing, and migration (Cabezas 2009). If self-interest had historically shaped love and sex in Cuba, how do we explain Cubans' fixation on the demise of true love in the post-Soviet era?

A historical emphasis on marriage within revolutionary socialist proj- ects politicized intimacy as a lens through which citizens could map eco- nomic inequality and social decline. Elise Andaya (forthcoming) argues that, historically, love and marriage had been fundamental components of socialist nation building; in the post-Soviet era intimate relationships became a symbol for social unrest. In the 1960s and 1970s, Andaya ob- serves, revolutionary leaders politicized intimate relationships when they argued that love and marriage perpetuated the inequalities of patriarchy and capitalism through an unequal inheritance of wealth. Government leaders promoted an egalitarian society in which young people would build families based on sincere desire, not economic considerations.[31] The implementation of marriage campaigns also meant to formalize hetero-sexual relationships and lower the number of matrifocal families, which were particularly associated with poor and black families (Safa 2009).[32]

After suffering years of state homophobia, the extent to which urban gay men, lesbians, and *travestis* drew on socialist moral discourse to dis-parage the impact of neoliberal reform might come as a surprise. Since the 1959 revolution, socialist government officials, work brigade captains, and community leaders had accused homosexuals of laziness and used hard labor to "exorcise" homosexuality from citizens. In an example of reverse discourse (Foucault 1990: 101), urban gays drew on similar ideas about hustlers taking the "easy way out" and refusing "to work" as a way to criticize the materialism and self-interest they associated with the sex trade.[33] Likewise, *jineteras, pingueros,* and others trading sex for money or goods also made use of state rhetoric to criticize the growing inequali-ties that inspired their work in the sex trade. They described their labor as *luchando* or fighting, the word that leaders often used to describe the struggle for independence and freedom.

While people echoed socialist ideologies, however, their appropriation of official rhetoric did not indicate their uncritical support for the Cuban government. Like most Cubans, many of my respondents felt entitled to social safety nets such as free education and health care but had grown cynical and tired of state control in an era of national insolvency. This dy-namic echoes other postcommunist contexts in which resistance to state ideologies has not been automatic, even in situations where people had experienced the brutality of Soviet systems (cf. Bloch 2003; Grant 1995).[34] Their appropriation of state discourse also reflects what Michael Herzfeld has coined "cultural intimacy" between citizens and the nation-state, in which similarities reign between state ideologies and social life even when citizens oppose the state (2005: 3).[35]

Younger generations of Cubans raised under socialism criticized the rise of materialism and self-interest embodied by Havana's informal sex-ual economy, criticisms that could also be read as an attempt to impose standards of decorum that have long been associated with an elite class in the Caribbean and Latin America. As scholars have shown, notions of decency and respectability originating with the colonization of the Americas divided populations between proper and deviant subjects. Most often linked with an aspiration to whiten and thereby civilize the nation, nineteenth-century colonial ideologies naturalized European dominance through ideas about gendered virtue, the dangers of miscegenation, and the importance of formal marriage (Findlay 1999; Martinez-Alier 1989; Putnam 2002; Wilson 1969, 1973).[36] While radically transformed over time, ideas about respectability continue to inform sexual practices and conjugal relationships throughout Latin America and the Caribbean (Freeman 2007). By eliminating the church, leveling inequalities of social class, and working toward racial and gendered integration in the job sector, the 1959 Cuban Revolution complicated the interrelated tropes of class decorum, whiteness, and sexual purity but did not eradicate them.

Moral discourses of respectability across the Caribbean and Latin America often reflect changing modes of production.[37] In Caribbean Costa Rica, for instance, export booms and the rise of banana plantations in the late nineteenth century reshaped fundamental ideas about gender, race, and sex (Putnam 2002). Similarly, during this era in Puerto Rico, discourses about respectability, which shaped "sexual practices, racial meanings, and sexual regulatory strategies," were tied to developments in the sugar industry (Findlay 1999: 6). Prostitution has often played a central role in igniting these discourses as elite observers reinforce class hierarchies and notions of gendered virtue that stigmatize working-class women as outside of the reach of honor and decency. Likewise, in Cuba a shift from a communist to a mixed-market socialist economy, and especially the introduction of foreign tourism to Havana, produced new norms and expectations in regard to sexual propriety and the public sphere.

At first glance, criticism of the sex trade might echo these morality discourses that seek to denigrate the moral turpitude of street culture in favor of propriety. Yet it is critical to recognize that gay, lesbian, and *travesti* Cubans were not necessarily promoting an adherence to traditional forms of decency. While privileges of color, class, and culture still informed people's perspectives of what counted as proper forms of labor and commodification, they did not do so in a straightforward manner. First, many sex workers whom they criticized were also white or light-skinned and shared similar class and family backgrounds. Second, criticism could be seen as an attempt to undermine burgeoning class inequalities rather than an instantiation of elite economic rule. Finally, urban gay critics defended same-sex unions and households against an endemic heteronormativity by idealizing same-sex liaisons, in opposition to sex workers' materialistic trysts; urban gays could thus position their

Figure I.1. The Yara cinema theater in Vedado.

identities and practices within the mainstream. Urban gays presented their genuine feelings of love in ways that naturalized nonnormative desires while questioning rising inequalities, by describing their intimacies as "natural," "normal," and "true."

CHRONICLING QUEER ENCOUNTERS

Havana boasts no formal "gay neighborhood" with bars, clubs, bookstores, theaters, and shops, so my entrée into the daily lives of my respondents began in the informal, ad hoc nightly gatherings that Abel Sierra Madero (2006) has described as an "ambiente homoerótico" or homoerotic scene. My initial exposure to Havana's queer nightlife in 2001 focused on an area called *La Rampa* (the Ramp), which is bookended by the Malecón sea wall at one end and the Yara cinema theater at the other.[38] In the 1990s, La Rampa had been renovated to accommodate travel agencies, hotels, and restaurants catering to foreign tourists. Every night, around 10 PM, gay men and women, sex workers, *travestis,* and tourists would convene on the brightly lit corner outside of the Yara theater. An hour later, police officers would herd the crowd down toward the Malecón, where everyone would drink cheap rum from shared plastic cups, gossip in rapid-fire street slang, and make out in same-sex couples.

I returned to La Rampa and followed the lives of the Cubans and foreigners whom I met there for nearly a decade, encompassing the sum-

time of research

mers of 2001 and 2002, thirteen consecutive months from December 2003 to January 2005, and the springs of 2005 and 2007.[39] By connecting with respondents' friends, lovers, and families, I conducted approximately 100 formal and informal interviews with gays, sex workers, and foreign tourists.[40] I spent time with my collaborators at home, at work, running errands, and waiting in endless lines. Difficult days led me to the police station or the hospital, good days to the beach or the ballet. I shared in birthdays and breakups, and witnessed countless nights of cruising as my friends scouted new lovers or clients in queer gatherings in Vedado and Centro Habana. The majority of queer respondents, fifty-two in total, were gay men and lesbians, with a smaller group identifying as *bisexual* or *travesti*. Among the people with whom I spoke, at the time nine openly acknowledged their work as *jineteras* and sixteen as *pingueros*. While the women worked predominantly with heterosexual male tourists, they frequented queer enclaves with their boyfriends, who were hustling gay men.[41]

The generational context of this study is especially important to highlight. My respondents belonged to a certain generation in terms of their relationship to Cuban national history—they were raised under socialism and experienced the crippling economic crisis during a moment in which they understood the dramatic impact it had on their daily lives and futures. Yet, most important, I encountered them at a certain moment in their life cycle. Male and female sex workers, in particular, would typically age out of sex trade or simply retire and establish families in their late twenties and thirties. I met these young men and women at a particular moment in their lives that should be interpreted as a reflection of the decisions and perspectives of a chapter in a much longer and more complex life story.

Given the changes in a life cycle, my long-term engagement was important to counteract superficial accounts of Cuban homosexuality that often circulate internationally. For decades, Cold War politics prevented U.S.-based scholars from conducting fieldwork in Cuba, and scholarship was limited to an analysis of statistics, interviews with officials, and studies of government documents. Even as Cuba has opened to foreigners, visitors often make assessments about homosexuality based on short trips to the island. Cuba, however, is a particularly complicated place, and the quotidian workings of Havana are especially opaque to outsiders. A perspective from the ground reveals the complexity of people's lives in a way that surpasses reductive politicized representations that reduce gay Cubans to victims of state oppression or exemplars of social-ist liberation.

A handful of pioneering studies on Cuban homosexuality, some eth-nographic (La Fountain-Stokes 2002; Leiner 1994; Lumsden 1996; Young 1981) and others literary (Bejel 2001; Quiroga 2000) have provided an invaluable foundation for my own research. I aim to offer an important counterpart to this scholarship by emphasizing the lives of lesbians and bisexual women.[42] In part, the dearth of scholarly attention to lesbian-ism reflects the erasure of lesbianism within revolutionary discourse as the Cuban Revolution itself remained silent about female pleasure and desire (Davies 1997). I thereby join a second wave of scholars focusing on homoerotic sexualities in Cuba, including Jafari Allen (2011), Carrie Hamilton (2012), and Tayna Saunders (2009a, 2010a, 2010b), who have used ethnographic techniques to consider the relationship between non-normative gender and sexuality. More than including women for the sake of equity, I uncover how gender normativity played a role in deciding what counted as socially acceptable forms of homoeroticism.[43]

While I met many people, my greatest insight into their lives came from integrating myself into the daily routines of households for months at a time. In this book, I focus on three households that embodied trends within queer enclaves, which allows the reader to imagine my collabora-tors as I knew them, within their social and kin networks.[44] My emphasis on the ramshackle apartments and modest houses that sheltered my re-spondents also stays true to the context of Havana, where private social scenes have flourished in people's homes, given the absence of gay public space (Arguelles and Rich 1984: 697). When people could secure privacy in their home, it immediately became the grounds for alternative networks of love and support.

As I collected stories on Havana's sexual margins, I did not single out people with specific racial identities, such as black or white Cubans, but skin color and ethnicity played an important role in my analysis. For the most part, I found that homoerotic relationships occurred between people of similar skin colors, and this kept with larger trends among heterosexual white Cubans, who tended to be endogamous (Fernandez 2010). In Ha-vana, race was talked about more openly than in the United States, but racism was discussed less. Describing people by their racial characteristics was so common that nicknames were often based on racial appearances—many people, for example, shared the same nickname, such as "*la negra*" (the black woman) or "*chino*" (the Chinese-looking man). People also openly discussed their sexual types with reference to color, unabashedly declaring that they preferred a certain color over another. I seize on these references to race in the stories I present to understand how people reinforced forms of racial privilege at a moment of shifting social hierarchies.

I focused primarily on relationships between Cubans, but I also wanted to understand the encounters between foreign tourists and Cubans and to consider how tourists viewed their presence in Havana's queer social life. Tourists often confided in me as an equal, as our position as mutual outsiders inspired them to tell me detailed stories of their experiences with Cubans. I spent time with gay tourists in their hotels, on group dates with their Cuban partners, at restaurants, city tours, and nightclubs, and often maintained e-mail contact after they returned home.[45] The twenty-two foreign tourists I interviewed were primarily gay men from Spain, Mexico, Canada, England, and the United States, with a few from the Bahamas, Aruba, and Scotland. I befriended fewer lesbian than gay male tourists because there were fewer foreign lesbians who participated in Havana's queer nightlife. Those from Canada and the United States were predominantly white, with a smaller number of black, Latino, and Jewish respondents. The majority of the tourists considered themselves middle- to middle-upper-class in their home countries, although all were wealthy by Cuban standards. Most were repeat visitors and had been traveling to Cuba for more than two years in a row. Just like Cubans, gay tourists did not conform to any particular type—they represented an array of sentiments toward Cubans and forged radically different relationships with the people they met. For instance, some maintained friendships with Cuban lovers that spanned decades, sending money for hustlers' families, while others arrived in Havana eager to find the cheapest sex in the Caribbean. To subsume all gay travelers under the same "tourist" category threatens to erase the tenderness and humor in many of these relationships and collapse important national and ethnic differences between visitors to Havana's queer enclaves. Hence, I use the term tourist as a placeholder to discuss how Havana's tourist industry structured their experiences, while using ethnography to attend to their unique differences.

MY ROLE IN QUEER ENCOUNTERS

In part, my sensitivity to the diversity of foreigners in Havana's queer *ambiente* stems from my own experiences as an outsider who, at times, commiserated with other travelers and, at others, sought to distance myself from the racism and naiveté of some gay tourists. Analyzing the queer encounters between tourists, urban gays, and sex workers allows me to draw on my own experiences as a source of insight. I join with anthropologists who have long recognized the fundamentally subjective nature of ethnographic research, in which using the self as a tool of investigation prohibits any pretense of objectivity. Rather than see this as a limitation, I embrace reflexivity as a strategy to provide some degree of transparency. When it comes to studying gender and sexuality, these strategies of acknowledging our feelings toward those we meet in the field are all the more crucial (e.g., Behar 1996; Kulick and Willson 1995; Newton 1993).[46]

As my relationship with Ruso suggests, I was targeted by hustlers seeking hard currency, and, at times, I served as an intermediary for Cubans working foreign clients. My respondents' willingness to take something from me often made it easier for me to take their stories from them. But like urban gays who questioned the authenticity of friendships, I dealt with the reality that friends were using me for money or access to goods, and this helped to reveal my own cultural assumptions about intimacy and instrumentality, which I reflect on throughout the chapters. While I remained critical of the systems of inequalities that granted me privileges, I was often left exhausted by constant requests to provide cash, clothing, or access to services available only to foreigners. Rather than suppress my reactions, I include my own experiences in order to uncover something about the range of relationships between foreigners, gays, and sex workers within Havana's post-Soviet landscape.[47]

While "sharing" a queer identity might have put some of my respondents at ease, to be clear, it did not offer automatic acceptance or mutual understanding. In fact, claiming that you are "the same" as your collaborators can obscure power dynamics and justify forms of domination (Rosaldo 1980; Yanagisako and Delaney 1995). Indeed, much was lost in translation. I am confident that my questions often distorted the sentiments of my respondents, who grew tired of my probing and could occasionally have placated me with the easiest answer. I found myself in this position often as Cubans inquired about my own sexual and intimate preferences. The first night I met Ruso, for example, he agreed to take my girlfriend, a medical student from the United States, and me to an underground gay party on the outskirts of the city. He ushered us into a car and asked, "Which one of you is the man?" "Neither of us, we don't think of it that way," I said. "Okay, but really," he insisted. It seemed ridiculous to launch into discussion of the nuances of female sexuality over the blaring reggaeton, so I simply pointed to my girlfriend.

Likewise, I initially remained blind to the social class distinctions my gay friends and respondents emphasized. In my eyes, professional urban gays and sex workers were "poor" in that they suffered equally from diminished employment opportunities and dwindling state subsidies. Growing up working-class in the United States, I viewed economic security as the determining factor of social class, with cultural capital playing an important albeit subordinate role. Hence, my collaborators taught me to see important differences in marginality and respectability through their constant comments about my crossing social boundaries to foster friendships with more "marginal" elements of queer nightlife. Most important, being queer or from a working poor background failed to protect my work from the power dynamics inherent in ethnographic research, especially when working with communities more vulnerable to social stigma and state intervention.

In addition to class and sexuality, my skin color also played an important role in shaping my research experience. Because I am light-skinned and blue-eyed, Cubans in Havana's queer nightlife often assumed that I was the tourist client of my American girlfriend, whom they mistook for a *jinetera* because of her reddish brown skin and curly black hair, signatures of her Louisiana Creole heritage. My own ethnicity, a combination of French Canadian and Native American (Cherokee/Choctaw)-German heritage, was irrelevant to my Cuban friends, who had a specific notion of what being *indio* looked like and translated my identity as white or more commonly *americana*. Writing about the prominent role of race in determining their social position during fieldwork in Cuba, Kaifa Roland (2010) and Jafari Allen (2011) have reported being mistaken for hustlers by tourists and criminalized by Cuban security officers, who failed to recognize them as foreigners because of their blackness. These prominent racial dynamics undoubtedly influenced the relationships in numerous ways, for instance leading to more friendships with lighter-skinned Cubans and encouraging my focus on notions of "whiteness" often left unarticulated by my collaborators.

During my research, racial and class divisions were exacerbated by the pronounced segregation policies, which required that tourists inhabit distinct economies, living quarters, and forms of transportation. Known as

Figure I.2. Painted sign near my apartment in Central Habana.

"tourist apartheid" by their critics, these regulations were overturned by
Raúl Castro in 2008 but structured much of my fieldwork experience. The
Cuban government welcomed the hard currency of capitalist outsiders but
feared their influence. Suspicion toward foreigners was heightened by the
George W. Bush presidency, which escalated political tensions between the
United States and Cuba.[48] Cuban government posters and television com-
mercials superimposed Bush's face over Hitler, as rumors of an impending
United States invasion circulated. These political battles converged on the
Malecón, where billboards with the photographs of the victims at Abu
Ghraib implied that the United States could make Cuba its next target.[49]
More insidious than dramatic moments of political theater, however, were
how these suspicions structured and inflected my most mundane tasks—
determining how and where I could procure food, housing, transportation, and goods. The government required all tourists to stay in hotels or
to rent a room in a house with a Cuban family, so legal private apartments
were not available. After six months of searching, including spending a
month in an "empty" apartment where the landlady slept in the living
room and used the bathroom in my room twice a night, I found an apartment in the working-class *barrio* of Centro Habana, where the landlord
kept a locked room to keep the appearance that he lived there.[50] The longer
I stayed in Cuba, the more comfortable I became circumventing the legal
and cultural segregation between foreigners and Cubans. Yet the vivid
experiences of boundary crossing from privileged tourist enclaves to Cuban realities no doubt informed my decision to focus on the rise of new
class systems related to tourism.

Anti-Castro Cuban American activists have often cited Cuban state homophobia as part of their broader campaign to denounce the human rights abuses of the Cuban government. Hence, these representations of Cuban homosexuality politicized my research in ways that were out of my control. Often culturally conservative, these movements seem less interested in advocating for gay rights for Cuban Americans and more concerned with using Cuban state homophobia to advocate for U.S. military intervention. These ideologically laden representations of Cuban homosexuality often excluded the experiences and perspectives of gays living on the island.[51] Further complicating the issue is how gay rights organizations in the United States often support U.S. military efforts to "liberate" gays abroad (Puar 2007).[52] Hence, in exploring the Cuban case, I focus on the lives and stories of people with nonconforming genders and sexualities to uncover the experiences and concerns that define contemporary Cuban social life on its own terms.

TRANSLATING FLUID CATEGORIES

Same-sex practice does not automatically result in "homosexual" or "bisexual" identities, although it might in contemporary Anglo-European contexts (Allen 2011; Boellstorff 2007; Valentine 2007; Weston 1993). Michel Foucault, one of the most prominent analysts of sexual subjectivity, analyzed how medical, judicial, and psychoanalytic ideas about sexuality converged during the nineteenth century to give birth to the "homosexual" subject. Same-sex practice had existed before that point, but the idea that one's homoerotic practice would result in a "homosexual identity"—described as an essence of one's self—was a historical concept specific to the confluence of models of thought in Europe. Anglo-European definitions of homosexuality therefore reflect specific histories of industrialization and colonization, and link same-sex practice to a fixed identity in a way that contradicts the meaning of same-sex practice in many non-Western cultures.[53]

Since homosexual identities reflect specific cultural systems and historical moments, it is important to resist projecting them onto the Cuban context. At the same time, insisting that all categories of Cuban sexuality are unique to the island exoticizes Cuba and ignores the far-reaching transnational circulation of terms and categories over the last century.[54] Keeping these constraints in mind, I have developed an imperfect solution to translating categories of sexual practice and identity.[55] I use "gay" and "homosexual" as gender-neutral words to refer to gay men and women. I recognize that "gay" has, at times, implicitly meant "gay men" and therefore privileged a masculinist bias, but my collaborators used the Spanish word *gay* to mean both men and women. Similarly, female respondents in relationships with women most often used the word *lesbiana* to refer to themselves, which I translate here as "lesbian." Cuban scholar Norma R. Guillard Limonta (2009) maintains that the embrace of the term "lesbian" by Cubans helps to undo the invisibility of female sexualities, arguing that "avoiding the word that defines these relations provides more evidence of rejection" (Guillard Limonta 2009: 70). I maintain that these terms are not simply direct translations of Western or scientific discourses of nonnormative sexuality, but hope to show their shifting, flexible nature by remaining sensitive to how terms were used and transformed in practice.

I prefer the term "subjectivity" over "identity" because it describes the formation of a self through social and historical processes. Whereas identities are based on our identification with a concept—race, gender, sexuality, class, and so on—the notion of subjectivity implies that there is no fixed, inherent self. While our identities can offer a platform for political activism, they can also trap us in systems of self-definition in which we are judged against standards of authenticity. Subjectivities, in contrast, encompass the idea that we are not fixed selves beholden to racial, gender, or sexual "truths" about us, but rather shifting embodiments of the moment in history in which we find ourselves.[56] By observing how post-Soviet economic changes infused nonnormative desires, I hope to reveal how specific historical and political circumstances generated sexual practices and identities.[57]

I use the term "queer" not to impose a universal queer subject onto the Cuban context but to highlight the shifting nature of desire and the fluidity of sexuality that queer encompasses. Cubans did not use "queer," and there was no clear Spanish equivalent. Instead, this distinction developed out of my own experiences in U.S. gay communities, in which my generation found "queer" a helpful alternative to sexual binaries (fixed homo-, hetero-, and bi- sexualities). The term "queer" provides a critique of these essentialist stances because it allows for a more nuanced understanding of desire.[58] Hence, "queer" refers to contexts in which nonnormative sexuality dominated but people did not adhere to homosexual identities, including heterosexuals engaging in same-sex practices, such as male sex workers. For instance, the presence of heterosexual sex workers in predominantly gay settings changes "gay enclaves" to "queer enclaves."

The word *travesti* I leave untranslated because the term "transgender" for U.S. readers too strongly suggests a transition from one gender to another.[59] *Travestis* very rarely used the Spanish word "transgender" (*transgénero*), and when they did, they were referring to women who had sex change operations. *Travestis* saw themselves as distinct from these women and used the term to mark that difference.[60] Many of the *travestis* with whom I worked narrated their sexual development as an evolution beginning with their identification as gay men and increasingly adopting traditionally feminine modes of dress and affect. They sought and maintained romantic relationships with men, most of whom identified as heterosexual. Many *travestis* took estrogen acquired from tourists to develop breasts, but none that I met desired the surgical removal of male genitalia. Moreover, they distinguished themselves from *transformistas* (drag queens), who were often men, gay or straight, that dressed in drag for entertainment.

Throughout the text, I interchange *male sex worker, jinetero, pinguero,* and *hustler,* and *female sex worker* and *jinetera*.[61] Although occasionally distinguished in social scientific literature, these terms took on similar meanings within common usage, and through detailed description, I hope to tease out their nuances. When Cubans referred to the sex trade that emerged in the 1990s, they no longer used the term "prostitution" but more commonly referred to it as *jineterismo* or hustling. A *jinetero* is literally a horseback rider or jockey. Rather than a misnomer for prostitution, *jineterismo* framed sex workers outside of traditional dichotomies of victimized prostitute and oppressive client. Stephan Palmié has highlighted how *jineterismo* cast the *jinetero/a* as an agent who literally "whips the money" out of his or her client (2002: 282). Similarly, Kamala Kempadoo has suggested that *jineterismo* potentially countered the existing social hierarchies that have perpetuated racialized and class dominance (1999: 124). Because a *jinetero(a)* could engage in a number of black market activities, including sexual labor, I find this term akin to the category of *hustler* in the United States, which can mean someone who engages in sex work but also refers to those making a living through street smarts and shadow economies.

In a similar vein, *pinguerismo* emerged in the 1990s alongside the widespread development of same-sex hustling in the tourist industry and combines the Cuban slang term for penis, "pinga" with "ero," which in Cuba indicates a person who works in a trade, such as a *cocinero* (cook) or a *plomero* (plumber), which does not require a university degree.[62] The term *pinguero* is akin to an older term, *bugarrón*, which typically signified a heterosexual man who enjoyed clandestine male lovers. In theory, the *bugarrón* would always be the active, insertive partner during anal sex. Although a *bugarrón* may have some form of exchange with his partners, the term *pinguero* is distinct because it consistently carries the connotation of a who has sex with foreigners for money. The people with whom I worked often used *bugarrón* and *pinguero* interchangeably, allowing the context to determine whether a man expected pay for sex or not.

Similar to the complex relationship between sexual identities and desire, the racial classification of my friends and respondents proved difficult to translate. According to the official 2002 Cuban census, the racial composition of the population was 65 percent white, 25 percent black, and 10 percent *mulato*, including a small percentage of Chinese descendants. Confusing matters is the fact that in Cuba a correlation of skin color, hair texture, facial features, and eye color combine to determine one's racial status. Six categories were most prominent, listed from white to black in increasing degrees of color: *blanco(a), jabao(á), trigueño(a), mestizo(a), mulato(a),* and *negro(a).* Given the options of white, black, or *mulato,* most Cubans would likely place *jabao, trigueño,* and *mestizo*—all varying shades of light skin and mixed racial ancestry—into the "white" category. As Nadine Fernandez notes, these classifications are also in constant flux because the "race" recorded on a person's official documents could change in each incarnation because it is determined by the observer (2010: 18). My friends and collaborators spanned the spectrum, with the smallest groups identifying as black or white, more often choosing one of the mixed categories. In lieu of projecting a black-white racial binary onto my respondents, I have tried, throughout my book, to let them identify their racial category or described their appearance in a way that illuminates these distinctions.

Likewise, following the lead of Cuban historian Abel Sierra Madero (2001), I consciously refrain from using the term "gay community" in the Cuban context. Gay community refers to a collective entity, similar to an ethnic minority, in a usage popularized during the gay liberation movements in the United States during the 1970s.[63] It has since come to represent both gay people and a collection of gay spaces including neighborhoods, bookstores, cafes, and bars. The absence of private property in Cuba makes the conflation of a unified group with a social space inappropriate for a socialist context. In the United States, activists and journalists often describe gay Cubans as lacking the "freedom" to create gay communities because socialist laws prohibit gays from creating industries that cater to a gay clientele. Cuban trajectories of nonnormative sexuality reflect different histories, which I explore in greater detail in the next chapter. Even in the United States, however, dominant ideas of a gay community do not apply to everyone. Working-class and queers of color have often not sought autonomy from their families or social groups, which often provided nurturance and protection from discrimination. In Cuba, many urban gays were likewise incorporated within their neighborhoods, workplaces, and families, and did not express a need to establish a separate community to stave off isolation.

My findings offer insight into the experiences of queer Cuban social life, yet I was surprised to find that my collaborators did not discuss HIV/AIDS as much as I had expected. I often asked about safe sex practices, and the majority of gay and bisexual men, as well as sex workers, that I interviewed were aware of the risks and claimed to use condoms most of the time. Although it came up occasionally, HIV/AIDS did not dominate daily discussions. This absence can be explained by Cuba's low rate of HIV transmission (0.1 percent), between six and ten times lower than that of other Caribbean countries. The lack of emphasis on HIV/AIDS also reflected the fact that it did not emerge in Cuba with the stigma of a "gay cancer" as it did in the United States. The first cases of HIV were introduced through heterosexual soldiers who had served in Angola and infected their wives upon their return.[64] Homosexuality and sex work are often framed through the lens of HIV/AIDS in media representations and scholarly accounts, so by emphasizing other facets of nonnormative sexual subjectivity and practice I hope to honor the perspectives of my interlocutors and broaden the scope of scholarly understanding of their lives.

THE SCHEME OF THE BOOK

Attending to the contestations of queer intimacy in post-Soviet Cuba I aim to shed light on the politics and inequalities of love in a moment in which socialist and capitalist systems collided and cannibalized one another—each in perpetual crisis and fragile recovery.[65] To begin, in chapter 1,

I set the stage for gay critiques of the sex trade by contextualizing gay urban life within official campaigns of gay tolerance, which emerged after half a century of homophobic policies. Rather than assume a predetermined progression toward sexual equality, I link the rise of gay tolerance to wider governmental efforts to preserve fragile revolutionary accomplishments during the transition to mixed-market socialism. I present and analyze the birth of tolerance in state-sponsored medical and cultural agencies, along with the rise of an informal gay nightlife in Havana. I argue that the efficacy of tolerance campaigns largely depended upon advocates' ability to disassociate prostitution and homosexuality because the two forms of sexual "deviance" had been historically entangled. Understanding the stakes of political inclusion for urban gay men and lesbians helps to elucidate why they were so fervent in their criticism of commodified sex and affect and sensitive to increasing social stratification in the post-Soviet era.

In chapter 2, I introduce gay siblings, a brother and sister, raised in Havana, who lamented the contemporary transformations within queer enclaves. They and their partners shared a house on the outskirts of the city and sought to maintain their distance from the explosion of commodified sex. Yet I demonstrate how they believed that the changing economy inevitably impinged upon their relationships. Illuminating how the inversion of cultural and economic capital frustrated gays and lesbians, I argue that working-class and middle-class urban gays reprised state-sponsored moralism to criticize sex workers through tropes of decency, labor, and the body. I demonstrate how, as urban gays disparaged commodified sex, they inadvertently perpetuated certain forms of preexisting class, racial, and urban discrimination. I point out the irony of these critiques, since many urban gays also utilized relationships with foreigners for personal gain or hired sex workers themselves.

Not all urban gay men and women, however, sought to distance themselves from transactional sexual relationships; some reacted very differently to the rise of the sex trade. In chapter 3, I examine a household of gay men who hired and supported male sex workers on an ongoing basis. Access to hard currency offered the men a middle-class lifestyle, but they were not invested in discourses of decency, or distinguishing "upstanding" gays from criminalized participants in queer enclaves. They partook in commodified sexual relationships, often supporting hustlers for months at a time, while decrying the state of emotional "emptiness" they attributed to young *pingueros* whom they cared for. Ironically, some gay men adopted a market mentality of contracts, labor, and "heartlessness" in their domestic dealings with hustlers and one another, even as they criticized these characteristics in the young hustlers they supported.

In chapter 4, I delve into the daily lives of female and male sex workers sharing a household in Centro Habana. Sex workers speak back to the accusations of delinquency leveled by urban gays. Focusing on the woman who headed the household and her best friend, a *pinguero* from the provinces, I trace how sex workers undermined reductive readings of gender and sexuality yet still reinforced normative roles. I examine how hustlers understood sex work as a temporary fix to financial dilemmas and defended prostitution by detailing the realities of post-Soviet poverty.

While urban gays criticized sex workers, sex workers frequently disparaged their foreign clients. Hence, chapter 5 attends to the perspective of gay tourists in Havana. Little scholarly work has explored the experiences and perspectives of gay tourists looking to pay for sex while on vacation. By demonstrating how queer tourists often interpreted their sexual encounters in queer enclaves as a form of political solidarity, I analyze how the system of Cuban-foreigner segregation limited tourist knowledge about Cuban social systems and inadvertently eroticized tourist experiences. I demonstrate how a pernicious ethnocentrism often pervaded well-meaning attempts to forge solidarity, as international gay activists frequently projected U.S.-based sexual identities and politics onto the Cuban context.

In concluding, I argue that in order to understand the nuances of gay social life in contemporary Havana and to forge solidarity movements with gay Cubans, international scholars and activists must remain sensitive to the unique trajectories of Cuban sexual equality even when their strategies are at odds with our own. I revisit my initial argument that the structural poverty bred by the loss of Soviet subsidies limited the promise of sexual equality for gays in Havana. As the Cuban government hesitantly embraced limited neoliberal capitalist reforms in the 1990s after decades of orthodox communism, discourses and practices of desire and sexuality embodied these national transformations. Havana's queer enclaves were caught at the crossroads of political struggles over sexual equality and the widespread introduction of transactional sex, thereby providing a poignant example of the impact of social economic restructuring on the most intimate practices of ordinary life.

FLEETING ENCOUNTERS

As a witness to the many contradictions that plagued people's lives in the post-Soviet era, I often inspired self-reflection, denial, and humor among my friends and respondents as they struggled to make sense of their decisions. More important, they emphasized how making ends meet had become as important as making sense of their sexualities, if not more so. It was this erotic-economic perspective that inspired Ruso to deny his role as a hustler, even as I joined him on his many adventures. His response also signaled how he would not allow his foray into strategic sex to define him.

Ruso eventually left Havana. After five years, he had aged significantly. Partying with tourists' hard drugs, skipping meals, and spending his cash on things like gold teeth had morphed his schoolboy image into a wiry, tougher persona. Before he returned to the provinces, he sat in my living room and cried. Nothing was the same. He wasn't making money like he used to, he rented a cot from a cold and alienating family, and most of his friends had been arrested or sent back to the *campo*. Before, someone had always offered to lend him a dollar or to cook him a meal, but now he often went without food. My original questions about *jineterismo* and his sexuality seemed irrelevant as I watched him wipe his eyes with the back of his hand. I gave him enough money to buy his ticket home and then some.

A week later, I spotted Ruso lying on the Malecón. I remembered the many stories that I had heard about *pingueros* literally crying to foreigners about how they needed cash to go home as a ploy to get money. "They will kill anyone in their stories—even their own mothers—to say they need the money to go back to the *campo*, and then they stay in Havana," one friend had told me. I walked up to Ruso, ready to confront him about his lie. "Look," he said, anticipating what was coming. He opened his battered, grayed cloth wallet, with the two twenties tucked into the cash pocket for my inspection. "I just wanted to pick up one more trick before I went home." I took my place next to him on the wall. I didn't care if he was lying; he knew the answer that I needed and I found that comforting.

When Ruso finally returned to the *campo* he married a young woman who had been a childhood sweetheart, took a job doing manual labor, and eventually started a family. I heard through mutual friends that he still took male lovers in secret. I met him during a moment in his life that was so radically different from the rest that it feels unfair to focus on it. Yet, it illuminates why I emphasize desire rather than sexuality, because desires, unlike identities, accommodate fluidity and change. Our drives manage to reconstitute our life trajectories again and again. The experiences that I witnessed and shared with Ruso shaped who he would become, but in no way determined his future selves. At the time, when he had prompted me to take out my notebook and write down his answers to my questions about his sexuality, perhaps I had underestimated his response. Write the term "bisexuality" down, he implied, because it could change by the next time I saw him. The stories that I present here, like Ruso's, offer a snapshot of who my friends, collaborators, hustlers, and confidants were during the moment that our lives collided. Many would not recognize me now, nor I them. But by recounting these fleeting encounters, I hope to uncover something true about who we were, or at least who we hoped to be, and shed light on the changing social worlds that briefly brought us together.

CHAPTER 1

"Tolerated, Not Accepted"

THE HISTORICAL CONTEXT OF QUEER CRITIQUES

In January 2007, just hours before daybreak, Cuban police officers descended upon the Malécon and detained *pingueros, travestis,* and gays. The officers loaded the rowdy crowd into canvas-covered military trucks and drove through the dimly lit streets to the police station. To secure their release a few hours later, the prisoners were required to sign "warning letters" in which they promised to avoid the Malecón. Juan Carlos, a twenty-three-year-old gay housekeeper who was caught in the raid told me, "I'm not a delinquent, but what was I going to do? They said that the Malecón was a place of drugs and prostitution, and if I went back I'd go to prison for social dangerousness."[1] Juan Carlos resented how he had become guilty by association and expressed frustration with the government for failing to distinguish between law-abiding homosexuals and "criminals."

The outrage the raid sparked among urban gays was significant because it suggested a stark departure from previous decades in which homosexuals, by definition, were considered delinquent. The anger and disbelief expressed by young gays, lesbians, and *travestis* points to how their expectations for fair treatment by police officers had changed radically over the last two decades. Homosexuality was not illegal and no longer punished by laws of "social dangerousness." Many found it offensive to be lumped in with sex workers and other "legitimate" criminals. Most important, state intervention into queer public gatherings, such as the raid, raised the stakes for urban gays to differentiate their values and behaviors from those young Cubans targeted by police—namely sex workers.[2]

In this chapter, I analyze official forms of homophobic state repression that followed the 1959 Cuban Revolution and trace the rise of gay tolerance beginning in the late 1980s. In exploring the emergence of tolerance discourse, I focus on the forms of queer visibility that arose in state health and cultural agencies, national media representations, and within prominent public venues. Yet I highlight the fragility of these nascent gains at the start of the twenty-first century, especially focusing on the normative overtones of queer representations and the incisive impact of intermittent police crackdowns on Havana's queer nightlife. In doing so, I hope to elucidate why the commodification of sex, affect, and intimate bonds might have carried such high stakes for those on Havana's sexual margins. I argue that young gay Cubans on the cusp of a tenuous embrace by mainstream Cuban society sought to distance themselves from historical associations with delinquency and prostitution embodied by the post-Soviet sex trade. While urban gays did not overtly link their criticism of commodified sex to the slow ascension to tolerance that I outline here, this backdrop helps to explain why younger generations of Cubans with nonconforming genders and sexualities so often focused on distinguishing decent values from delinquency, erecting borders between those who had sex for pleasure or love and those who fostered intimacies for money and self-interest.

Understanding historical social exclusion as well as the rise of gay tolerance in the post-Soviet era demands a reconsideration of typical representations of a Cuban sexual minority oppressed by an unchanging, homophobic state. State homophobia, like homosexuality, reflects specific cultural and historical moments. Domestic tensions, transnational crises, and changing economic modes of production inspire new techniques for the regulation and control of gender and sexually nonconforming populations. Despite these nuances, the state often dons the aura of a unified, static entity, as if the state itself acts, rather than a collection of individuals who navigate conflicts and make decisions (cf. Sharma and Gupta 2006). Indeed, Cubans themselves often talked about the state as a singular entity that acted upon them and that reflected the will of Fidel Castro. For instance, people would offer the explanation of "Fidel" to explain government measures from the opening of a new school to trash collection policies. Working in Cuba, anthropologist P. Sean Brotherton (2008) suggests that we reconsider monolithic representations of the Cuban state to trace how "multiple actors, institutions, and bureaucratic processes" shape Cubans' experiences (2008: 260). Similarly, by tracing a genealogy of sexual regulation in Cuba, I highlight state agencies' varied and, at times, contradictory approaches to sexual practices and desires.

REVOLUTIONARY REPRESSION

While state homophobia intensified under communism, the conflation of homosexuality with national contamination began long before the 1959 revolution. In fact, the category of "homosexuality" first emerged along-side conceptions of the modern nation-state in the 1880s, in what Emilio Bejel has described as a "discursive matrix of Cuban hetero-national symbol system" (2000: 167). Cuban national identity in the late colonial and early republican eras posited the virility of Cuban men as a measure of their ability to resist Spanish and U.S. colonization. The problem of sexually deviant behavior dominated social hygienic discourse throughout the nineteenth and early twentieth centuries.[3] Even José Martí defended Cuba against imperialism by arguing for the strength of Cuban manhood.[4] National hygienic campaigns during the 1920s, as described by Abel Sierra Madero, also targeted garzonas (mannish women) who were said to embody U.S. colonization and suffer foreign contamination, both considered threats to Cuban independence (2006: 95).

These discourses linking the national body to sexual practices were deeply raced and classed. Elites, for instance, celebrated mestizaje or racial mixing but only in heavily sanctioned ways—through heterosexual liaisons between white men and women of color but not men of color and white women (Kutzinski 1993). In a similar vein, Verena Martinez-Alier (1989) examined conjugal and kinship practices in colonial Cuba, highlighting how marriage was a practice reserved for elites and denied working-class Cubans, who entered consensual unions, hence maintaining class systems of wealth and inheritance. This allowed an elite class to use marriage to juxtapose their own endogamous conjugal practices against a multiracial working class. These discourses of race, class, and sexuality fomented by social hygienic rhetoric linked social reproduction, racial engineering, sexual regulation, and the family as critical components of independent nation-building in ways that continued to resonate after the 1959 revolution.

Like many decolonization movements, the post-1959 revolutionary era suggested another shoring up of gender and sexual nonconformity in order to defend the Cuban nation against forms of U.S. imperialism. For decades leading up to the 1959 revolution, homosexuality had been associated with a depraved underclass of mafia, prostitutes, and criminals. Bars frequented by queers, even those who belonged to the upper classes, were often controlled by organized crime and existed alongside strip clubs, whorehouses, kinky cabarets, and live sex acts (English 2007: 217). Cubans also associated homosexuality with foreign imperialism because a large number of visitors and servicemen from the United States seeking homoerotic experiences had created a thriving gay sex trade in Havana (Arguelles and Rich 1984: 686). Leaders viewed homosexuals as part of an urban riffraff resulting from the vices of capitalist inequality.

Optimism among those in same-sex relationships for the possibility of inclusion in the new revolutionary society quickly dissipated in the face of repression and state violence toward homosexuals. The management of sexual nonconformity was institutionalized with the Cuban turn to Soviet communism in 1961, as was typical within communist contexts where the preexisting divisions between public and private realms eroded (Sharp 1996: 102). Neighborhood watch groups, Committees to Defend the Revolution (CDRs), were organized to monitor the domestic practices of citizens. Homosexuality was officially criminalized by the newly formed National Assembly, which put policies in place to prohibit gays from working with children or becoming members of the Communist Party—a prerequisite for basic career mobility. Unlike the direct attacks on male effeminacy, lesbianism was often erased from public denunciations of homosexuality. Yet women in same-sex relationships still suffered from state repression, as they were purged from universities, abused in prisons, and expelled from state-run boarding schools (Hamilton 2012: 41).

After 1959, nascent government agencies focused on regulating and eliminating what they saw as sexual deviants tied to foreign exploitation and bourgeois indulgence.[5] In 1961, the government conducted its first massive roundup as police forces attacked Havana's Colon neighborhood in search of what famed gay Cuban author Virgilio Piñera coined the Night of the Three P's: "pederasts, prostitutes, and pimps." The fact that this was one of the primary acts of the nascent government indicated that repressing sexual transgression was a priority. Fidel Castro gathered intellectuals and artists, many of whom were openly gay, in Havana's National Library, and presented his new policy that all art and culture would support the revolutionary effort. Speaking to the artists, Castro famously declared: "Dentro de la Revolución todo; contra de la Revolución, nada" (Within the Revolution, everything; Outside of the Revolution, nothing), establishing strict control over the public discourse surrounding sexual difference and ideological deviations more generally. Likewise, the nascent revolutionary government announced its first act of censorship when it confiscated *P.M.*, an experimental documentary that revealed the untamed side of Havana's nightlife and included scenes suggestive of male homosexuality.

Throughout the 1960s, state homophobia largely revolved around a fixation with masculine gender conformity as homophobic campaigns targeted effeminate men.[6] The homosocial bonds of revolutionary militaristic masculinity—love between soldiers and rebels—demanded the disavowal and suppression of male homosexuality in particular (Epps 1995). Psychologists enrolled effeminate boys in special schools where they were "virilized" through playing baseball and reenacting war games with swords and toy guns (Bejel 2001: 103).[7] In 1965, Che Guevara introduced the *Hombre Nuevo* (New Man), an idealized masculine citizen-soldier poised to confront the emasculating powers of U.S. imperialism through discipline and a strong work ethic (Behar 2000: 138).[8] While Guevara's attack on homosexuality was only implied, the New Man became an iconic emblem of proper heterosexual manhood. Government leaders maintained that homosexuals could become New Men through socialist reeducation and their integration into labor and military projects.[9] From 1965 to 1968, the military imprisoned gays in labor camps, called the Military Units to Increase Production (UMAP), charged with "rehabilitating" men of military age who were declared unfit to defend the country.[10] Along with other "detractors," homosexuals were forced to perform hard labor in the fields of Camagüey.[11] While more men were imprisoned than women, historian Lillian Guerra has noted that at least one all-female camp at UMAP imprisoned lesbians alongside female sex workers who refused to enter government retraining programs (Guerra 2010: 288). The camps gained a reputation for their harsh treatment of detainees and quickly became the center of international controversy as members of the Cuban Union of Writers and Artists organized protests.[12]

More than simply implementing homophobic policies and norms, the revolutionary government also institutionalized a cultural regime of compulsory heterosexuality defined by mutual respect between heterosexual men and women (Leiner 1994: 73; Smith and Padula 1996: 174). Heteronormativity was consolidated through state control over health and reproduction, marriage and divorce, and public housing arrangements, all of which intensified state intervention into private affairs. Moreover, institutional and cultural homophobia was often compounded by enduring gender and racial discrimination, placing white lesbians and darker-skinned gays at even greater risk for harassment and marginalization (Guillard Limonta 2009). Government leaders idealized the heterosexual, nuclear family as the backbone of revolutionary society. For instance, the government published the "Thesis on the Role of the Family in Socialism," which criticized promiscuity and upheld heterosexual marriage as the foundation for egalitarian gender relations (Hamilton 2012: 36). Similarly, the Family Code was established in the 1970s to guarantee that men and women shared equal responsibility for parenting and domestic duties in the household (Espín 1991: 11). The Family Code both implemented policies to ensure women's equality in the home, and, at the same time, encouraged conjugal ties over informal unions and female-households (Safa 2009: 46). This suggests that the Family Code both promoted equality and institutionalized conservative notions of what constituted a family (Bengelsdorf and Stubbs 1992: 155). As Jafari Allen points out, the institutionalization of family life through state policies meant that gender and sexual transgression, including public displays of homosexuality and prostitution, were thereby seen as a threat to the order of the family (2011: 114).

Homophobic campaigns and heteronormative policies were complicated by the fact that socialist programs improved the lives of many gay Cubans, especially working-class and black men and women, who benefited from the redistribution of wealth and policies of racial integration. The government greatly reduced many social inequities common in Latin America and the Caribbean, including malnutrition, unemployment, illiteracy, gender disparities, and massive poverty (Burchardt 2002: 57). Socialist programs also addressed the discrepancies between urban and rural dwellers by bringing citizens from the countryside to live in cities and urban residents to work programs in the *campo* and to serve as literacy teachers. Through intensive government programs, Cuba would come to enjoy a highly literate and educated citizenry, as well as a generally healthy population with infant mortality rates on par with or exceeding the world's wealthiest countries. Similarly, many lesbians benefited as the government challenged domestic roles for women, sending them to work as brigade leaders, teachers, agricultural workers, administrators, machine operators, and managers of state enterprises (Perez 1988: 371).

State leaders reconfigured gender and kinship ideologies, which had previously equated women's moral authority with their confinement to the domestic realm (Andaya forthcoming). These significant improvements in the quality of life for a significant number of gay men and lesbians complicated how gays interpreted homophobic policies of the revolutionary government.

Despite the benefits of socialist programs, decades of state homophobia and social exclusion left gay men, lesbians, and *travestis* more dependent on intimate social networks for survival. In Havana more generally, tenderness and affection served as a form of "network capital" as a resource that was as important as, if not more important than, money (Fernández 2000: 106). Especially the case for those marginalized by the state, the importance of social bonds had primed urban gays to respond critically to the commodification of intimacy in the post-Soviet era, which they felt threatened to undercut crucial social ties. Participants in Havana's queer *ambiente* expressed concerns about changes in intimacy, not because they ascribed to traditional or neocolonial notions of middle-class respectability found throughout the Caribbean, but rather because many believed that changes in love were diagnostic of a dystopic future in which everyone faced the challenges of daily life and state control alone.[13]

THE RISE OF TOLERANCE

In 2010, Fidel Castro made international headlines when he publicly apologized for the detention of homosexuals in work camps during the late 1960s, acknowledging responsibility for the camps but claiming that he personally harbored no homophobia. The apology offered a monumental reversal of Castro's famous proclamation in 1967 that a homosexual could never "embody the conditions and requirements of conduct that would enable us to consider him a true revolutionary, a true Communist militant" (Lockwood 1967: 124). Castro's mea culpa represented the most significant nod toward gay tolerance among a series of public laments from high-ranking functionaries such as Ricardo Alarcón, president of the Cuban National Assembly, and Ruben Remigio Ferro, the head of the Cuban Supreme Court.[14] For the first time in Cuban history, some gays and lesbians could embody the "requirements of conduct" that qualified them as respectable citizens despite their nonnormative sexualities.

Castro's proclamation symbolized the culmination of a slowly mounting movement toward gay tolerance within prominent government agencies.

While major shifts toward official gay tolerance among state leaders did not materialize until the late 1980s, hints of leniency coexisted alongside homophobic policies as early as the 1970s. In 1975, the National Assembly repealed Resolution Number Three, which excluded homosexuals from obtaining positions of power. Likewise, the government established the National Working Group on Sexual Education (Grupo Nacional de Trabajo de Educación Sexual), codirected by a Cuban physician and an East German sexologist. The group publicized progressive research findings on sexuality, publishing the widely read *El hombre y la mujer en la intimidad* (Men and Women in Intimacy), which argued that homosexuality was a natural variant of human sexuality (Arguelles and Rich 1984: 693).[15] In the 1979 Penal Code, the National Assembly decriminalized private forms of same-sex practice, although public displays of homosexuality were still outlawed (Article 303a, Act 62 of the Penal Code, April 30, 1988). Neighborhood CDRs, once the bastion of surveillance, began to focus on distributing mundane information regarding health, education, and sanitation. By the late 1970s, many gay Cubans described a general feeling that discrimination stemmed from individual attitudes, not from official policies (Leiner 1994: 51). Yet, despite these advances, in 1980 the government encouraged gays and criminals to leave the island for the United States during the Mariel exodus, in an effort to purge the "scum" of Cuban society.[16]

In the late 1980s, government leaders sought to protect Cuba from the growing acceptance of capitalist ideologies and practices that had transformed communist societies in Asia and Europe (Domínguez 1993: 106). Between 1986 and 1989 leaders reversed many market-oriented reforms and initiated the "Rectification of Errors and Negative Tendencies," an economic and social program that sought to recentralize state power and return to moral incentives (Mesa-Lago 2000). The sense that Cuba was vulnerable to capitalist cultural influences inspired leaders to become more inclusive in their efforts to fortify a homegrown Cuban culture. In 1988, as part of the rectification process, Cuban vice president Carlos Rafael Rodríguez challenged literary censorship and criticized "intolerance and dogmatism" during a speech to the Cuban Union of Writers and Artists (Domínguez 1993: 114). Cuban artists were encouraged to produce a local cultural renaissance that would stave off capitalism. After years of extreme control, a new generation of artists and writers generated a number of significant gay-themed art exhibits, literary publications, and public dialogues.[17]

Figure 1.1. Government billboard that reads, "Our Human Capital Is Most Important."

As Cuba suffered devastation following the loss of Soviet subsidies in the 1990s, the political leadership faced unprecedented vulnerability and sought support from previously ostracized communities, including gay Cubans. As one Cuban film professor explained, "It no longer mattered who you had sex with, only that you supported Fidel." The introduction of foreign tourism and the opening to capitalist mass culture exacerbated the need to fortify Cuban culture against contamination. For instance, the minister of culture, Abel Prieto, intensified ongoing efforts to raise citizens' cultural literacy so that they would "recognize the spiritual dimensions of the Revolution" and successfully ward off the "superficial mass culture introduced by foreign tourists" (Prieto 2004). Likewise, President Castro announced the "Battle of Ideas" and plastered the island with billboards that read, "Socialism Is Stronger than Ever," "Our Greatest Asset Is Our Human Capital," and "The Weapons of the Revolution Are Our Ideas."[18] State leaders moved away from traditional rallying cries, terms such as "sacrifice" and "struggle," and instead relied on what they defined as classic cultural heritage and real Cuban values (Frederik Meer 2005: 402). Gay Cubans, and queer cultural producers in particular, could assist in the battle for the nation's consciousness by promoting revolutionary values during a moment of fragility.[19]

Official discourses of gay tolerance emerged in the midst of these efforts, as Cuban government agencies collaborated with formerly excluded social groups to promote a post-Soviet revolutionary culture. Cuban leaders instituted a broad attempt to become more inclusive after the crisis, which included, but was not limited to, tolerance toward homosexuality. For instance, the National Assembly lifted the ban on religious organizations, and the Office of Religious Affairs worked with Christian groups to promote revolutionary morality (Ayorinde 2008: 144). Similarly, the Ministry of Culture established the Brothers Saiz Organization to recruit rap artists who critiqued U.S. imperialism, a sharp departure from previous accusations that rap artists were antisocial delinquents (Fernandes 2003). As Sujatha Fernandes points out in her study of Cuban cultural industries, government leaders tolerated greater freedom of artistic and cultural expression, including artistic works critical of the government (Fernandes 2006: 40). Anthropologist Aihwa Ong has found that "neoliberalism as exception," or the embrace of pockets of capitalism in a communist context, often leads to the inclusion of previously ostracized groups (2006: 5). Indeed, the incorporation of social groups and topics that had been previously excluded from the purview of state sponsorship was welcomed into state-run organizations.

The reintroduction of tourism and global capital to the island not only impacted domestic policies, but also placed Cuba on an international stage in a new way. As the Soviet bloc pulled its support, Cuban leaders had to answer to a new international audience. This occurred during a historical moment in which gay rights were becoming diagnostic of a government's embrace of modern values—similar to historical rhetoric of women's rights. As Jasbir Puar (2007) has pointed out, same-sex equality increasingly serves as a signifier of progress, democracy, and civilization. As Cuba sought to market itself in a post-Cold War world, international opinions about the government's record on social issues translated into investors' perceptions about the Cuban government's stability.[20] Moreover, the rise of gay tolerance in state-sponsored agencies reflected a maturation of the Cuban Revolution. The revolution was not a singular event but an ongoing process, and inevitably, the principles of justice could be applied to sexual difference.

TOLERANCE TOWARD HOMOEROTIC THEMES IN THE ARTS

Queer intellectuals, writers, and artists who had historically been associated with bourgeois decadence were no longer viewed as impediments to building a distinctly revolutionary culture. New themes, including nonnormative sexualities that had qualified as taboo, emerged in state-sponsored artistic arenas, including the performing and visual arts, dance, theater, film, literature, and music. Most iconic among the new symbols of tolerance toward homosexuality was *Strawberry and Chocolate (Fresa y Chocolate)* (1994), a feature-length drama produced by the Institute of Cuban Art and Cinematographic Industry (ICAIC).[21] The appearance of a sympathetic homosexual protagonist who championed Cuban culture in *Strawberry and Chocolate* served as evidence of the state's changing attitudes toward gay citizens because the national film industry had been explicitly used to shape national consciousness. Rebel leaders had established ICAIC immediately after the triumph of the revolution, and during the 1960s and 1970s, ICAIC sought to redefine class, gender, and racial hierarchies and establish Cuban revolutionary nationalism through the power of film.[22] By financing *Strawberry and Chocolate* during the crisis of the Special Period, ICAIC sent a powerful message about counteracting Cuba's international image as homophobic and broadening the public's perspective toward homosexual citizens.

Strawberry and Chocolate dramatized an unlikely friendship between David, a handsome, macho revolutionary studying at the University of Havana, and Diego, a gay, effeminate intellectual. Diego was a passionate expert about Cuban high culture who was forced to leave the island after officials blacklisted him for homosexuality. The film suggested greater tolerance toward a particular type of compatriot—a patriotic, intellectual queer who would champion Cuban culture, but could not persuade young militants to swing his way. For instance, in Senal Paz's short story on which the screenplay was based, Diego explains, "If it's a choice between cock and Cuba, it's Cuba all the time" (Paz 1991: 55–56). While David's heterosexuality is duly reinforced through a romance with Diego's neighbor, as literary scholar Jose Quiroga has pointed out, the script desexualized Diego's character (2000: 141). Despite the stereotypical representation of male homosexuality, *Strawberry and Chocolate* portrayed a homosexual protagonist dealing with issues of political repression in unprecedented ways. The codirector, legendary filmmaker Tomás Gutiérrez Alea, said that he had wanted to use *Strawberry and Chocolate* to critique intolerance or the "ostracization of the person who is different" (Gutiérrez 2002). The film opened the way for several national Cuban film productions, often coproduced with Spain, that have portrayed cross-dressing and queer protagonists, including award-winning films such as *Lista de Espera* (2000), *Suite Habana* (2003), and *Barrio Cuba* (2005).[23]

Tolerance toward representations of nonnormative sexuality in the state-funded performing arts far surpassed the queer iconography that developed in the film industry. Writers and directors in Havana's state-funded performing arts could offer more radical representations of queer visibility since theater reached a smaller audience.[24] Popular theatrical productions such as Carlos Díaz's Teatro El Público (Public Theater) mixed drag, camp, and *choteo*, a popular form of comedy that relies on sarcasm and teasing, to forcefully question traditional gender and sexual roles, as well as political authoritarianism. Díaz's *Las viejas putas* (The Old Sluts), a play based on a pornographic Argentinean comic strip, starred a horny lesbian grandmother, a *travesti* nephew, a *jinetera*, and a promiscuous bisexual alien. Male and female actors cycled through each role, irrespective of gender. More than a simple transgression of gender norms, the piece tested the boundaries of political criticism.[25] Unlike the national cinematic representations of homosexuality, which tended to portray a cultured, upstanding socialist citizen who suffered because of intolerance, theatrical performances more directly attacked normative values.

While theatrical representations of lesbianism were not as prevalent, some important advances in terms of lesbian visibility were also being made in plays such as *El último bolero* (The Last Bolero) by Ileana Prieto and Cristina Rebull, in which a lesbian leaves Cuba because she was expelled from the university, and Héctor Quintero's play *Te sigo esperando* (I'm Still Waiting). In 2007, the Ministry of Culture sponsored *De hortensias y de violetas* (Of Hydrangeas and Violets) through the Center of Theater in Havana. The play featured the ongoing dilemmas of a lesbian couple trying to conceive a child. While the script dealt with themes such as "the sperm bank," a nonexistent entity in Cuba, the message was more universal and focused on common struggles to build a family. One of the lesbian protagonists had a sister who struggled with infertility, a narrative device that universalized the lesbians' predicament. Written by sociologist Esther Suárez Durán, the play offered themes of the family as a bridge to encourage tolerance toward sexual difference. Rather than reject traditional values and promote social and sexual transgression, the characters wanted to fit into mainstream Cuban society. This type of normative approach might seem reconciliatory, but key moments in the play still addressed lesbian oppression in quite incisive ways. For instance, one of the primary characters proclaims: "The straight men discriminate against straight women, the heterosexuals discriminate against homosexual men, homosexual men discriminate against homosexual women, and homosexual women discriminate against themselves."[26] The unique freedom of expression offered by the arts in Havana, even mediums that tended to condone more normative or stereotypical versions of homosexuality, fostered an important space for many urban gay men and women who could witness their daily lives portrayed on stage.[27]

HOMOSEXUALITY IN A STATE-PRODUCED TELENOVELA

State-run television remained the last cultural frontier for tolerance toward homosexual themes. Whereas the film industry historically maintained its autonomy, the Cuban Institute of Radio and Television (ICRT) was directly governed by Cuba's primary censorship agency, the Department of Revolutionary Orientation (DOR), making it a much more conservative medium. Viewers could choose among four channels, two of which would often broadcast the same educational programming or political roundtables. The programming schedule was meant to order viewers' days around appropriate times for work, politics, and leisure. For instance, daytime programming featured fish darting around their tank because viewers were meant to be working, not lounging in front of the television.[28] On this tightly monitored stage, censors limited gender and sexual transgression to the cross-dressing of straight male comedic actors or to a brief mention in educational health programs.[29] Even as *Strawberry and Chocolate* screened in movie theaters in Havana, it was years before it would air on television.[30] In this environment of highly ideological low-budget broadcasts, telenovelas from Brazil, Argentina, and Mexico were extremely popular as characters and plots became standard fare in daily conversations.[31]

Hence, when a homoerotic love affair appeared on a novela produced in Havana, *La cara oculta de la luna* (The Dark Side of the Moon) became the most watched television show in Cuban broadcast history.[32] *The Dark Side of the Moon* appealed to viewers because it portrayed a realistic version of the struggles of contemporary life, from overcrowded housing to family breakdowns. The state-produced telenovela charted the fictional infection stories of five protagonists—three men and two women—living with HIV. Through melodrama, the writers aimed to teach citizens about high-risk sexual behaviors that might lead to infection. Marlon Brito López, one of the writers, articulated the goal of the series as to "alert the public of the dangers of the HIV pandemic" and to eliminate "prejudices regarding those who live with HIV and AIDS, especially related to the family" (Brito López 2006).

Although the writers and producers intended to inspire a public dialogue around AIDS, most viewers focused their attention on Yassel's segment—almost twelve hours—in which a handsome and hard-working hero is seduced by Mario, an openly gay attorney. In the first half of his story, Yassel appears as a strong and caring husband to his wife Belkis and a sensitive father to his seven-year-old daughter. Belkis's friends jealously comment that she has married the perfect man. Through extensive scenes too racy for Cuban primetime, audiences witnessed the romantic magnetism between Belkis and Yassel. The emphasis on his manly desires for his wife left audiences unsuspecting of his homosexuality and heightened the drama surrounding his "demise."

Ironically, Yassel meets Mario while daydreaming about having sex with his wife. Perched at his construction site, Yassel absentmindedly lets a rock fall from the building, and it lands on Mario walking below. Motivated by guilt, Yassel visits Mario to help him during his recovery. Yet Mario senses what viewers could not—Yassel harbored homoerotic desires beneath a happy, heterosexual façade. In response to Mario's advances, Yassel initially storms out, pushes Mario down, and calls him a fag. But like a "*mariposa* to a flame," as Mario puts it, Yassel cannot stay away.[33] Finally, Yassel gives in to Mario's advances. (Unlike the explicit love scenes between Yassel and his wife, Mario and Yassel only share a glass of wine and gaze into each other's eyes; the homoerotic sex is left to the spectator's imagination.) Yassel pays a high price for his transgression. His marriage ends in a bitter divorce, and he loses his home and custody of his daughter. He never establishes a relationship with Mario, and, as spectators knew from the outset, he contracts HIV from his brief affair.

In an interview, the series director Rafael González explained his approach to the scenes between Mario and Yassel. "We have to deal with these [scenes] very carefully," González told a Cuban reporter, "avoiding exaggerations, so nobody thinks we are being negative about this sexual orientation. Everyone needs to live according to his or her own personality. But they must do so with protection, that is what matters (*La Jiribilla* April 28, 2006). As González suggests, gay tolerance was not the first

Figure 1.2. Yassel admits his romantic feelings for Mario in the state-produced telenovela *The Dark Side of the Moon*.

priority of the writers and producers. Instead, they wanted to craft a public health message that would reach the widest audience to preserve Cuba's low HIV transmission rate, which at the time was only 0.1 percent, lower than the United States (0.6 percent). The novela offered a medium for disseminating safer sex information as Cubans encountered a sharp increase of foreign visitors to the island and the release of Cubans living in sanatoriums, where HIV-positive Cubans had previously lived in mandatory confinement. Moreover, there was a growing public health concern about sex work and HIV transmission.

The Dark Side of the Moon had some unintended consequences. It medicalized same-sex practice, encouraging men who have sex with men to adopt a homosexual identity in a way that contrasted with local identities. Consistent with the *bugarrón* stereotype, Yassel shirks any identification with queer categories and admonishes Mario for forcing him to discuss sexual identities. Many Cuban viewers might recognize Yassel as a *bugarrón*, a heterosexual who acted as the penetrative partner in sexual liaisons with men, but the *bugarrón* identity was unavailable to Yassel. When Yassel refuses a homosexual identity, Mario responds, "No of course not, you're a man who has sex with men if that makes you feel better." Mario's use of the term "men-who-have-sex-with-men" was uncommon in Cuban parlance and suggested a public health framing of same-sex practice. The term was the latest in a series of categories that tried to adapt the *bugarrón* identity to HIV prevention models.[34] Instead of maintaining a heterosexual identity, his character left his wife because he discovered a "true" homosexual identity.

Many gay men and women I spoke to about the series were critical of the depiction of Mario as an isolated individual, with no family or friends, who endangered the hero. For instance, one gay advocate felt that *The Dark Side of the Moon* encouraged people's attachment to Belkis, not Yassel, and mobilized a latent homophobia. To illustrate his point, he told me how he had been getting rice in the bodega while everyone was gossiping about Mario. He heard an older woman exclaim, "You have to watch those fags! Your husband used to have a sweetheart, now he has a boyfriend." Acknowledging that the overall message to have protected sex was important, he wondered why the producers had decided to portray "gay romance in such an unrealistic way." But not all urban gays reacted negatively to the representation of homosexuality. I watched the dramatic climax of the serial with a group of gay men and, as Belkis discovers that her husband has been unfaithful with a man, my friends stood and yelled at the television, "Finally women will realize that we're sleeping with their husbands!" Even as the narrative reinforced dominant ideologies, it allowed for subversive readings and created opportunities for social critique (Mankekar 2004: 19).

The refined gay protagonist who had relinquished the handsome young revolutionary in *Strawberry and Chocolate* had finally managed to seduce the masculine everyman in *The Dark Side of the Moon*, yet only to serve as a parable for the growing threat of AIDS. Similar to historical attempts to eliminate institutionalized racism and sexism beginning in the 1960s, cultural agencies only hinted at a shift in consciousness regarding sexuality. Nevertheless, queer visibility differed significantly from previous government campaigns because the state-funded films in the 1970s and 1980s had presented the legacies of slavery, colonialism, and sexism as impediments to building an independent society. In contrast, contemporary cultural productions hailed a male homosexual who was still not a revolutionary icon, but whose attraction to the mythic heterosocialist hero would be tolerated. Worse yet, the cultured effeminate man posed a formidable threat to the stability and longevity of the heterosexual family unit. *The Dark Side of the Moon* embodied the contradictions of national visions of homosexuality in the post-Soviet era by making male homosexuality visible and galvanizing public debates but also imposing restrictive norms regarding same-sex identities and reinforcing negative stereotypes.

TOLERANCE OF NONNORMATIVE SEXUALITIES IN PUBLIC HEALTH

In addition to queer-themed artistic productions, officially sanctioned appeals for gay tolerance also emerged in public health discourse during the 1990s. Building on earlier progress made in 1972 by the National Working Group on Sexual Education, some psychologists and medical professionals in national health agencies promoted the normalcy of same-sex desires.[35] By 1989, the working group had been reorganized into the Centro Nacional de Educación Sexual (National Center for Sexual Education), known as CENESEX. The organization conducted workshops that addressed parenting, family planning, STD prevention, and gender and sexuality, and produced the most significant public proponents of gay tolerance. Quite radically, it implemented police sensitivity training to prevent the unlawful arrests of *travestis* and gays in Havana. Promoting the idea that homosexuality was a biological reality, rather than a culturally induced state, the CENESEX website declares that being homosexual or bisexual is "a sexual orientation that is not provoked by seduction at any age, nor is it contagious, nor is it acquired by educational defects or bad examples in the family."

The center's innovative approach reflected the pioneering leadership of Mariela Castro Espín, a psychologist and the daughter of acting Cuban president Raúl Castro and Vilma Espín, the founder of the Federación de Mujeres Cubanas (Federation of Cuban Women, FMC). Castro Espín positioned the struggle for gays within the revolution's humanistic framework and argued that Cuban society needed to develop a "healthier culture of sexuality, one that is fairer, that helps to erode old, erroneous beliefs and prejudices that emphasize sexual orientation" (Castro Espín 2004). Many gay men and women celebrated CENESEX's efforts. This was especially the case during police sweeps, when many gays credited Castro Espín with personally securing the release of *travestis* and others who had been wrongly imprisoned. In our conversations, people expressed relief in having a powerful ally in Castro Espín to defend their cause.

Whereas international gay rights organizations emphasized pride around minority rights, Cuban advocates preferred to focus on rooting out homophobia rather than promoting a politicized gay movement. When I asked José, a bright and handsome gay thirty-year-old who worked with CENESEX what had inspired the opening toward homosexuals in the early 1990s, he confidently responded, "The Cuban Revolution." Although José worried that government censorship had stymied real public debate in Cuba, he opposed what he described as "militant" gay movements that would depart from revolutionary values. Advocates insisted on a socialist, egalitarian framework that would seamlessly integrate gay citizens into mainstream, state-run programs rather than question governmental control. For instance, in 2008, CENESEX sponsored the first annual International Day Against Homophobia, emphasizing the eradication of homophobia rather than the promotion of pride. The event included gay themed performances, lectures, panels, and book presentations. At the conference, attendees wanted to march into the streets and create a spontaneous gay pride parade, but Castro Espín warned against it. (In later years, they would march down the Rampa.) In another telling example, CENESEX denounced a fundraiser for gay Cubans held by a Spanish gay rights organization in Barcelona because the organization politicized Cuban homosexuality and used the image of Che Guevara in its ad campaign.

Rather than breaking with socialist logics to position homosexuals as a political bloc, advocates expanded on the idea that the domestic sphere and the heterosexual family were legitimate and productive sites for state intervention. For instance, in 2007, CENESEX joined with the Federation of Cuban Women to propose legislation that would outlaw discrimination on the basis of sexual orientation or gender identity, extend social programs for *travestis*, and allow transgender Cubans to change their identity cards without undergoing sexual reassignment surgery.[36] The law proposed to work by reforming the Family Code to mandate that family members treat homosexual, bisexual, or transsexual relatives equally, making it the responsibility of parents to love and support their sons and daughters (Guillard Limonta 2009: 72). According to Castro Espín, the policy would help homophobic and sexist fathers that "many times think that they have to conform with a pre-established cultural script— to be macho, they should reject their gay son[s]" (Castro Espín 2004). As a vehicle to secure equality for gay Cubans, the Family Code ironically naturalized the heteronormative, nuclear family to advocate for the legitimacy of homosexuality.[37]

While not entirely uncritical of contemporary politics, gay advocates at CENESEX sought to promote the incorporation of sexually marginalized groups into mainstream society and ongoing socialist state projects. This strategy, however, has had its detractors. Abel Sierra Madero has argued that CENESEX remains too focused on instating normative gender and social roles for gays. Similarly, Puerto Rican cultural critic and filmmaker Frances Negrón-Muntaner (2008) has criticized the reconciliatory tone of CENESEX's efforts. Rather than an evacuation of state control, critics argue, the medical and mental health discourses around homosexuality suggest new platforms for biopolitical regulation.[38] Yet, in response to these critiques, doctor and CENESEX staff member Alberto Roque Guerra (2009) has criticized scholars for insisting on a "politicized" focus regarding gay rights in Cuba.

CENESEX's approach to equality reflected the specific history of homophobia in Cuba, as psychologists, educators, and health advocates attempted to divorce same-sex practice and desire from traditional associations with criminality and prostitution. Gays were encouraged to denounce what had been deemed forms of criminality and eschew a politics of separation, embracing integration into mainstream society and the nuclear family. For example, in 2004, Castro Espín appeared on television advocating for gay tolerance by reassuring viewers that homosexuals were "not delinquents, weren't prostitutes and were not participating in socially unacceptable behavior." Similarly, an article in CENESEX's journal *Sexology and Society* celebrated the growing number of gay Cubans who had arrived in Havana to study or work and distinguished between homosexuals and the "economically motivated" migrants in gay enclaves (Robledo Diaz 2001). Yet, by the time gay advocates appeared on national television assuring the public that homosexuals were law-abiding citizens and educated socialists, Havana's queer nightlife had become overrun with sex work and "delinquency."

THE FRAGILITY OF QUEER PUBLIC SPACE

Rather than chart a narrative of progress from repression to visibility, intermittent police crackdowns on Havana's queer nightlife implied the state's more oblique approach to gay citizens, who were both increasingly tolerated and subject to greater scrutiny. An informal queer nightlife emerged in prominent neighborhoods in the 1990s.[39] Gays congregated outdoors, in public areas such as the Rampa.[40] While these gatherings remained ad hoc and unofficial, the spots held symbolic value because the government had controlled public space as a way to implement social policies. Hence, the mass presence of homosexuals in popular parks and cafes, outside cinemas, and along the Malecón could be read as a sign of increased tolerance.

Shortly after urban gays laid claim to informal public spaces, however, sex work exploded in many important sites of queer nightlife, such as the Rampa, Parque Central, and outside the Payret Cinema.[41] As efforts to contain the influx of sex tourism gained momentum, nascent queer enclaves suffered. In 1998, the Ministry of the Interior introduced *Operativo Lacra* (Operation Vice), a special police force dedicated to eliminating prostitution around the tourist trade. In January 2003, Fidel Castro signed Decree 232, which confiscated any property used for prostitution, including underground nightclubs, and that same year, the Ministry of National Commerce converted nightclubs that hosted drag shows and had a large gay clientele into vegetarian restaurants (Sierra Madero 2006: 103). Police patrols became an ordinary part of nightlife on the Rampa, as well as other sites known for queer gatherings. Officers would ask everyone for identification cards, sending Cubans from out of town scurrying from police, and officers would detain unauthorized migrants and occasionally disband the gatherings. Despite the constant presence of police forces on the Rampa, the state's exercise of power tended to be arbitrary and inconsistent, fostering a paradoxical sense that the Rampa was a zone of tolerance and state surveillance. Participants who held a Havana address dismissed the officers, ignoring their orders to move off the Malecón until police physically pushed them along. Moreover, police officers seemed unsure of how to balance the simultaneous privileges of foreign tourists against the highly regulated ways they were meant to interact with Cubans.

Interestingly, the widespread nature of state interventions into Havana's nightlife suggested that the government was not targeting homosexuality. Arrests were ordinarily made under the law of "social dangerousness" (*un estado peligroso* or *peligrosidad social*), defined as "the special proclivity to commit crimes, demonstrated by the conduct that contradicts [. . .] the norms of the socialist morality" (Artículo 72, Código Penal). The ambiguity of the law empowered officers to arrest anyone, and yet gays were usually spared. Instead, police used the decree to detain rural migrants and sex workers. Because gays residing in Havana legally felt protected from police detainment, many found the raids frustrating but described the sweeps as a necessary means of managing the rise of criminality.

Even though police weren't primarily criminalizing homosexuals, the raids ignited a tacit homophobia in public praise for crackdowns. Before one police sweep on the Malecón, an opinion piece appeared in the *Tribuna de La Habana* (Havana Tribune) in which a Cuban described walking along the Malecón and observing a "transgressive" space (Sierra Madero 2001: 102). With a nod to tolerance discourse, the author declared his respect for diverse sexualities and claimed, "They have all the right in the world to enjoy their practices." But he went on to suggest that the "public manifestation of behavior that belonged in an intimate and private space" stood in direct contradiction to the spirit of "work, of struggle, and the Cuban way of having a good time" (qtd. in Sierra Madero 2006: 102). The commentator ignored how heterosexual desire, expressed through *piropos* or catcalls along with public displays of affection were omnipresent in the city, and implied that same-sex relations were meant to remain "private." This attitude illuminates how the raids could reinforce public homophobia by suggesting that homosexuals should not enjoy the same access to public spaces as heterosexuals.

The development of an *ambiente homoerótico* in Havana indicated official tolerance toward homosexuality, yet government leniency was tested by the influx of foreign tourism and sex workers to queer nightlife. By detaining rural migrants and sex workers under the law of "social danger" and establishing a constant vigilance over queer enclaves, police officers contributed to public perceptions that urban gays were transgressing social norms and deviating from shared political values. Most important, urban gay men and women had to distinguish their values and beliefs from those of sex workers in order to defend themselves against the renewed stigma of criminality.

THE LIMITS OF TOLERANCE

Urban gay anxieties about the rise of the sex trade can be partially explained by the unique trajectory of gay tolerance in Cuba. Gay men and women had made important strides toward social and political acceptance because they had managed to shed long-standing associations with criminality. When gay tolerance rhetoric began to appear in state-run arenas in the 1980s, gay advocates emphasized that homosexuals were respectable citizens who defended revolutionary values and embraced

Cuban culture. Yet the prevalence of the post-Soviet sex trade threatened to unravel these hard-won victories by tethering homosexuality to forms of "deviancy," links that had haunted gays in Cuba since the dawn of the 1959 revolution. In order to claim a place in the nation, they had to distance themselves, both discursively and physically, from enduring associations with an underclass of delinquents and prostitutes—those who failed to conform to socialist moral standards.

While tolerant attitudes toward homosexuality reshaped state-funded artistic productions, national television broadcasts, public health campaigns, and the nightlife of prominent urban neighborhoods, these developments should not be conflated with actual feelings of inclusion on the part of gay men and lesbians in Cuba.[42] For gay men and women in Havana, the reality of increasing tolerance was complicated. Urban gay men and women often responded to questions about the shifting attitudes toward homosexuality with the refrain: "We are tolerated, but still not accepted." Mainstream Cuban society still did not see gays as equal to heterosexuals, and more insidious forms of discrimination often replaced outright harassment in many neighborhoods, workplaces, and families. Many described newfound social gains as fragile. Some felt that these cursory gestures toward inclusion were swiftly undermined by the realities of post-Soviet poverty, as widespread unemployment and material concerns overshadowed the benefits of cultural advances.

By describing their status as "still not accepted," urban gays implied that tolerance could be a stage on a longer journey toward acceptance. Yet political theorist Wendy Brown (2008) has warned of the dangers of tolerance discourse within neoliberalism, arguing that tolerance fixes the identities of marginalized people against a norm in a way that prevents their total incorporation. To be tolerated, one must be and remain different from those doing the tolerating.[43] In post-Soviet Havana, discourses of tolerance threatened to fasten homosexuality to an outsider position that could never be fully integrated into socialist norms and values.

By tracing the historical contours of repression and tolerance, I have offered a backdrop for the various forms of urban gay nostalgia for "true" intimacy that I present in the following chapters. This particular history of revolutionary state repression followed by a tenuous, conditional embrace of homosexual citizens helps to explain the judgments and dilemmas of young urban gay men, lesbians, and *travestis*. In these next chapters, I explore how the realities of daily life for participants in Havana's queer nightlife often overshadowed the benefits of rising sexual tolerance discourse in state arenas. Moving away from narratives of gay progress, I turn to the issues that young Cubans with nonconforming genders and sexualities identified as most central to their lives—the erosion of "authentic" love and intimacy, and the challenges of navigating a rapidly shifting social and economic landscape.

CHAPTER 2

"A Normal Fag with a Job"

THE COMPLICATED DESIRES OF URBAN GAYS

In Havana, I spent much of my time with two gay siblings, a brother and a sister who lived, together with their partners, in a house about twenty minutes from downtown Havana. Lisette was a boisterous thirty-year-old who barely reached five feet tall and had fine features, ochre skin, and kinky auburn curls. Her brother, Osvaldo, was a witty twenty-six-year-old with cool blue eyes, a dark tan, and a shaved head. Both were sharp, resourceful, and charismatic. Osvaldo enjoyed a reputation for seducing straight men he met on the street and Lisette had earned the nickname *jefa* (boss) because of her knack for accomplishing the seemingly impossible through black market connections.

Post-Soviet economic restructuring had derailed the siblings' career plans and left them at the whim of nascent dollar economies.[1] Lisette had abandoned college to take a job cleaning houses. Lisette's girlfriend, Dalia, a thick, milky colored twenty-three-year-old, earned a more substantial monthly salary than Lisette—$60 versus $10—because she qualified for work in the tourist industry. Dalia had studied English since she was ten years old, and this made her a good candidate for management positions. So when Dalia moved into the house, she encouraged Lisette to quit her job. Lisette expressed some anxiety about the arrangement. "Dalia tells me I don't have to work," she said, "so I do everything in the house for her. I cook, clean, wash all the clothes; I let her sleep in because I know she's tired from working nights. It's not that I'm lazy." Similarly, Osvaldo had abandoned his career as an upper-level medical technician, which paid a meager salary in Cuban pesos, for a more lucrative job as a night watchman at a German businessman's sprawling estate. The businessman lived with his Cuban boyfriend, a former sex worker, and the couple hired gay staff members as a way to protect their privacy. Osvaldo worked the graveyard shift and sometimes slept on the floor on a piece of cardboard. He used his salary to support his boyfriend Pedro, in his early twenties with chestnut-colored skin and an easy smile, who had no access to hard currency as a student at the University of Havana. Even though they had secured jobs that guaranteed a lower middle-class standard of living, the sudden erosion of state-sponsored safety nets left Lisette and Osvaldo more vulnerable to poverty than previous generations.

Lisette, Osvaldo, and their partners built a stable family life in which their sense of humor, sexual freedom, and intimacy created a safe haven away from the impact of chronic disappointments and dwindling opportunities. Their father had built the house in the 1960s, when he moved back to Cuba from Miami with the hope that the revolution would improve the lives of working-class Cubans. It was a simple, comfortable structure with concrete floors and sparse furnishings, a bathroom without hot water, a large eat-in kitchen, and a narrow living room facing the street. The house shared an overgrown backyard and a phone line with extended family that lived upstairs. When their father died, their mother remarried and moved down the street, leaving the house to the siblings. While the house originated as part of the revolutionary government's push to promote nuclear families, Lisette and her brother used it to build a different kind of family that included same-sex partners, extended kin relations, and, occasionally, gay friends needing a place to stay.

Their mother stopped by nearly every afternoon, and while she was in the house, everyone refrained from showing affection with their partners out of respect. Similarly they would shut their windows and doors to prevent their extended family upstairs from hearing politically sensitive or overtly sexual conversations. The attempt to tone down the otherwise demonstrative and bawdy tenor of the household in the presence of older familial generations conveyed the mix of tolerance and inequality that typified many kin networks. Lisette and Osvaldo had been open with their mother and father about their sexual preference from a young age, and they sympathized with their parents' struggle to accept their homosexuality. "My mom had a much harder time than my dad accepting that both of us were gay," Osvaldo said. "Can you imagine? First you find your fifteen-year-old daughter going down on the girl next door, and then, a month later, you walk in on your eighteen-year-old son having sex with a boy," Osvaldo said. "But my dad just stood there and said, 'Call me when you're done,' and shut my door." Like many Cuban families, they followed a general principle in which no one directly discussed being gay, but their identities were implicitly condoned.

On the weekends, the house bustled with friends who escaped their overcrowded family apartments to drink rum, play dominoes, meet for sexual liaisons, and watch movies. Informality prevailed, as people walked around in their underwear, smoking each other's cigarettes and napping on any bed that happened to be free. Friends relied on one another for both emotional and financial support in ways that might qualify them as gay kin in the United States. But the closeness of these relationships was more common among friends in Cuba, where socialist solidarity combined with economic hardship to promote unprecedented interdependence. Friends lived with Lisette and Osvaldo for extended periods of time, sharing their beds, eating their food, and using their bedrooms for affairs and trysts when they lacked privacy in their own homes. In her research, Kath Weston (1997) found that gay kinship did not supplant what gays in California described as their "blood" relatives, but urban gays did suggest that procreation was not the only way a family could be made. Lisette and her friends did not draw on kin terminology in such prominent ways, yet, like many urban gays in Weston's research, the intimacies between friends often surpassed those shared by family.[2]

In this chapter, I explore how Lisette, Osvaldo, and their friends and lovers sought to distance themselves from queer enclaves because of what they described as "social decline." In part, their harsh reaction to the changes they described reflected how they had also had to acquire hard currency in ways that challenged their values and beliefs—through intimate relationships, Cubans living abroad, foreigners, and black markets. I highlight how the economic crisis forced Lisette and Osvaldo to embrace contradictions between their critical attitudes toward sexual commodification and their increasingly strategic personal relationships. In defending their perspectives about appropriate forms of labor and love, they challenged homophobic ideas that equated homosexuality with criminality and impropriety. Yet, at the same time, their appeals to decency often drew on and perpetuated forms of racial, urban, and gender privilege. Through a snapshot of two years in the life of the siblings' household, we witness how Lisette's and Osvaldo's efforts to distance themselves from the increasing pull of market relations and self-interest ultimately prove futile.

EASY MONEY

One afternoon we sat at the kitchen table, eating chorizo with yellow rice, when the conversation turned to sex workers, as it often did. "They don't want to work," Lisette said. "Cuba is one of the few places where you can live without really working. They just make $20 here and there and they have enough to last them a couple of weeks. Ten dollars can take care of a lot of things in Cuba." When I asked why some young men worked as *pingueros,* and others found legitimate jobs, Osvaldo said, "They don't have the head for it. They're not smart enough or they don't want to work. They're lazy. They can earn in one night with a *yuma* what I earn in two months. They don't want to sacrifice." Osvaldo's boyfriend agreed. Pedro explained that he had participated in a group of psychology students at the University of Havana that conducted an unpublished investigation on *jineterismo.* After interviewing nearly fifty young hustlers, they found that the majority cited the absence of high paying jobs as the inspiration to turn to the sex trade. "Hustlers could make in one night what they would make in a year working for the state," Pedro said. "The situation is impossible. They want things and have no way of getting them." Similarly, Dalia told us about two of her female cousins who had worked as *jineteras* and married Italian men. Her cousins could not imagine why Dalia would refuse to have sex for money when she had unlimited access to foreign tourists at a resort where she worked. "I would have a van full of foreigners," Dalia said, "and my cousins would tell me, 'Just go with one of them to earn $300!' But why have sex with them when I'm smart and can work for my pay and the tourists will leave me good tips without the sex?"

Lisette, Osvaldo, and their partners disparaged the motives and work ethic of hustlers, but not their risqué sexual behavior. Notably, their condemnation did not reflect a moral judgment about promiscuity; both siblings exercised a certain degree of licentiousness in their own sexual lives.[3] This distinction was important because it suggested that they did not seek to reinforce traditional standards of respectability typical throughout the Caribbean, such as sexual restraint and formal marriage (Freeman 2007).[4] Likewise, Lisette and Osvaldo included friends and neighbors who engaged in sex work in their social circle, and Osvaldo treated a few *pingueros* in the neighborhood for sexually transmitted diseases when they felt embarrassed to go to the clinic. Instead of excluding sex workers from their personal social circles, their criticism perpetuated the notions that affection and desire should remain untainted by material interests, despite the fact that their own relationships often involved negotiations over housing, salaries, and work outside the home.

While Lisette and Osvaldo did not judge sex workers for acting outside of the bounds of traditional sexual decorum, like many working- and middle-class gays they drew on discourses of industriousness to accuse sex workers of suffering from a lax work ethic. Ironically, government leaders had historically used similar communist rhetoric to accuse homosexuals of turpitude and weakness. Rather than attack nonconforming gender and sexual populations directly, government leaders had often coded homophobic attacks through labor rhetoric that accused gays of being unfit for revolutionary duties or part of a lazy bourgeois intelligentsia. Lisette and Osvaldo appropriated discourses of respectability that had been used against them. Foucault has called this reverse discourse, or a process through which homosexuality has demanded its legitimacy often through the exact vocabulary by which it was stigmatized (Foucault 1990: 101). When applied to the Cuban case, the concept of reverse discourse cues us to the ways that homosexuals, who had long suffered from ideas about labor, drew on these same discourses to defend themselves.

Their reinvestment in socialist work ethics and ideas of self-sacrifice did not, however, indicate an uncritical embrace of the Cuban government. The siblings often expressed frustration over anachronistic policies that forbid privatized employment and wealth, given the dominance of gray and black markets in Havana. Raised by staunch communists, they belonged to a generation that had grown extremely cynical toward outdated political slogans. They had not witnessed capitalist exploitation firsthand and had suffered through the post-Soviet crisis when their adult lives were just beginning. They often expressed frustration that the Cuban government could be an obstacle to earning a living and wanted more opportunities to make money in a free market environment. Despite their cynicism toward the Cuban government, however, they maintained mainstream socialist ideas about what it meant to be decent and hard working.

Urban gays protested the inversion of cultural and economic capital and lamented how the crisis had devalued education and hard work. Lisette, Osvaldo, and their partners felt frustrated by growing income disparities as living standards were increasingly disconnected from labor (Espina Prieto 2001). They leveled their criticisms in an environment in which sex work easily surpassed earnings in legitimate state-run sectors. One sex worker would stand to earn ten times the salary of Lisette's household combined, through just one visit from a tourist. Urban gays recognized how post-Soviet poverty gave rise to the sex trade but resented how sex workers could access hard currency while young urban gays scraped together a living with reduced government subsidies. Working a few hours to make the equivalent of an annual salary seemed facile within a context in which many young urban gays like Lisette and Osvaldo had more casual notions about sex.

"NORMAL" SEXUALITIES

The siblings felt comfortable with their sexual identities; both claimed that they had always known that they were gay. Growing up, they had experimented with homoerotic relationships with neighbors and felt confident in their sexual prowess. Lisette prided herself on the fact that she had never had sex with a man. Her friends admired Lisette's strong sense of her lesbian identity, and she delighted in the fact that she had inspired a number of her former girlfriends to "become lesbians" by introducing them to same-sex eroticism and love. With great self-satisfaction, Lisette told me how she had seduced Dalia before they'd even met. A mutual friend had introduced them over the phone, and after three weeks of sweet talking Dalia, Lisette took the three-hour bus trip to see Dalia in her hometown. According to Lisette, the day she arrived they had sex, and two days later, Dalia told her parents that she was a lesbian and moved to Havana to live with Lisette. "That's how we do it in Cuba," Lisette told me. "Women get right down to business." She often described herself as a lesbian *normal*, which meant that she shunned strict butch and femme roles. She and her friends often gossiped about how difficult it would be to maintain a relationship with a butch woman who would not let her more feminine partner touch her in bed. "They just make them lie there, while the masculine one does everything," Lisette often complained. She and her friends implied that their style—not too masculine or too feminine—and their sexual preference for women who were similar made their lesbianism more contemporary.

Figure 2.1. A group of lesbians gather at a friend's house.

Lisette and her peers were proud of their lesbian identities, which challenged heteronormative sexual ideals, but were critical of gender nonconformity in which women performed masculine styles of dress and demeanor.[5] Lisette, slightly darker than her brother with kinky hair, also openly discussed her sexual preference for light-skinned women—white, olive, and light brown—over *negras*. In her analysis of oral histories among "women who love women," Carrie Hamilton identifies a similar prejudice against *mujeres fuertes* (strong women) that often manifested itself along the lines of race and social class. Hamilton argues that this bias reflected an internalization of institutionalized homophobia, which often targeted masculine looking women. Also, she found that women who had been exposed to transnational models of feminism and lesbianism were more likely to eroticize sameness and be suspicious toward gender roles among lesbians (2012: 189). Lisette's strong feelings about what comprised "normal" lesbian sexuality were inflected by certain racial and class distinctions, which encouraged her to seek out similarities rather than differences.

Osvaldo often embraced the identity of the effeminate gay *pasivo*, and he did not discriminate when it came to his lovers' skin color. While not the only way that men interpreted homoeroticism in Cuba, the notion of the *activo* (active/insertive) and *pasivo* (passive/receptive) male sexual partners continued to have a strong presence in sexual encounters.[6] Osvaldo adhered to a perspective similar to gay Cuban author Reinaldo Arenas, who criticized same-sex relationships in the United States for straying away from a masculine and feminine model. "The ideal in any sexual relationship," Arenas wrote, "is to find our opposite" (Arenas 1992: 133).[7] Like his sister, Osvaldo took satisfaction in his ability to sexually arouse heterosexuals and win their attention, but unlike Lisette, Osvaldo did not seek to transform the men through the homoerotic encounter. Heterosexual masculinity was a key component of Osvaldo's desire for men, hence he did not wish to uncover or incite a gay identity beneath their heterosexual façade. Likewise, racial differences rather than similarities could become part of the erotic attraction.

Osvaldo challenged the idea that his masculine counterparts were more shrewd or powerful than he. In the stories Osvaldo told about his sexual adventures, he often appeared as the powerful seducer of heterosexual men. One evening, Osvaldo, wearing his signature lime green bikini briefs, washed dishes and told me about his years of military service. "I was the boss," he said, "and all the men were having sex. We'd do it in my office, the sugar cane fields, or on *guardia* (overnight shifts) when no one was around." Osvaldo continued:

> One time I saw a guy having sex with a goat. You know how military pants have those deep pockets on the side? Well, he would put the goat's hooves into the pockets on the side of his pants so the goat would wiggle and try to get free. That motion would make him ejaculate. When the guy realized that I was watching, he got really scared.

Osvaldo's description of military service disrupts the idea that as the *pasivo* he lacked power, while also challenging the dominant representation of effeminate men as the victims of militaristic revolutionary campaigns. His narrative encourages us to reconsider the homoerotic practices that existed within the Cuban military, rather than to only see the military as a force that oppressed and imprisoned gay men excluded from service.

The siblings' perspectives regarding their sexual desires led them to distrust the claims of male sex workers who maintained that they were heterosexual.[8] "I physically cannot get an erection with a woman," Osvaldo often said. "If a *pinguero* gets hard with a man, he has some desire." Other urban gays also claimed that male sex workers were hiding homosexual desires, but often debated the relationship between homoerotic sexual practice and identity. In one typical exchange, Alberto, a dark-skinned thirty-two-year-old gay family doctor, insisted that any man who had sex with men had to be gay. Osvaldo agreed that the men had to have desire to maintain an erection but did not feel that this desire qualified him as gay. Osvaldo suggested that a man could have sex with other men and still be straight (*cheo*) as long as he was the penetrating partner (*activo*). Alberto challenged these categories:

> I can't have sex with a woman because I'm gay, it doesn't work.
> [The *pingueros*] must have some desire that makes them bisexual,
> at least. *Bugarrón, pinguero*, they're all gay. They call themselves
> this or that or say they are just doing it for the money, but how
> can a man get an erection for money? He has to feel something; he
> has to have some desire. They just don't want to admit it.

I sensed Alberto resented how the men could maintain heteronormative privilege while enjoying homoerotic relationships. Whereas he lost family support once he revealed his gay identity, heterosexually identified men who had sex with men could enjoy a range of sexual experiences while preserving their standing within gender hierarchies. Alberto's reaction also reflected his position as a doctor influenced by medico-scientific categories of homo- and bisexuality onto same-sex practices. In addition, Alberto tended to be attracted to other dark skinned, gay-identified men rather than heterosexuals, so the idea of finding his "opposite" played less of a role than it did for Osvaldo. As their disagreement suggests, money could simultaneously be interpreted as a cover for real homoerotic desire or the impetus to feign desire in order to access cash—in either case, they both believed that what was once simple, physical attraction had been distorted by the new market economy.

Ironically, Osvaldo's partner Pedro, like many of the *pingueros* they criticized, struggled to maintain a "heterosexual image," as he described it. In addition to his relationship with Osvaldo, he sustained romantic relationships with a young woman at the university and one in his hometown. Osvaldo often expressed resentment regarding the arrangement, but told me that he consented because Pedro was younger and handsome. Commonly described as *tapando la letra*—literally to cover the letter, or hide one's sexual identity—Pedro insisted that he was not hiding anything and instead described himself as *bisexual*. Whenever Pedro would describe himself as *bisexual*, however, Osvaldo was quick to remind him that he failed to achieve an erection during sexual encounters with women. Osvaldo often retold the story of their first encounter to emphasize that he was the true object of Pedro's desire. They had met at a film matinee, when Osvaldo sat down and started rubbing Pedro's leg. "We went to a park and talked for a while, but he was crazy to fuck," Osvaldo said smiling at Pedro, "So we ended up fucking in the stairwell under his aunt's house." Pedro seemed embarrassed by this story and averted his eyes as Osvaldo talked. Even after they had been together a year and purchased commitment rings, Pedro refused to take photographs with Osvaldo for fear that people could tell that they were partners.

I found that many of Lisette's lesbian friends similarly distrusted female sex workers who claimed a bisexual or lesbian identity, but for the opposite reasons to those of urban gay men who remained suspicious of male hustlers. Rather than an indication of suppressed homosexuality, lesbians often questioned the true desires of women who discovered lesbianism through the sex trade. For example, Clara, a white twenty-two-year-old with waist-length black hair and bright green eyes, was a close friend who lived in Lisette's neighborhood. She identified as heterosexual when she began working with tourists, but after a number of male tourists hired her to perform in threesomes, she discovered that she could experience sexual pleasure with women and began to identify as "*bisexual.*"[9] She agreed to quit the sex trade after she met a young, attractive white lesbian willing to support her financially. After two years, an Italian ex-client invited Clara to a beach resort, and she accepted against her girlfriend's wishes. Lisette told me that she had expected this to happen. "This guy is young and handsome," Lisette said, "Clara likes him, and she's using the money as an excuse to cheat. Once they've been in that world, they always fall back on it." Authentic lesbianism emerged as a form of selfhood into which one was born, not an identity discovered through the sex trade. Whereas true same-sex love could be inspired by the seduction of lesbians, as was the case with Lisette and Dalia, it could not arise from market forces.

In part, the mistrust of women who had worked in the sex trade and now maintained homoerotic relationships also reflected unease about *bisexualidad* (bisexuality), which many Cubans associated with the introduction of commodified sex.[10] The absence of a discussion about *bisexual* identities in the comprehensive works by scholars of male homosexuality in Cuba such as Ian Lumsden (1996) and Marvin Leiner (1994) indicates that Cubans were not using the term *bisexual* in the early nineties. The link between sex tourism and *bisexualidad* means that people who engaged in erotic encounters with both men and women before the early nineties did not adopt the label. Many gays described *bisexual* identified Cubans as hiding behind the label to avoid the loss of privilege associated with identifying as gay.

While heteromasculinity maintained its privileged place at the top of the social hierarchy, urban gays like Lisette and Osvaldo found ways to creatively twist these systems to enhance their own personal and erotic power. Unlike popular perceptions of the victimized male *pasivo* or the shunned lesbian, they described their sexualities as a source of their charisma and influence over others, even heterosexuals. Osvaldo's ability to entice straight men to participate in anonymous sex and Lisette's power to transform heterosexual women into lesbians served as evidence of their confidence. Yet the extent to which they could challenge their place in sexual hierarchies was limited, particularly for Lisette, who faced gendered constraints. In particular, Lisette and her friends felt comfortable questioning sexual norms but also policed one another's gender performativity and reinforced racial endogamy by rejecting lesbians who were dark skinned or "too masculine." Whereas men could cross gendered and racial boundaries and adopt a *pasivo* gay identity, women who too radically transgressed gendered norms were considered failed "men" or *machos*. Hence, women were often confined to gendered norms and racialized notions of attractiveness even among other lesbians.

THE DECLINE OF *EL AMBIENTE*

Like most other gays in Havana, the siblings' social lives consisted of going to the Malecón on the weekends or, if they had cash to spend, attending underground gay parties or drag shows hosted in someone's home. Yet, as they struggled with an explosion of commodified sex and low-level violence in Havana's queer nightlife, they described a decline in the class of people that comprised Havana's queer *ambiente* and slowed their involvement. As queer public nightlife became associated with sex tourism, many homosexuals distanced themselves from the sexual subculture of the city (Sierra Madero 2006: 101). One night, sitting on the Malecón, a *pinguero* punched an older gay man in the face. The police detained the young hustler and disbanded the gathering. On the way home, Lisette complained about the loss of social space for what she referred to as "respectable gays." "We used to have places to go, nice places," she said. "When I was younger we all used to go to these teahouses, you'd stare at someone and then maybe talk or flirt. It was much more civilized." Likewise, Osvaldo nostalgically characterized Havana's queer enclaves as less vicious before the rise of the sex trade. "Now, everyone is trying to get something out of each other," he said. "They compete for the attention of the tourists. The whole attitude used to be freer. It didn't matter what clothes you wore or how much money you had. Everyone was just out to have a good time." The siblings described how hustlers from the provinces used tightly knit gay social worlds for profit, often disrespecting gays and disrupting otherwise calm queer social settings.

Although the changing ambiance affected both gay men and women, many lesbians felt more vulnerable to the physical violence of straight hustlers. Lisette's comments about the lack of "civilization" reflected a common sentiment among her female friends, across the color spectrum, who told me that they had become too scared to sit down on the Malecón. My familiarity with the hustlers often inspired comments, and Lisette would entertain her friends by telling them how a "delinquent" would approach us, and she would prepare to run, while I greeted him like an old friend. Lesbians had a separate party circuit, known as the *fiestas de las mujeres* (women's parties), that often took place in cramped living rooms with a small stereo playing music. The parties lacked the cosmopolitan flare of the more professional gay parties, often held outdoors with a live deejay. Many lesbians described the women's parties as "*de nivel muy bajo* (low class)" and complained of the constant brawls that broke out. Lisette, in particular, warned me that when "the *hombres* (masculine women) start drinking, they're worse than men." Although the lesbian gatherings were less influenced by the influx of foreign tourism and sex workers, many women did not see them as a sufficient alternative to hangouts like the Malecón.

In addition to the changing dynamics in queer enclaves, Osvaldo and Pedro reported problems with police who confused them for sex workers. According to Osvaldo, police had a difficult time distinguishing male sex workers from law-abiding homosexuals. In order to attract foreign gay clients, hustlers had appropriated queer stylistic codes, such as tight-fitting jeans, snug polyester T-shirts, and designer tennis shoes. Osvaldo told me about a police crackdown on queer nightly gatherings that had begun in March 2007, when officers detained Osvaldo outside the Payret movie theater, a cruising spot for *pingueros*. Police officers transported him to a makeshift holding cell on the first floor of an abandoned building that had been established to deal with the overflow of arrests during the sweeps. Osvaldo told me that he recognized a number of people being held, including two pingueros and a *travesti* neighbor that lived on his block. After Osvaldo spent three hours in jail, his arresting officer apologized. Outraged, Osvaldo scolded him for wasting his time. In part, Osvaldo's outraged response was also informed by his whiteness. Unlike his black peers, who routinely experienced police stops for their identification cards, Osvaldo was unaccustomed to detentions and thought that police should recognize him as a proper, hard-working citizen. Later, making light of his detention, he told me, "I was looking so good, so hot, and so young with my tight jeans and brand new shirt that the police thought I was a hustler. They didn't realize I was just a normal fag with a job!"

Unwanted propositions from tourists also made Osvaldo and his gay male friends uneasy about the informal nightly gatherings in Vedado and Centro Habana. Many gays told me that they felt humiliated when foreign tourists assumed that they were sex workers because prostitution had become so rampant. For instance, Juan, a childhood friend of Osvaldo's, was a twenty-seven-year-old gay geneticist with ecru-colored skin who had won a research fellowship to Western Europe. A number of times foreign tourists on the Malecón had offered him money for sex, even after he explained that he was a scientist. One time, a prominent sixty-year-old European doctor visiting Havana for a conference had propositioned Juan as he showed him around the Malecón. Juan felt the advance was an awkward by-product of perceptions about Cuba. "I'm not up for the *lucha* (struggle/hustle)," he said, laughing. "Since I didn't take the deal, now the doctor wants me to find him boys. I'm supposed to make sure he doesn't get ripped off." We laughed at the thought of studious, soft-spoken Juan acting as a bodyguard to ensure that the hustlers didn't run off with the doctor's money.

For some urban gay men, artistic and cultural events offered an alternative to the informal nightlife in Havana. Their participation allowed them to contrast their "cultured" sensibilities against those of sex workers. Osvaldo often attended the ballet, theater, art openings, and film festivals, made affordable through state subsidies. When I attended the premiere of the ballet *Romeo and Juliet*, Osvaldo's gay acquaintances packed the auditorium. He proudly pointed out the men he had slept with over the years. I recognized a few from the Malecón, but most circulated in what they described as more "cultured" social worlds, echoing the split that La Fountain-Stokes (2002) identified between respectable gays in the arts and those who participated in the sex trade. Even though a number of Osvaldo's lovers who circulated in the arts were *mulato* or darker, traditional discourses typically associated high culture with whiteness and being "civilized" and blackness with street culture and *"folclórico,"* the racially tinged term that many Cubans, including Osvaldo and his friends, used to refer to African-based spiritual practices. Osvaldo and his peers believed that the government had made traditionally highbrow culture populist. Since no one was priced out of attendance, participation in cultural events stood as a democratic measure of decorum. Hence, urban gays who longed for a "civilized" queer social world benefited from the birth of official rhetoric celebrating queer intellectual and artistic production. Artistic and cultural arenas had historically served as sanctuaries for gay intellectuals, artists, and audiences and continued to do so in the post-Soviet era.[11]

FOSTERING INSTRUMENTAL FRIENDSHIPS

Normally, Lisette and her peers sharply criticized Cubans who hustled foreigners for what many urban gays described as "easy money." Like many urban gay men and women in their twenties and thirties, they strained to keep their private lives separate from the rampant rise of commodified sex and raffish behavior. Yet, even as they criticized the hustlers, I was struck by how easily they could play into tourist expectations for a possible payoff. One scorching weekend at Mi Cayito, the gay beach near Havana, I introduced Lisette and Dalia to a group of wealthy gay men from Los Angeles that I had met on the Malecón. Adept at dealing with well-to-do foreigners from her stint as a server at a tourist resort, Dalia invited them over for an "authentic Cuban barbeque." On our way home, as the Chevy rumbled past green rolling hills and the sea, Dalia explained her thinking, "You never ask them for anything. At the resort, I would even refuse tips from one Canadian couple and eventually they came to like me so much, they offered to adopt me and take me out of the country. If you convince foreigners that you are not after their money, they will really want to take care of you."

The next night, Dalia took charge, ordering Lisette to set up the kitchen table in the backyard, next to the cage of squealing pigs. Osvaldo barbequed his month's salary in pork and chicken. Pedro traded in a favor with a neighbor who worked at the Cohiba factory for black market cigars. They filled the washing machine with sodas and I bought bottles of high-end rum. They pulled out the dominoes and replaced Elton John with salsa music. Upon the tourists' arrival, Dalia offered the men postcards of Cuba to take home as keepsakes.

Unaware of the differences between the Malecón and the less commodified spaces of gay friendship, the tourists treated the barbeque like any other event in Havana's gay nightlife. Assuming that all gays were part of the same social scene, the tourists invited four of their Cuban "boyfriends" to attend. Although Dalia and Lisette were accustomed to socializing with *pingueros* in queer public gatherings, their presence at the house created an awkward tension. Everyone had to keep up the façade that the hustlers were gay to respect the relationships that the young men had established with their foreign clients. In the kitchen, Lisette confessed to me that she felt that the young hustlers were *muy bajo* (low-class) and untrustworthy.[12] From her perspective, they could not leave soon enough. Adding to the confusion, Lisette's mom was shocked by the tourists' unabashed behavior and incessantly asked if they were U.S. spies. "No Mom," Lisette finally told her, "They're just fags; that's why they're so weird."

The show of wealth more generally put the gay Cubans that Lisette had invited in an awkward position. One of the tourists, a handsome white forty-five-year-old editor, bet $40 on a game of dominoes—more money than the entire family earned in a month. From the tourists' perspective, living *la vida loca*, as they called it, meant that Cubans were generally for sale. For instance, Juan, the young geneticist, felt especially confused when Robert, a fifty-year-old entertainment lawyer, expressed an interest in him. Even after I explained that Juan only dated Cubans, Robert insisted that he did not need sex but felt a real connection and wanted to help him. Robert offered him a pair of Gucci loafers and $50. For weeks afterward, Juan joked with me about how he had been treated like a hustler.

The barbeque exemplified an impulse to perform *cubanidad*, or authentic Cuban culture, for wealthy foreigners and reflected how many young urban gays raised in socialist Cuba were caught between the ideals of industriousness and the realities of the post-Soviet economy. Despite their earnest efforts to mitigate the impact of the new mixed market, many urban gays engaged in the very types of tactical relationships that they belittled. While I never directly asked my friends what motivated the barbeque, at the time it seemed too obvious to question. It is possible that they did not know specifically what their welcoming embrace of the wealthy gay tourists could garner. In general, an ongoing friendship meant that foreigners would offer gifts or cash when they returned to Cuba.

Dalia, in particular, had been trained in the forms of "niceness" and friendship required by the service sector through her experiences in tourism.[13] While she and her peers sought to delineate between private authentic affection and commodified forms of intimacy in the marketplace, her work in tourism had reshaped her subjectivity, readying her to interact with foreigners in particular ways that would inspire patronage. These transactions were not limited to the hotel, resort, or restaurant but manifested in the "private" domestic life of her gay family. Indeed, by inviting the men into their home, Dalia and the others provided an amicable intimacy that the travelers would recognize and appreciate. If the foreigners felt at home with Lisette and Osvaldo, they were likely to remember them fondly and include them in their future itineraries. While no one articulated a specific payoff, there was an implicit understanding that rich friends would come in handy.

Hearing Dalia's approach to foreigners—that to inspire their generosity, you never ask for anything—definitely brought to mind my own relationship with the siblings, their lovers, and their friends. While I might have been more sensitive to the realities of urban gay life than the tourists from Los Angeles, my friendships were no more immune to instrumentalism. One of the reasons I felt so comfortable with Lisette and Osvaldo was that, unlike many of the sex workers whom I came to know, demands for money or goods were fewer and more subtle. In general, they were extremely generous and our friendship felt reciprocal. Likewise, I engaged in the same contradictions that my friends did by delineating between authentic and strategic intimacies, while constantly blurring these boundaries in practice. Our friendship could be described as instrumental on both ends as they gained access to currency and goods, while I gained access to life stories and experiences. Yet, because this trade was accompanied by sincere affection on my part these strategic aspects were downplayed. The coexistence of instrumental and authentic affections alongside our ongoing attempts to discern between these categories spoke to the entrenchment of cultural ideologies of intimacy within my own thinking as well as that of my friends.

TACTICAL SEX WITH FOREIGNERS

As the barbeque illustrates, lesbians and gay men occasionally initiated strategic friendships with foreigners, but more striking were times when gays who criticized sexual commodification themselves engaged in sexual relationships with tourists for hard currency. One night on the Malecón, Dalia and Lisette met two Mexican lesbians who invited them to dinner. One of the women offered Dalia $100 to travel to a beach resort for the weekend and sleep with her. At first, Lisette agreed to the arrangement and Dalia made plans to go with the woman. The day before their trip, however, Lisette decided that she was no longer comfortable with the idea; in addition to feeling jealous, she viewed the affair as a lapse in values. Dalia insisted, and a heated fight ensued. Although Dalia agreed to cancel, the incident remained a touchy issue in their relationship.

I wondered how Dalia had rationalized her desire to sleep with the Mexican tourist after describing Cubans who engaged in commodified sex as low class, but it felt inappropriate to ask her. Lisette had told me the story, and I worried that both Dalia and I would feel embarrassed if I questioned her because it would mean disrupting the self-image that she had presented to me. After spending time with Dalia, I could imagine a few ways that she might justify the affair. It seemed easier to differentiate herself from *jineteras* because it would be a one-time act rather than a way to make a living. Similarly, commodified relationships between women were rarer and therefore did not fit the dominant stereotypes that people associated with sex tourism. It was possible also that she was attracted to the woman, flattered by the attention, and excited about the possibility of spending time in a luxury resort. The money had served as an excuse to overstep the bounds of her otherwise monogamous relationship with Lisette.

It was the possibility of Dalia's mutual attraction to the tourist that seemed to spark Lisette's indignation. If Dalia had felt no attraction to the woman, she would simply have refused. The inconsistencies in Dalia's perspective on tactical sex led Lisette to question Dalia's true feelings. The conflict brought up particularly strong anxieties for Lisette because her last girlfriend had emigrated through an invitation from a lesbian living in Switzerland. Reflecting on her past relationship, Lisette told me, "She was the love of my life. She was always crazy to get out [of Cuba] and I would never stand in the way of that. We never fought; we always understood and trusted each other. But I wasn't going to stop (*frenar*) her from what she wanted." Lisette and her ex-girlfriend remained close, and every time the woman returned to Cuba she showered Lisette with money and expensive gifts. While Lisette had supported her ex-girlfriend's decision to leave Cuba, the experience had left her anxious about being abandoned.

The option to engage in sexual relationships for money or goods was so pervasive in Havana that some, like Dalia, considered partaking when the opportunity presented itself, despite their critical attitudes toward the sex trade. For instance, Lisette's neighbor Javier reported a similar proposition from a tourist that led him to experiment with strategic sex. Javier was an olive-skinned, wire-thin, gay eighteen-year-old with black hair and deep-set brown eyes who shared a cramped two bedroom with his grandmother, aunt, uncle, sister, a newborn nephew, and three young cousins. A regular at Lisette and Osvaldo's, he planted himself in their kitchen every afternoon, smoking cigarettes and helping Lisette cook and clean. When boredom prevailed, Lisette would dress Javier in women's clothing, apply make-up, and encourage him to lip-sync to her favorite Celine Dion album. In the mornings, he attended a continuation high school—a project that he believed Fidel Castro had started for young people "who don't work or study, to channel their energies into something useful." Javier characterized the $4 he received monthly for attending continuation school as "enough to buy a pizza, a soda, a ham sandwich, *or* a stick of deodorant."

Javier often told me that the *pingueros* at his school bullied him, and he felt pressured to live up to impossible material standards set by sex workers. "I've been marked down in school for wearing a baseball cap in class," Javier told me. "But I wear a cap because I don't have the money to buy shampoo and hair gel. I would be embarrassed with my hair like this. All those *pingueros* on their cell phones, with new clothes, hair gel, and cologne. I'd rather keep it on and get bad grades." Perhaps a product of envy, he often described *pingueros* as materialistic and superficial. Yet once he had sex with an older white Canadian tourist for a possible payoff. He admitted that he did not find the man attractive, despite his preference for older men, and expected the man to give him money or gifts. He told me:

> We did sexual things, but not penetration or anything. He gave me $10 to get a car home and two shirts and an electric shaving kit. I haven't gone with foreigners again. I didn't like being with him. I felt bad. It wasn't me. I wasn't ashamed, because no one had seen. I kept thinking, "What am I doing?" It just wasn't me.

The anonymity of the experience prevented Javier from feeling the shame he associated with transgressing the social border between sex workers and gays. Despite Javier's whiteness, which often protected young Cubans from being seen as sex workers, the police had stopped him when he was with the tourist and demanded to see his identification, which had left Javier extremely nervous. Ultimately, his experience allowed him to craft his identity in opposition to *pingueros*, declaring: "It just wasn't me." Javier's boundary crossing denoted the realities of poverty and demonstrated the extent to which the option of tactical sex permeated gay urban life.

Some lesbians who adamantly criticized sex workers also participated in strategic sexual relationships with foreigners. The most striking example of this contradiction was Amanda, an attractive, bronzed olive-complexioned twenty-one-year-old lesbian computer student, who had originally introduced me to Lisette. Amanda vocally criticized the "trash on the Malecón" and warned me about *pingueros* "invading" Cuba's gay nightlife. At one point, she and I fell into an intense argument because I maintained friendships with *pingueros* and *jineteras* that she insisted were "dangerous." "You can't see that they are bad people because you're a foreigner," she told me, "but I can see what they're up to and I don't think it's right for you to be hanging out with them." For Amanda, I belonged to an upstanding social world because I was white, a student, and a foreigner, making my relationship with the marginal elements of Havana's queer enclaves a lapse in social boundaries. Yet, less than one year after our argument, Amanda met and married a young Italian male tourist and emigrated. After a few months in Florence, Amanda's new husband discovered her in bed with a woman and demanded a divorce. Even after marrying a man for emigration—the goal of many *jineteras* in Havana—Amanda would never describe herself as a *jinetera*. Amanda maintained the divisions between decent, hard-working gays and the delinquents preying on queer enclaves even after she donned a heterosexual persona to marry a foreigner.

As for lesbians who stayed on the island, some of the most financially successful received support from abroad, often through relationships with foreign men. For example, Lidia, a trim twenty-three-year-old with chestnut hair and milky skin, owned a number of luxury items like a cell phone and a car. She had worked briefly in the sex trade and invested her earnings in a car, which she rented to tourists for $40 a day. Lidia described her forays into the sex trade as a short-term sacrifice for a longer-term business investment. While some like Lidia worked briefly in the sex trade, others maintained ongoing relationships with foreigners. Always decked out in gold and emeralds, Josefina, a chubby twenty-nine-year-old lesbian, had lily white skin and pink cheeks. She always picked up the tab with friends, plucking dollars from a wad of cash as wide as a toilet paper roll that she carried in her denim fanny pack. Her money came from a Spanish businessman with whom she had a four-year relationship. They had a three-year-old son who lived with Josefina and her girlfriend, while the man lived in Madrid with his wife and children. "How did you meet him?" I asked her. "Not *jineteando*," she answered quickly and laughed. Since we had only recently met, it seemed important for her to disavow *jineterismo*, acknowledging that I would likely view her relationship with the Spaniard through that lens. "He was doing business with my brother, who introduced us," Josefina clarified. Even though they would never consider themselves *jineteras*, some prosperous lesbians secured their living through relationships with foreign men.

In a similar vein, *travestis* who consistently relied on sex work to earn hard currency would similarly distinguish between their work and hustling and criticize what they saw as the materialism and superficiality that had spawned the sex trade. Cooking dinner with Dulce, a twenty-two-year-old *travesti* with long black hair and fawn colored skin, in Lisette's kitchen, I chopped an onion as she hunched over a pressure cooker full of kidney beans. Dulce told me that her father had kicked her out when she was fifteen and she had moved in with her great-grandmother, who had died and left her the house. Her father could not accept that she was a *travesti*. "It was a total shock because I had always been a Daddy's boy," she told me. "He wanted me to be a *gay normal*, a gay who didn't dress like a girl or anything like that." Embedded within her father's discomfort with *trav-*

estis was, ironically, a tolerance for certain types of homosexuality that qualified as "normal," along with the stigma of *travestismo*.

Dulce had previously held a state job at a gas station, but once she began cross-dressing she felt too uncomfortable to return. She described herself as uninterested in the flashy spectacle of *travesti* drag competitions and private gay parties replete with transnational queer tourists. Dulce advocated for her *travesti* identity but remained critical of sex work. One Sunday morning, Dulce sat on the edge of her bed and told me that she had risked arrest the night before to earn $20 by performing fellatio on an Italian tourist. "I'm not prostituting myself or hustling," she said. "From my perspective I haven't done either. I'm *luchando* (struggling). Struggling to survive, struggling to get ahead, do you understand me?" Dulce continued:

> If I had another way to make income, I wouldn't (*jinetear*) any more. There are people that yes, they like it. They like to go out every night, I don't. I prefer the tranquility of my house, so I only do it when I need some money, when I'm totally broke.

Distinguishing herself from what she saw as more materialistic hustlers by stating that she only goes out when she needs to, Dulce emphasized that she preferred to live a "normal" life, staying home with her boyfriend and avoiding delinquency.

The inherent contradictions of young gay men, lesbians, and *travestis* engaging in strategic sexual relationships with foreigners even as they criticized the sex trade reflected how personal values continued to be informed by preexisting socialist norms despite the fact that everyday realities of the post-Soviet crisis made these realities an impossibility. Whereas communism had promoted egalitarianism and cultural over financial capital, post-Soviet socialism had fractured this system and created an uncertain reorganization of social and sexual classes. The economic transition represented a break in preexisting social hierarchies, and those who rejected socialist values and cultural investments could prosper. Sex work became a dominant theme with which urban gays could contrast their own beliefs and experiences against others.

REINSCRIBING SOCIAL HIERARCHIES

I wondered why Osvaldo and Pedro were not more sympathetic to the structural disadvantages that could lead young Cubans to sex work. Although urban gays did not comment on race directly in their criticism of sex workers, they often overlooked how their skin color afforded them greater opportunities in the new mixed market. The leisure industry, especially in the Caribbean, is organized around gendered and racialized sexual constructions, and racial-ethnic profiles play a tremendous role in one's position within tourist economies.[14] "How did you get a job that pays in dollars?" I asked, hoping to understand their thinking. Osvaldo said:

> You have to know someone to get a job that pays in dollars. We call it a *palanca* (lever), the thing you use to shift your car. For instance, my friend had my job before me, and when he quit, he offered me his position. There was no application process; it's all about who you know. On top of that, there aren't many jobs that earn dollars here.

Despite their sensitivity to how job security rested on personal networks, lighter-skinned and white urban gays often ignored the reasons why some could remain within the boundaries of "decent labor." Scholars of Cuban tourism have noted the absence of darker-skinned Cubans in positions such as the front desk at hotels, where they would have direct contact with foreigners. (Cuban workers in Havana's tourist industry that I interviewed identified this trend as a by-product of the foreigners' preference for white staff.) Black Cubans often worked in lower-paid industry jobs, including state-run hotels for Cubans, as performers in cultural shows, or as maintenance, security, and hotel kitchen staff. Lighter-skinned and white gay critics often failed to account for the realities of occupational segregation that would make legal positions within the tourist economy all the more difficult for dark-skinned Cubans to secure.

In a similar vein, Cubans did not assume that white and lighter-skinned lesbians who engaged in tactical sexual relationships with foreign men were *jineteras* because they didn't embody the popular stereotype of the Cuban *mulata*. Within Cuban popular culture, relationships between white foreign men and darker-skinned Cuban women were automatically perceived as motivated by money or access to immigration, despite the cultural and educational background of the couple.[15] The lesbians I spoke to were better able to disavow a sex worker identity because they imagined *jineteras* as poorer, darker, and less educated than themselves, even though they admitted that the relationships with foreign men departed from their "true" homoerotic desires.

In addition to perpetuating racial inequalities endemic to the new mixed market economy, Lisette, Osvaldo, and their friends also reincarnated urban and rural divides to attack the provincialism of sex workers from the countryside. Typical of urban gays, they often suggested that Cubans from the provinces lacked intelligence and culture. These stereotypes were especially pronounced with stories about *Orientales,* Cubans from the Eastern provinces who have historically migrated to Havana in search of employment. In one striking example, Lisette insisted that boys from the countryside developed larger penises by "rehearsing" sexual intercourse with animals when women were scarce. Her lesbian friends in the room all agreed that bestiality "made it grow." As evidence, Lisette offered a childhood story about Osvaldo's trip to the Eastern provinces. "Osvaldo went one summer," she said. "My cousin invited him to have sex with some of their sheep, but he didn't do it. My brother, being from [Havana], had more education, he knew better." She maintained that men in the countryside had limited access to women and that this drove them to bestiality. Lisette's comments were emblematic of tropes of sexual perversion that gays recounted about migrants, often contrasting the civilization of urban queers to the ignorance of *guajiros* (country folk). The provinces, which revolutionary leaders in the 1960s had represented as a space of masculinity that could purge homosexual tendencies from the national body, were remade as sites of sexual perversion. Circulating tropes of rural ignorance, gay narrators could exert ownership over an urban landscape within which they held a marginal presence.

While some lesbians and gay men negotiated relationships with foreigners while maintaining their distance from sex worker identities, other queer Cubans were structurally positioned to rely on the sex trade. In particular, *travestis* had difficulty securing state employment due to homophobia, and their ongoing association with prostitution often led to greater police harassment. Cuban *travestis* had gained visibility during the 1990s yet continued to face tremendous discrimination and limited career options. During my research, the National Center for Sexual Education (CENESEX) had established *travesti* employment training programs, but the results of these efforts were slow coming. Many *travestis* dropped out of school due to harassment and found it difficult to hold jobs in state-run industries, where they often faced hostile coworkers. If they stayed within their residential neighborhoods and out of tourist zones, police did not routinely bother them. However, once in tourist zones, they often faced censure under the vague "social danger" laws that empowered police crackdowns.

In certain respects, urban gays who criticized the sex trade reinforced post-Soviet class hierarchies. I maintain, however, that these criticisms did not arise from a place of pretentious indifference or recourse to dominant ideas about sexual respectability. My urban gay respondents did not exclude friends and neighbors who engaged in sex work from their social circle, but forms of racial, gender, and urban privilege were opaque in their accounts. By questioning sex workers' capacities to sacrifice hard work in pursuit of high-minded goals, urban gays leveraged their newly won cultural capital to unwittingly perpetuate structural inequalities.

BREAKING UP

When I visited in 2007, the house that had once been brimming with laughter and raucous antics had settled into an empty calm. Although Lisette and Dalia had worked to maintain a loving and supportive union, Lisette's financial dependence on Dalia made her insecure and needy, creating stress in the relationship. Although Dalia had encouraged Lisette to stop working, she often felt smothered by her care and attention. After two years together, Dalia began spending more time with her cousin, who had worked as a *jinetera*. Everyone emphasized that the woman was a threat to the relationship. "The thing is," Osvaldo said as he cut into an avocado, "The girl is not *really* Dalia's cousin, she's the ex-girlfriend of Dalia's male cousin. She is a *jinetera*, which means that she's slept with women before for money and maybe she's into it." For months, Lisette ignored the rumors that Dalia was having an affair. When it became too obvious to deny, Dalia and Lisette spent two days fighting and Dalia moved out of the house. Lisette was devastated. After her breakup, Lisette met an older, closeted lesbian who worked for the Communist Party and moved into her house in the affluent Miramar neighborhood. Through her girlfriend's connections, Lisette found work conducting background checks to verify the political allegiance of applicants for government jobs. The irony of determining the communist loyalties of other Cubans was not lost on Lisette. Aside from the constant traveling around Havana on a bicycle to interview the neighbors of applicants, however, she liked her job and the prestige it offered. The position paid in pesos and provided one meal a day, so Lisette was saving money to buy a hard drive to start a black market movie rental business that she hoped would bring in hard currency.

A month after Lisette moved out, Osvaldo returned home from work to discover that Pedro had left without warning. Osvaldo found out through mutual friends that Pedro had emigrated to the Dominican Republic through a letter of invitation from the family of his hometown girlfriend. After a few months, Pedro moved to Miami, where he was living with his girlfriend's parents and working at a car wash. When Osvaldo called, Pedro was overcome with paranoia that his girlfriend would find out about his past and he demanded the Osvaldo never contact him again. "He said that the life we had together was dead to him," Osvaldo said, explaining how being abandoned left him depressed and alone. Every time Osvaldo talked about Pedro, his face crumpled in frustration and he held back tears. He understood that Pedro wanted to leave Cuba, but Osvaldo felt deceived by Pedro's dishonesty and his rejection of their life together. "If you really love someone, how can you just forget about them?" Osvaldo asked. Osvaldo took on a second job as a medical lab technician as a way to keep his mind off Pedro. He told me that he grew tired of wasting his talents and college education as a low-skilled night watchman. He returned to working days at the lab and nights as a guard. He explained that one job was his passion and the other offered him a way to make ends meet. Nevertheless, his grueling schedule meant that he slept sporadically, a few hours in the afternoon between his shifts and on weekends. Once known for his popular presence at queer-dominated cultural events such as the ballet and film festivals, Osvaldo spent little time socializing.

Soon after Pedro left the island, Javier, who had been the other permanent fixture in the household, also left Cuba, for the United States. Javier's father had migrated illegally on a homemade boat when Javier was eleven years old, and Javier had been waiting to join him in the United States ever since.[16] Frustrated by hiding his homosexuality at his grandmother's house, Javier imagined that life in the United States would mean he could "live with a boyfriend, be more free, and buy things." In 2006, Javier moved to Philadelphia to live with his father.[17] He called me when he arrived, but I could barely recognize his voice. He spoke in deep, strained flat tones to portray a "manly" image in front of his father. After three months in Philadelphia, Javier moved to New Jersey to live with his aunt and her three teenagers in a one-bedroom apartment. He secured a job unloading food shipments in a warehouse an hour's bus ride from his aunt's apartment, and he shared a bed with his older cousin, who Javier described as a "delinquent." After a few months in New Jersey, Javier wanted to return to Havana. He felt lonely, and "acting straight" was wearing him out. "I never realized what I had there," he told me during his lunch break at work. "I was so excited to come to the United States, but now I would give anything to be sitting on the Malecón with my friends again."

Even though Lisette and Osvaldo had tried to stave off the impact of macroeconomic shifts, the rise of poverty and growing inequalities had disrupted their family life and contributed to the demise of their relationships. As financial security could be guaranteed primarily through access to foreigners, tourism, and migration, same-sex relationships suffered from new opportunities for betrayal. Finally, government officials were beginning to promote homosexual tolerance, but by the time prominent leaders decried institutionalized homophobia, urban gay men and women found their lives irrevocably transformed by financial instability. The experiences of Lisette and Osvaldo over the course of a few years reveal how structural economic shifts wreaked havoc on personal relationships as stories of faithlessness and abandonment were given new life in the post-Soviet era. Urban gays represented these changes as defining moments and described how economic challenges shaped their feelings about love and desire, and vice versa. In doing so, they constructed distinct realms of a private, domestic sphere that was meant to remain outside the clutches of global capital and material incentives. Rather than shelter their household from negotiations over money and migration, their home and queer kin networks were profoundly shaped by financial obligations and expectations, both acknowledged and unacknowledged. The embrace of cultural capital and traditional values of hard work and decency could not protect urban gays from a changing social landscape in which intellect and culture failed to translate into social status or financial security.

In this chapter, I have explored what it meant to embrace a *gay normal* subjectivity, and traced how critiques of commodified sex helped Lisette and Osvaldo to represent themselves as resourceful and dynamic in contrast to those taking the "easy way out" of post-Soviet hardships. I have also demonstrated how their ideas about gay normativity—both in terms of sexuality and social decency—challenged homophobia, but inadvertently drew on and perpetuated the privileges associated with whiteness, cosmopolitanism, and gender conformity. Far from being a removed observer, my presence in Lisette and Osvaldo's household and the ongoing flow of cash, commodities, and access to other foreigners that I provided helped keep the house afloat. Our friendship symbolized the blurred boundaries between affection and instrumentality that characterized intimacy in post-Soviet Havana. How might their lives have looked had they embraced the commodification of culture and bodies that had become endemic in Havana? What if they had more openly acknowledged their participation in strategic friendships and tactical sexual relationships? In the next chapter, I explore the daily lives of gay men who embraced relationships with sex workers and contributed to the commodification of sex. Through an exploration of their negotiations with sex workers, I highlight how they, like Lisette and Osvaldo, found their own desires and values at odds with the realities of their daily lives.

CHAPTER 3

"Tell Me You Love Me"

URBAN GAY MEN NEGOTIATE COMMODIFIED SEX

Our neighborhood had been enjoying forty-eight hours of continuous electricity for the first time in months. Just as Fidel Castro was addressing the electricity crisis on television, the power went out again. The unending darkness was exacerbated by the oppressive heat without the relief of fans and the precious amounts of meat and milk spoiling overnight in refrigerators. Candles were scarce and, if found, cost ten pesos each—one tenth of many Cubans' monthly salaries. I walked out onto my balcony to cool off. The bright lights of the Hotel Habana Libre sign loomed over the shadowy neighborhood. Powered by generators, the hotels never lost power, and the sign served as a stark reminder of the dramatic inequalities that separated Cubans and tourists. Antonio, my neighbor, hunched over his railing, shirtless and gnawing on a cigar stub. He smiled and offered the familiar refrain, "No es fácil" (It's not easy).

Out of the shadows, I heard Oscar calling my name from the street. Like most buildings in Havana, our buzzer system was a relic of the prerevolutionary past. I threw him the key to the building entrance and waited by the door as he marched up four flights of stairs. We dragged rocking chairs onto the balcony, hoping to catch an ocean breeze. In the dim light, I could see that Oscar was wearing eyeliner and mascara. Cubans often mistook him for a tourist—white, tall, in his late thirties, well fed, and dressed in name brands, he stood out on the street. He wiped his wide forehead with a rag and propped his feet on the railing.

"Ivan's dead," Oscar said, "I don't know what happened, but he never came home. We went to the Malecón to look for boys. I lost track of him and went home around one in the morning. Ivan had the only house key, and he wasn't at the apartment. So I had to walk half an hour to get the landlord's key. If he isn't dead, I'm going to kill him and then throw him out of the house."

"What if something really happened to him?" I asked.

Oscar lowered his voice and leaned in toward me. The neighbors were perched on their balconies, and we knew they were listening as always. "Well, I called one of the gay twins, and he saw Ivan on the Malecón with a young *pinguero*," Oscar whispered. "They were making out until five in the morning. Ivan bought a beer with a $10 bill, which means that he had some money, but not enough to pay the *pinguero* and get a room for two days. The *pinguero* probably killed him," he said only half-joking. "I'm going to wear a big black sun hat to the funeral and dark glasses. How I love dramatic hats," Oscar said, raising his voice again.

Friends for over ten years, Oscar had invited Ivan, a skinny thirty-four-year-old with blond highlights and sandy colored skin, to move from their hometown to live with him in Havana. Oscar worked as a stylist in a black market photography studio and made enough money to pay for food and rent, but hated to be alone.

I thought about all of the stories that I had heard about hustlers who had drugged, robbed, assaulted, or even killed gay clients.

"I'm not going to worry," Oscar said, as if reading my expression. "Ivan's mom wasn't worried. She said he takes off like this every so often." He asked if I had any cookies. I returned from the kitchen with his favorite caramel biscuits, unavailable in the peso stores.

"When I called Ivan's sister," he continued, "she didn't care either. All she could talk about was a *yuma* (foreigner) that she let *meterle pinga* (fuck her) for $10 and a case of lemon lime soda. She told me that she couldn't talk because she had to go to bed to rest her pussy. The tourist had promised her $30 for another go at it." Oscar laughed and reached for another cookie: "So, I'm not going to worry."

For the next six days, Ivan's whereabouts dominated our conversations. On the phone, over dinners of yucca and pork, during pirated broadcasts of CSI: Miami, and sitting on the Malecón, we retold the story to one another, emphasizing different details as if we had overlooked some clue. "The house key." "The hustler." "The $10 bill." We knew that someone should go to the police, but Oscar couldn't afford to be investigated since he lived in an illegal apartment and worked in the black market. Instead of going to the police, Oscar called the morgue. They had received four old people and one thirty-something man with a beard. Luckily, Ivan was clean-shaven.

On the seventh day, worry overwhelmed Oscar. He visited all the major police stations and called me from a pay phone. "Ivan's been in prison this entire time," Oscar said, relieved. "He bribed a police officer. 'Insubordination,' they called it." There would be no trial; Ivan only needed someone to pay his bail, and he would be released. Oscar couldn't visit Ivan because he wasn't a relative, so he called Ivan's mother. Sitting in the visiting room, crying, Ivan told his mother that he had offered a police officer $3 to prevent his own unlawful arrest. She borrowed 600 pesos ($30) from Ivan's sister to pay for his release.

The morning after Ivan returned home, he showed up at my apartment, his already wiry frame noticeably thinner. Drinking sugary espresso and chain-smoking, Ivan admitted that he had lied to his family and really had bribed the officer in order to save a hustler he had hoped to sleep with. Instead, the policeman had arrested them both. Being the victim of a wrongful arrest would garner more sympathy than going to jail to protect a *pinguero*. In prison, Ivan had shared a cell with two prisoners; one stole a nun's car and the other had assaulted a police officer. "My cellmates told me that nothing bad would happen," Ivan said, "but when the guards brought in another gay prisoner, everyone started shouting, 'Look at the *pato* (fag).' I decided to keep my mouth shut, because if I spoke they would know I was gay." Ivan paused to take a drag from his cigarette. "My nerves gave me constant diarrhea and vomiting. They never allowed me to bathe. Imagine how I stank, with shit on my pants," he said, pinching his nose between his fingers. "They let me out [of the cell] once a day to see a psychiatrist. He knew I wasn't a delinquent and said that he would help me. I think he was *medio pájaro* (half fag)."

"What happened to the *pinguero* you were with?" I asked.

"The *pinguero* was released on the second day," he said. "We weren't allowed to talk, but as he was walking by, I threw him a crumpled piece of paper with Oscar's phone number and address. I begged him to make contact." Oscar never heard from him.

The night of Ivan's release, Oscar invited a new *novio* (boyfriend) to dinner and told him to bring another hustler as a homecoming present for Ivan. When Ivan walked into the living room, he "let out a scream like a woman." The *pinguero* with whom he had been arrested sat on the sofa. Unaware that it was Ivan's house, he was practically trembling when he saw Ivan. The hustler swore that he had tried to contact Oscar. Ivan didn't believe him but didn't argue. After a dinner of *picadillo* and rice, they had sex. "He said he's going to marry me," Ivan said, laughing.

From Ivan's perspective, the story had a fairytale ending because he had suffered for the man he desired and was ultimately redeemed by the marriage proposal. Ivan's tragicomic dealings with the young hustler exemplified the mix of desire, betrayal, and redemption that typified many gay men's relationships with *pingueros*. As I demonstrated in the last chapter, many urban gays resisted the commodification of sex in queer enclaves, but some gay men pursued the young, handsome, heterosexual men who inhabited their sexual fantasies. In this chapter, I focus on Oscar, Ivan, and their friends, to tell the stories of light-skinned gay men who either hired young hustlers for discrete sexual acts or provided the domestic and affective labor hustlers needed to survive in Havana. Although the gay clients I discuss recognized that hustlers lacked sexual desire, the live-in relationships that qualified *pingueros* as *novios* or boyfriends fostered gay men's expectations of mutual caring and tenderness. I describe how gay men felt torn between their sexual attraction to young *pingueros* and their distaste for the bald-faced commodification of sex and affect. By exploring how gay men coped with the betrayals implicit in tactical erotic-economic relationships, I demonstrate how effeminate gay men's desires for masculine, heterosexual men led them into relationships that contradicted their ideas about fundamental values. I also trace the contradictions in their ideas about a division between a realm of market-based self-interest and a private sphere of genuine affection as they came to embody certain forms of emotional detachment and market logics that they disdained in hustlers. Likewise, I suggest that the suffering gay men described actually helped some to construct feminine subjectivities as hopeless romantics who could not resist caring for young hustlers, hence offering a means for gender and sexual expression.

"THE BIRDCAGE": MAKING HAVANA HOME

Oscar explained that he always knew that he was gay but had married a childhood girlfriend to avoid disappointing his mother, who had been devastated when Oscar's father, a police officer and a strict communist, left the family to be with a younger woman. Wanting to spare his mother grief, Oscar concealed his desire for men and married his best friend from the neighborhood. While married, Oscar spent a number of years in the military as the assistant to a high-ranking military official. "I would sit on my porch and watch all these young guys pass by my house," he told me. "I couldn't take it any more. I knew it would kill my mother, but I had to do it." After two years of marriage, Oscar admitted his homosexuality to his family. His mother cried for six days and refused to get out of bed. Slowly, she accepted it. Oscar confessed to me that he believed that despite their volatile past, he had become his mother's favorite child. "Maybe because I don't have a family or she feels as if she has to defend me. I always tell her that when she gets old, she's going to live with me and I'll take care of her."

Following his divorce, Oscar moved to Havana, where he met and fell in love with a young, handsome Italian tourist. "Fabio," as Oscar's friends nicknamed him for his resemblance to the Italian fashion model, invited Oscar to Milan. Oscar accepted, and planned to stay in Italy illegally. He contacted a childhood friend, a *jinetera* who lived with her Italian husband in Milan. But Oscar's boyfriend became overbearingly jealous. "I was like Rapunzel locked in that high-rise apartment building all day," Oscar told me, "I was so lonely. In Italy it's all work, all the time." After three months, he honored his tourist visa and returned to Cuba.

Back in Havana following his Italian adventure, Oscar found a job as a hair and makeup stylist in a black market photography studio that paid roughly $200 a month. His salary afforded him a solidly middle-class lifestyle that Cubans without access to hard currency could not manage—a cell phone, brand-name clothes and shoes, cologne and toilet paper, taxis instead of public buses, and meat on a regular basis. Like many Cubans navigating new informal economies, Oscar had found his job through personal connections.[1] While Oscar lacked a source of income from abroad, his boss received money from family in Miami that supported the photography studio, which in turn supported Oscar.

Now financially secure but balding and a little pudgy around the middle, Oscar felt that he had wasted his prime years hiding his homosexuality, and he paid handsome hustlers to recover what he felt was his lost youth. In describing the logistics of paying *pingueros*, Oscar seemed at once sympathetic and self-interested. Like many gay clients, he criti-

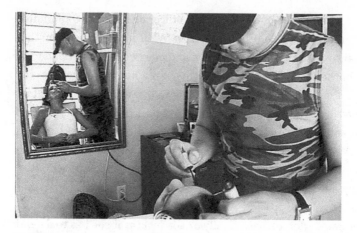

Figure 3.1. Oscar prepares a girl for her *quinceañera* photos at the black market salon where he works.

cized the commodification of affect and sex but also hunted for a bargain. Oscar explained where he found the best "boyfriends." In front of the Sotija store, the men were the cheapest. "They'll go for thirty pesos, which is a little over $1, or even a plate of food. They're cheap, and *muy baja* (trashy)." Men at the Payret cinema, across from Parque Central, would have sex for $10. "Sometimes even $5 if they're desperate enough," he added, meaning that it was late in the evening and they needed a place to stay. On the Malecón, the *pingueros* were the most handsome and the highest paid, charging Cubans $25 for sex. "But toward the end of the night," Oscar said, "you can get someone, someone pretty, for $15 when they realize that they're not going to get any work."

Oscar rented a two-bedroom house, a converted Catholic convent, in Centro Habana. After the revolution, with the church banned under communism, religious buildings had been appropriated for public housing. In Oscar's unit, the owner had added an upstairs loft that held the two bedrooms. The apartment retained its original ornate copper ceilings, and two marble pillars awkwardly divided the kitchen. Oscar enjoyed access to hard currency and greater sexual freedom but often suffered from loneliness. Living alone was considered unnatural in Cuban cultural mores, and Oscar was accustomed to being surrounded by friends and family. He would prefer to share overcrowded living conditions, squeezing four people into his double bed, than face his daily routine alone. He occasionally had hustlers as live-in boyfriends, but these relationships were fleeting and failed to provide the emotional intimacy he craved. So Oscar invited Ivan to move in with him.

An unemployed hair stylist, Ivan agreed to cook, clean, and keep house while Oscar worked. Ivan dreamed of starting his own salon or beauty school but hadn't worked as a stylist in over a year. Positions at black market salons were extremely competitive, and Ivan had trouble making a living in the peso economy. He periodically cleaned houses that rented rooms to tourists, and he occasionally resorted to theft. One time, he admitted that he stole $200 from two tourists staying in the house that he cleaned. "I don't know what came over me," he told me. "I just saw all the money sitting there, and I grabbed it." Although Oscar claimed to have a stricter moral code than Ivan, he never judged Ivan's indiscretions. Oscar often said that he was willing to support Ivan because "she is my *amiga*, my *hermana* (sister)," blurring the lines between kin and friendship. Serving as a caretaker and companion to Oscar offered Ivan the opportunity to live in Havana, but it also meant that he had to submit to Oscar's authority. Unequal access to hard currency fostered a power dynamic between Oscar and Ivan, who donned the role of a traditional "housewife." Their distinctions between authentic bonds of friendship and commodified liaisons with hustlers helped to downplay how their own friendships involved financial support.

In addition to Ivan, Oscar also invited his lifelong friend Ruben to stay for extended periods of time. A tan forty-six-year-old chef with bright blue eyes, a long face, and platinum blond hair, Ruben still resided in their hometown and, like Oscar, made a decent salary, as a chef for a Canadian company. In the late 1970s, Ruben had become a local hero in their provincial town when he became the first person to openly acknowledge his homosexuality. Ruben had counseled Oscar when he was young, and now Oscar could repay his generosity by inviting him to stay in Havana for weeks at a time. Ultimately, the men bonded over the experience of hiring hustlers, replete with betrayals and the dilemma of being attracted to men who did not care for them.

The house served as a space of emotional support and a lively escape from the boredom of daily life. Oscar and his friends affectionately called it "the birdcage" after the French film *La Cage aux Folles* (The Birdcage) and always said, "This place is a cage full of crazy *pájaros* (literally birds, slang for fags)!" It wasn't unusual for Ivan to turn up the music and create elaborate dance routines while doing chores—frequently converting his mop handle into a makeshift stripper pole. Oscar and Ivan nicknamed all of their major appliances, and when the washing machine began to whine under the strain of too many clothes, someone would shout, "Becky's screaming for more!" During overnight visits from *pingueros*, there were often mishaps with everyone sharing beds, and Oscar and his friends openly discussed the awkward details, which often included tales about snoring, bed sharing, and morning erections. During the weekends, Oscar, Ivan, and Ruben spent hours gossiping, dying each other's hair, and scouting for attractive young hustlers. Their closeness and constant banter created an important camaraderie that urban gays missed in their relationships with hustlers. They relied on one another for companionship while meeting their sexual needs with *pingueros*.

Spending time at Oscar's house allowed me to maintain friendships with sex workers while integrating myself into a gay household. Whereas Lisette and Osvaldo had protectively encouraged me to avoid sex workers altogether, Oscar's social circle fully incorporated mutual friends that other urban gays considered too "low class." My role as a third-party observer to their relationships with sex workers allowed me to befriend hustlers without being pegged as a potential client. While I paid Oscar's rent when his work permit was delayed and bought gifts for him and his friends, for the most part Oscar did not depend on me for monetary support. His financial independence allowed me to feel as if our friendship was more trustworthy, which was ironic because it suggested that I harbored assumptions about true friendship as removed from the market that were similar to Oscar's. In hindsight, it is clear that the realities of our relationships were neither purely innocent nor solely market driven, given that I was using his life story to write a book and I felt genuine affection for Oscar and his friends. Oscar and Ivan had few female friends and frequently explained that they disliked lesbians because they had little in common with butch women, so I served as a novelty. As a white foreigner, I also enhanced their standing as cosmopolitan Cubans who were more familiar with international gay culture and fluent in brand names and practices that circulated outside of Cuba. While travel restrictions and financial hardship kept them from fulfilling their wish to travel the world, relationships with foreigners compensated.

The introduction of a mixed market economy had inspired Oscar, like numerous other gay men and women, to move to the capital to find work and escape the harsh criticism and homophobia that plagued their small towns. Urban gays frequently celebrated the cosmopolitan anonymity of Havana, which allowed them to entertain a number of lovers without being subject to the judgment of nosy neighbors. The socialist government's strict control over migration and housing had previously forced many gays to live with or near their families in the towns where they grew up. Because Oscar's hometown was close to Havana, he could reside in the city legally and did not worry about routine police checks for undocumented migrants from outside Havana.

The rise of black markets in Havana also created new employment opportunities for some urban gays, who established financial security and greater independence.[2] Moreover, in the post-Soviet economy, jobs that paid in hard currency supported a breadwinner's family and friends. As state leaders dissolved safety nets, personal networks of income redistribution materialized in ways that cushioned the harsh realities of high unemployment. While some of Oscar's money went to his mother and brother in his hometown, he also created a gay family in Havana for which he was the primary breadwinner. This family, like many other kin networks in post-Soviet Cuba, became a primary locus of financial support and stability in a context of shrinking state subsidies and safety nets. "Family" or "sisterhood," in the case of Ivan and Oscar, was prized as safe from market forces but actually involved good amounts of invisible domestic labor and the exchange of food and housing for emotional and affective work. Likewise, while Oscar imagined his household as built around intimacy and love, as opposed to his relationships with *pingueros*, which were formed around mutual self-interest, he came to manage his domestic life with strategies of authority and contract labor endemic to the new mixed market economy.

"WE LET THEM WIN"

Oscar and I made a weekend trip to his hometown, so that I could meet his mother and see the small coastal city where he had grown up. During our visit, we climbed a narrow staircase to get to Ruben's two-room apartment, which had served as a sanctuary for gays and lesbians in the town for decades. In the absence of a living room, we sat in Ruben's bedroom surrounded by red curtains covering the walls. Fidel Castro appeared on a tiny television hanging in the corner, which Ruben had muted when Fidel launched into a speech about the energy crisis. Ruben proudly showed us the new items he had purchased with his most recent paycheck—a stereo with a remote control, a new backpack, and a cordless phone. As we lounged on his bed, the conversation turned to their love lives and they began to discuss the slang that *pingueros* used to describe sex with gay men. In the discussion that ensued, I found that they succinctly articulated many important aspects of their mixed feelings toward hustlers.

OSCAR: Killing the game (*matando la jugada*) that's what the *pingueros* call it when they have sex with us. That's how they like to think about it, like it's work, so they call it that.

RUBEN: There are boys who don't work, so they make their living charging for sex and they call it their "game."

O: The game is their work. However long "the game" lasts, one hour or half an hour, and they have their money.

R: And we let them win. Even though we know there isn't any love, pleasure, or emotion, but to satisfy our desire, we accept it. But it's sad, very, very sad.

O: It's very, very sad.

R: To know that you're with someone who is doing it for money and not for love. If you don't know that, you can enjoy it and feel happy. But we're conscious of the fact that it's for money— not love, or a minimum amount of pleasure. Nothing.

O: Nothing, they don't feel anything. You realize that they're empty. There's nothing inside, they are simply empty.

R: It's only *por interés*, for money. There are very few who aren't like that.

O: We've lost a lot of important values, human values.

N: Before it was different?

O: Yes, before it was for love or because they liked you, understand me?

R: Or for pleasure.

O: Not any more. We've lost all of those beautiful values that we carry inside that make one human, we've lost them.

R: We say the men working the street are heartless.

O: We've come to the conclusion, because we've talked about it a million times, that they come from the interior of the country to Havana. They leave their heart there, and arrive without emotions, empty.

R: But that's life today in Cuba.

o: We live in a bad situation. It's a different era, a harder time. Sometimes I tell them, that their way of making a living is easy, the easiest way—not the right way. The right way would be to study, to work.

r: We work.

o: We work, but they just hit the street. I don't know. But how sad, this whole thing. I hate it.

In their dialogue, they commented on their own complicity with the changes that they lamented. Oscar and Ruben were dismayed that *pingueros* described sex as work or *la jugada* or "the game," but as Ruben concluded, they let *pingueros* "win" in order to satisfy their own sexual appetites. In their youth, they had commanded personal power in their love affairs with straight men. According to Oscar and Ruben, before the post-Soviet crisis, straight men had sex with gay men for pleasure. The camaraderie and mutual affection that could exist between two men engaged in a clandestine affair embodied the tenderness and empathy that often characterized relationships between Cubans during socialism. The trysts they enjoyed with masculine men allowed effeminate gay men to access the brotherhood that the revolution had been built upon. To engage in sexual relations with men who were seeking only money eroded this sense of sexual prowess, which had characterized their liaisons with straight men in the past.

Oscar and Ruben prided themselves on the fact that straight men had *wanted* to sleep with them, a reality that helped to ease the burden of social rejection. To suffer homophobic attacks by a man who would later become one's lover lessened the sting of public homophobia and counted as a personal triumph. Moreover, their resignation to "the game" struck an emotional chord because Oscar and Ruben had always demanded respect, even in their provincial hometown. For instance, when Ruben's neighbors called him a "faggot" in the street, he began hanging his lovers' clothes in his front yard while they slept in his apartment after sex. "The best," Ruben told me, "was a naval officer's uniform. It shut up the neighbors for weeks. All the old biddies started to worry they'd see their husbands' clothes on the line!" On numerous occasions, Oscar and Ruben commented on the difference it would make if homophobic, gossiping women knew that they were sleeping with their husbands.

In post-Soviet Cuba, Oscar and his friends suggested that the eruption of capitalism transformed young men into zombie-like creatures absent of sentiment or affect, whose fixation with earning cash precluded the possibility of pleasure. Like zombies, the hustlers were dead inside while appearing to be alive. Oscar and Ruben used the compelling notion of "emptiness" (*vacíos*) to describe the internal state of *pingueros* when they arrived in Havana, suggesting that they left their "hearts" in their hometowns. Emptiness becomes a symptom of the introduction of capitalist values in which relations *por interés* vacate an emotional self and leave a money-seeking shell. Oscar and Ruben viewed this state as the internalization of a broader decline in Cuban society, in which values fundamental to personhood, or what Oscar described as the state of "being human," were eroding.

The specific types of affective and sexual commodification that *pingueros* offered were fostering the false expectations and frustrations that Oscar and Ruben described. The ideal encounter with a *pinguero* was not a purely sexual one, which would then leave intimacy and caregiving to the domain of noncommodified bonds. Instead, they wanted the young men to perform tenderness and intimacy, even if emotional attachments were feigned. Hustlers would become live-in *novios* for whom gay men would care like a cherished husband—cooking, washing clothes, cleaning, mending, and giving love and attention. The illusion of love was also reinforced by the exchange of the relationship for room and board, rather than cash for discrete sexual acts.[3] This prevalent manner of dealing with live-in boyfriends enjoys certain parallels with the "girlfriend experience" in the United States in which heterosexual men seek a more involved relationship with female sex workers. Elizabeth Bernstein (2007) traces a shift from modern-industrial prostitution in which consumers bought a "quick sexual release" that was emotionally void and postindustrial sexual commerce in which consumers craved "bounded authenticity," a girlfriend experience, in which intimacy is part of the market transaction.[4] For instance, male clients now sought mutual sexual stimulation, kissing, and cuddling. Where Oscar and his peers departed from this model of bounded authenticity was that men purchasing the "girlfriend experience" in the United States gained comfort in knowing that intimacy would remain within the boundaries of a market transaction and there were no ongoing emotional obligations, whereas this dynamic was precisely what inspired disappointment among gay Cuban clients who criticized the sex trade.

By pursuing white *pingueros* close to their own skin color, gay Cuban men could perpetuate the fantasy that the hustlers were *novios*, since relationships in Cuba tended to be endogamous. Oscar and his friends did not partake in the fantasy of the hypersexual black or brown masculinity and preferred white or lighter-skinned sex workers. Unlike the exoticism that often characterized white Anglo-European foreigners' desires of Cuban men and fueled transnational interracial fantasies, Oscar and his peers discriminated along the lines of color, but by preferring light-skinned or white hustlers. Because racial and color preferences were attributed to the realm of desire, and desire understood as something innate, these preferences could be easily detached from accusations of racism. According to the logic of desire, you cannot control whom you want.

While poetic in their assessment of contemporary homoerotic straight-gay connections, whether the decline in these relationships could be blamed entirely on the rise of market relations was unclear. Their aging process had coincided with the emergence of the sex trade, but they overlooked how getting older might have limited their sexual prospects. Some men like Osvaldo, for instance, who were five or ten years younger also described dramatic changes due to the sex trade but still enjoyed unpaid sexual relationships with heterosexual men. Many older gay men were more cognizant of how their age excluded them from sexual liaisons and did not blame the rise of commodification to the same degree. For instance, Oscar's fifty-six-year-old gay uncle Victor had framed four eight by ten airbrushed photographs of a young woman in black lingerie revealing her breasts in his bedroom. Victor noticed my confusion as I stared at the photographs and explained, "It's so the hustlers can focus on her while they're having sex with me. It helps to get them excited when they come over." It was true; there was a direct line of view from the mattress to the wall. As is evidenced by his efforts to keep young sex workers aroused, Victor openly recognized the absence of hustlers' desire.

Homoerotic liaisons had indeed become commodified in new ways, but strategic sexual liaisons existed before the 1990s. In the 1960s and 1970s, gays described "*el palestinismo*" or young heterosexual men (referred to as *palestinos*) who moved from the provinces in search of better living conditions and lived with gay men in Havana. In the 1980s, some gay men enjoyed a higher standard of living than others, so gays from different economic backgrounds and generations would often live together in a trend that became known as the *etapa de titimania* (era of the sugar daddy).[5] The era of *titimania* also applied to older heterosexual men who were well connected in the government and kept young women as "trophies." Along with the introduction of the mixed market economy in the 1990s, new dynamics of privilege often reduced these ambiguous, longer-term, live-in affairs to straightforward sex for cash transactions.[6] Oscar and his friends had live-in relationships as well as occasionally paying for discrete sexual transactions with *pingueros*. The coexistence of these systems inspired Oscar and his friends to debate what constituted a "real" or "normal" relationship. Hence, transactional sex did not simply replace previous social ties, but rather both systems intermingled in ways that fostered undefined boundaries between affection and transaction, giving rise to moral uncertainty and anxiety.[7]

For Oscar and Ruben, their criticism of the new capitalist "game" suggested their attempt to erect and maintain boundaries between a domestic sphere of pleasure, desire, and camaraderie, and a public sphere of incentivized transactional relations. They disparaged *pingueros* for "not working," but also complained that hustlers understood sex with them as a "game," or a type of labor. This inconsistency illuminated ideas about the moral boundaries of commodification. According to Oscar and Ruben, some acts such as emotional caretaking and sexual gratification should not be considered labor, while other activities such as their own jobs in the service industry cooking and styling could be rightfully commodified in the marketplace without threatening the values *humanos* of revolutionary society. Ironically, in their dealings with sex workers they came to see their caretaking and financial support as types of commodities and sought to impose "rules" as part of the unspoken contract they shared with their live-in *novios*.

DIFFERENT APPROACHES TO *PINGUEROS*

Urban gay men measured their attraction to and desire for young hustlers against a pragmatic cynicism, and most often concluded that their desire justified the emotional risk. Oscar tried to maintain a skeptical detachment with the hustlers who became his live-in boyfriends. In particular, his relationship with Juan Pedro, a twenty-two-year-old *pinguero* with coffee-colored skin and a faint moustache, embodied his stern philosophy. Juan Pedro was quiet, mature, and handy around the house. Although he was from Havana, he had escaped a one-room apartment that he shared with his mother and five siblings to live with Oscar. He generally followed Oscar's instructions to stay home during the day while

Oscar worked, but he took to drinking, sometimes finishing an entire bottle of rum by himself. One night, Oscar refused to have sex, explaining that when drunk, Juan Pedro never reached orgasm and would penetrate Oscar for hours. "We messed around instead. Juan Pedro gave me a blow job, and you know, we licked a little ass," Oscar told me:

> Then, when I was ready to go to sleep I could tell that he was wound up and wanted to go out. I told him to go out, have a couple of beers, and come home, that it wasn't a big deal. He said no at first because he didn't want to make me mad. He eventually went. I didn't care if he found some girl, but it was a test to see if he could handle himself.

But Juan Pedro didn't come home until the next night. By the time he arrived, Oscar had packed all of his clothes into a navy blue backpack that sat propped up by the door. For Oscar, betrayal meant violating his rules. Oscar said to me, "He's the one who lost. He had a great setup. A house, food, clothes. He didn't have to work or do anything all day, and he messed it up. His mother's place is total squalor and he hates it, but now he'll have to go back." Juan Pedro cried and pleaded with Oscar not to force him to return to his mother's apartment, but Oscar refused to forgive him.

Ironically, Oscar adopted the very emotional stance that he criticized in young *pingueros*. One could easily describe Oscar's unyielding attitude with Juan Pedro as "heartless." As much as Oscar sought to erect boundaries between a public sphere of commodified affection and a private realm of true love, I found that he came to approach his domestic life with market logics that included certain ideas about contract labor, firing, and authority. His status as the primary breadwinner afforded him authority over Ivan and the hustlers who lived with him. He was "the boss" not because he was the older patriarch of the household, but because of his status as the primary earner. Not only did he demand sexual and domestic labor from those in the house, but at times he also required forms of emotion work such as exhibiting the proper "attitude" and, in the case of Ivan, being cheerful and fun—efforts commonly associated with late-capitalist service industries. For all of the value he placed on intimacy and affection, Oscar, like many gay men I spoke to, expressed pride in his ability to remain reserved, if not "professional," with his live-in boyfriends. Mastery over his emotions represented his best defense in the new world of commodified sex and affect and symbolized his fluency in the contemporary language of self-interest.

Nevertheless, there were times when Oscar let his emotional guard down, bought into the fantasy that a handsome young man was in love with him, and suffered the consequences. For instance, when Oscar met Paul, a charming seventeen-year-old from the Eastern provinces with blonde curly hair and light green eyes, there was trouble from the start. Paul's mother, worried that he was running with the wrong crowd, demanded that he return to Pinar del Rio. When he didn't come home, she took the bus over 100 miles to stand outside Oscar's house and scream: "You cock suckers should be arrested!" "I'm going to have you faggots put in prison for raping my son!" Fearful of his mom, Paul moved in temporarily with his aunt in Havana. While there, Paul called Oscar four times a day telling him, "I don't love you a lot because we just met," he told Oscar, "but I love you." Oscar took my arm, "Oh *chica*, I know it's a lie, but lie to me, lie to me, *tell me you love me!*" he shouted. To want Paul to declare his love, despite the fact that Oscar knew it was a lie, illuminates how Oscar could accommodate both the knowledge that their relationship was based on money and legitimately indulge in the fantasy that Paul adored him. Neither wholly commodified nor entirely sincere, the relationship with Paul suggested how his desire to be the object of Paul's affection overwhelmed Oscar's typical detachment with sex workers. In Oscar's desire for Paul to declare his love, even if it was a "lie," the possibility of a different kind of love emerges. Rather than the strict divisions between commodified intimacy and authentic, noncommodified bonds that Oscar and his friends typically discussed, it suggests that in certain circumstances performances of love could satisfy the longing for emotional attachment, even in the context of transactional sex. This notion of love echoes the notion of love that Denise Brennan describes among Dominican women in Sosua, who described being "in love" as a process that required savvy and determination, in contrast to love as an elation of "losing control of one's senses or wits" (2007: 204).[8]

When Paul's mother left Havana, he moved back in with Oscar. One evening, Oscar returned from work to find Paul missing. Ivan, stirring a pot of boiling towels on the stove, said Paul had gone out with an older man who was "recruiting him for a boy band." Immediately, Oscar became suspicious that Paul was keeping clients. "He can't even sing!" Oscar said to me. "I'm going to ask him if he put the microphone in his mouth." As we sat down to eat, Paul came through the door. Oscar asked Paul what had happened to the $5 he had given him. Paul dutifully listed his purchases. After dinner, Oscar told Paul to take a shower and Paul refused. "Listen to me, we're going to have a mellow evening. I worked all day, I want you to take a bath and then we're going to watch a movie," he said to Paul in a calm, paternal tone. But Paul was already in the living room playing house music at such a volume that it blared into the street. "I already had a talk with him yesterday about playing the music so loud," Oscar told me, "but look at this, he's doing it again. Tell him to turn it down?" A week later, Paul left Oscar for another gay man who was Oscar's age but had more money and government connections. Oscar seemed crushed, both at the loss and because of his own lapse of vulnerability.

While Paul had broken through Oscar's protective guard, the majority of the time Oscar defined himself by the fact that he had little tolerance for disrespect. Rather than expect his boyfriends to feel desire or love, Oscar believed the appropriate attitude in the new transactional world was respect—to honor the unspoken contract between them. Oscar had trained himself to accommodate the illusion that he was the object of the young man's desire along with the reality of self-interest that structured the encounter. Oscar required regular sex in exchange for financial support and domestic caretaking and remained cognizant of the mutual incentives that structured the boyfriend relationship. It struck me how Oscar's emphasis on "the rules" echoed the approach of the *pingueros* whose "game" he condemned.

In contrast, Ivan saw himself as a helpless romantic and wanted to remain caught in the fantasy that there was mutual love and desire between him and the *pingueros* to whom he became attached. Since these relationships were domestic and lasted for a few weeks at a time, Ivan held out hope that the hustlers would feel genuine affection. This meant that Ivan did not enforce rules like Oscar and sought to mystify the transactional nature of the exchange. The most extreme case was Ivan's obsession with Antonio, a handsome twenty-two-year-old with thick black hair, broad shoulders, and sandy skin that offset his bright green eyes. Within two days, Antonio moved into Oscar's house, and Ivan cooked, washed and mended Antonio's clothes, and helped him get ready for his dates with male clients.

Antonio continually defended his heterosexual prowess and was careful to tell stories about his successful womanizing in Ivan's presence—

offering a reminder that Ivan did not live up to his standards. As he bounced Ivan on his lap he told me about his love of women, "I fuck my girlfriends all night. We start at midnight and fuck until six in the morning. Women—young ones, old ones. I've been invited to leave the country three times but I didn't want to go. Once to Italy, once to Canada, and once to Holland. I didn't want to leave, but now I have to find a little old lady who will take me back to her country and support me. I'll just stick it in her (*meter*) every night and she'll take care of me." In addition to emphasizing his womanizing skills, Antonio denigrated male clients in front of Ivan. For instance, one afternoon Antonio lay in bed as Ivan sewed a rip in his jeans. Taking a drag off his cigarette, Antonio said, "I've got to go kill a bunch of cockroaches tonight." He ran his hand over his bare chest, adding, "There's a ton of them. That's how they are, if there's one, there will be more. I'm going to kill them good with my big dick, so I can get some cash." "*Ay, chico!*" Ivan replied, chastising him for being so crude. Antonio's emphasis on how much he liked women and how little he thought of gay men preserved his heterosexual status and reinforced his position of power over Ivan.

Antonio obviously did not reciprocate Ivan's romantic feelings, but the more Antonio rejected Ivan, the more obsessed Ivan became. Ivan called Antonio's mom, pretending to be a state employer to see if Antonio had lied about his life. "It's true," Ivan reported, "he works as a technician. His mom wanted to know if I knew where he was, I said that I hadn't seen him."[9] Another time, Ivan came to my house depressed that Antonio hadn't called. "I saw him last night with his *yuma* (foreigner)," Ivan said with a beer in his hand, "and I tried to talk to him under my breath because I felt embarrassed, since the *yuma* understood Spanish. He said he'd call me at 1 PM, and at five past one, I was crying. It wasn't his body or his big dick, or any of that, but he was so affectionate and caring," Ivan said. He then confessed that he was wearing Antonio's underwear. He pulled out the edge of Calvin Klein boxer briefs from his pants. "They're not even clean," he said. "I need to find someone gay and start a real relationship."

For Ivan, the fact that Antonio refused to identify as a *pinguero* fueled the fantasy that their relationship was real. "He said that I was his second experience with a man," Ivan told me. "He must be a *pinguero*, and he just doesn't want to tell me. He just says he's *loco* (crazy)." An investment in a homoerotic, binary gendered system was most apparent with the terms *loco* and *loca* that Antonio and Ivan used to characterize their personality

Figure 3.2. Ivan follows Antonio on a walk along the Malecón.

and sexual types. Carlos Paz Pérez, in his study of Cuban slang, defined the *loco* as a man or woman who behaves in an "extravagant form during the sexual act" (1998: 126). Urban gay men and hustlers extended Paz's definition to characterize *los locos* as men who would "fuck anything." Heterosexual men who traded sex for cash inhabited the top of a gendered chain of command in which their girlfriends and gay men would care for them. Young hustlers often relied on an overtly macho and sexualized attitude toward women, and, occasionally, used violence toward feminized queers to reinforce their heteromasculinity. This gendered hierarchy had become more entrenched with the rise of commodified sex. *Los locos* offered a counterpart to *las locas*, the slang term used throughout Latin America to describe effeminate, flamboyant homosexual men. The *loca,* or fag, was not merely a derogatory term originating outside the gay community, but rather gay men often embraced and inhabited it self-consciously.

The terms perpetuated traditional gender hierarchies because *las locas* or "crazy women" described men who acted like women, reinforcing notions of appropriate masculine and feminine behavior. *Los locos* or "crazy men" described a conventional Cuban masculinity in which men harbored an unrestrained sexual desire to penetrate their object of choice. At first glance, *el loco* may appear to challenge gender and sexual systems because men can desire to penetrate either women or other men. While this is partially true, upon closer inspection, the category reinforces the privilege of masculinity while disavowing queer practices and performances. Despite a man's homoerotic encounters, he can maintain his masculine status if he conforms to gendered norms, whereas the *loca* transgresses gendered expectations and is thereby stigmatized. While both participate in sexual and emotional bonds, unlike *la loca* who is stigmatized, *el loco* is never queered.

While the commodification of intimacy greatly impacted the gender and sexual subjectivities of gay Cuban men, it did not impact them in the same way. In part, the differences between urban gay attitudes toward the sex workers with whom they formed extended relationships reflected various gendered versions of queer male identity. Oscar saw himself as homosexual, "but a real man," and he maintained strict boundaries with sex workers. In contrast, Ivan described himself as more "feminine," a hopeless romantic who allowed his emotional attachments to cloud his decision making, such as going to jail to protect a sex worker whom he barely knew. Similar to Ivan's arrest, which opened this chapter, his relationship with Antonio embodied his more permissive attitude. From my perspective it seemed that Ivan's subjugation to his "boyfriends" fed into his ideas about gendered norms. By accepting hustlers' disrespect, he could serve as the feminine sexual and emotional counterpart to masculine, heterosexual men. The introduction of market capitalism not only resulted in commodified sexual and affective homoerotic relationships between men, but also provided an opportunity for redefining expressions of gender and masculinity. Moreover, uneven access to wages in the new economy also influenced how they approached hustlers, with Oscar and Ruben often criticizing Ivan as "hopeless."

CONFLICTING IDEAS ABOUT LOVE AND SEX

Ivan's relationship with Antonio began to cause arguments in the household. Oscar grew tired of supporting Antonio and felt Ivan was too affected by the situation. He began to pressure Ivan to get rid of Antonio. One evening, Ivan stirred chopped chorizo and garlic into a pressure cooker full of garbanzo beans. Oscar hovered over the pot and chided Ivan, "Antonio comes to sleep in your bed and eat our food and never gives you any *cuchi-cuchi* (sex) at all. He leaves and you cry all day." Ivan shook his head and agreed, "I know, it's time I left these *pingueros* behind."

After two months, Oscar kicked Antonio out of the house. Oscar arranged for Antonio to rent a cot at a friend's house in the neighborhood, but Ivan disgustedly told me that Antonio could not stay there because there were "too many blacks." In his conversations with Oscar, Ivan appealed to a mutual cultural racism to try to convince Oscar to change his mind, but he refused. A few days after Antonio had left, I arrived to find Ivan mopping the building stairs using buckets of water to wash away condom wrappers, animal blood, and small piles of dog shit. Antonio was sleeping in the bedroom. He had arrived at 3 AM suffering from an asthma attack, so Ivan had taken him to the hospital. Antonio kept his duffle bag with his things in Ivan's room and returned to change his clothes, but normally slept elsewhere. "What about Oscar?" I asked. "He was fine about it, they even talked this morning. He's loosening up about the whole thing."

Ivan told me that he felt Oscar's disapproval resulted from hidden jealously. According to Ivan, Oscar wanted Antonio to himself. Ivan told me that he now thought of Antonio as a friend, nothing more. His mouth curled into a distorted smile, and I couldn't tell if he was lying or about to cry. I had assumed that Ivan's lovesickness had caused his paranoia about Oscar's interest in Antonio. But, shortly after Antonio left Havana, Ivan found nude photographs of Antonio on Oscar's phone. Ivan felt certain that Oscar had sex with Antonio and then kicked him out when Oscar became jealous of Ivan's relationship with Antonio. Ivan was devastated. "Oscar knew how I felt about Antonio. It was foolish for me to feel that way, but I did. Why would my best friend do that to me?" Ivan moved out of Oscar's apartment, and although he never confronted Oscar, he pulled away.

Personal conflicts arose not only in regard to the moral boundaries of commodification, but homoerotic ties also fostered ethical quandaries when different gay men had conflicting interpretations of what these new relationships meant. Gay men might have contrasted their bonds with *pingueros* to "real" relationships, but the impact of these hookups on Oscar and Ivan's friendship was irrefutable. Since Oscar viewed his affairs with straight hustlers as outside of the realm of "real" or sincere relationships, he could easily transgress sexual boundaries with Antonio that he would consider immoral had Antonio been Ivan's boyfriend. In the case of Oscar and Ivan, one was playing the game of transactional sex and the other approached his encounters with *pingueros* as love affairs.

As urban gay men made sense of their ties with hustlers, their perspectives about loyalty and betrayal varied. These distinctions bled into their relationships with each other. Oscar's role as the breadwinner also made Ivan more vulnerable and, hence, more likely to tolerate indiscretions. Ironically, the fact that their friendship did possess elements of domestic labor and material support, although unrecognized as such, opened opportunities for increasing conflict. The changing economic landscape raised the stakes of these distinctions in ways that ignited conflicts over the meaning of love and intimacy, straining the ties between lifelong friends.

On the one hand, affairs between gay clients and *pingueros* challenged traditional sexual hierarchies because urban gay men "employed" straight male sex workers. This new market relationship meant that gay clients theoretically controlled the parameters of their sexual and emotional bonds. On the other hand, these ties also reinforced the heteromasculine privilege of homoerotic male hustlers, who openly denigrated gay men and reduced previously affectionate straight-gay trysts into sex for pay. What these relationships meant in terms of gendered and sexual identities was similarly complex. Some gay men like Ivan lamented the absence of mutual respect in the relationships, but their suffering and subordination to macho hustlers also reinforced their effeminate sexual identities and intensified feelings of romantic fixation. Being an object of desire, for some gay men, meant submitting oneself to the abuse and betrayal of straight lovers. Payment for sexual services presented an extension of the insult. Rather than a deviation from erotic and romantic attachments, these bonds were indispensable to the very sexual and gender roles that some gay men inhabited. Homoerotic hustlers were conjurers who brought gay male fantasies and identities to life.

In post-Soviet Cuba, sex could be considered appropriate for commodification, while traits like empathy, friendship, respect, and tenderness were placed beyond the bounds of the market. Gay men who engaged in transactional sex often found their hopes for intimacy and respect at odds with their sexual desires for young, attractive masculine men. As is typical in postcommunist contexts, urban gay men remembered socialism as a system of reciprocity and obligation and felt that privatization threatened to undercut social relations through a new emphasis on individualism (Buyandelgeriyn 2008: 239). Yet, in practice, the bounds between the market and the intimate realms of the domestic sphere blurred in important ways as new formations of authority, caregiving, and emotion work emerged. Moreover, at times, declarations of love and tenderness within transactional relationships could be enough to satisfy the needs for tenderness that gay men expressed. Some gay men drew on gendered and sexualized explanations to make sense of what they described as betrayals. Rather than chafe at the duplicity of young hustlers, many urban gays felt that their unrealistic romantic fantasies about hustlers warranted mistreatment. For instance, instead of holding a grudge against the hustler who abandoned him in prison, Ivan felt an otherwise tragic story ended happily because he had consummated the relationship.

LOCAL PRACTICES OF COMMODIFIED SEX

Gay Cuban and tourist clients viewed transactions with *pingueros* differently, revealing how sexual labor and the moral limits of the marketplace reflected cultural values. Foreign tourists and Cuban clients both blurred the boundaries of commodified sex through the boyfriend experience, but many North American and European travelers believed that hustlers were young gay men in need of financial help. This perspective reflects common Anglo-European ideas about homosexuality as a relationship between two gay men. In contrast, Cubans openly acknowledged that hustlers maintained wives and girlfriends. In fact, sex workers' family lives reinforced the mystique of heterosexual masculinity and thereby enhanced gay desire. Racial and ethnic exoticism also played a different role for Cubans and white foreigners.

In terms of other types of social hierarchy, gay men in Cuba were not automatically more privileged than the sex workers they hired. Whereas foreigners wielded greater financial and social privilege than hustlers, many Cuban clients only fared marginally better economically than the sex workers. Likewise, *pingueros'* performances of heterosexuality placed them above effeminate gay men in Cuban gender and sexual hierarchies and, unlike tourists and sex workers, gay Cuban men often shared racial and ethnic identities with *pingueros*. More broadly, the dynamics between gays and sex workers suggest an unforeseen consequence of transnational capital upon the intimate practices of desire. These exchanges are especially pronounced in contexts that rely heavily on tourism. For instance, similar to Cuba, as gay tourism increased in the Dominican Republic in the 1980s, Dominican gays felt that they could no longer afford *bugarrones*, who preferred higher paying foreigners (De Moya and García 1998; Padilla

2007). Attention to these gay-*pinguero* relationships challenges popular misconceptions that the Caribbean sex trade is fundamentally hetero-sexual, being the neocolonial conquest of brown women by white men.

Just as urban gays tried to distance themselves from the impact of mixed market economies but found themselves sleeping with foreigners, many Cuban gay clients decried the rise of self-interest, but sustained the sex trade by providing the domestic labor needed for young hustlers to survive in Havana. The sex trade depended upon men like Oscar and his friends to house, feed, clothe, and care for the young hustlers that arrived from the provinces. Often providing the invisible domestic labor needed to sustain sexual laborers, Oscar and his friends lamented the extent to which relations had become motivated by money to the exclusion of tenderness and friendship between gay and straight male lovers. They forcefully criticized the "heartlessness" and "emptiness" that they associ-ated with the rise of sex tourism but coped with these changes in ways that put them at odds with their own beliefs. Ironically, some men like Oscar mimicked the emotional mastery and distance that they criticized in *pingueros* as rules of the market economy manifested in their daily lives and reordered the expectations of the domestic sphere. Moreover, through discussions of lax work ethics of hustlers, Oscar and his friends ignored how they gained access to hard currency through legal and black market service industry jobs, where their urban origins and light skin offered an advantage. Likewise, they often insisted on the differences between gay and sex worker desires for commodities and money, which helped to obscure how their own friendships and kin networks had been influenced by money and status. Material interests informed Oscar and Ivan's friendship in ways that shifted interpersonal power dynamics, despite their feelings that friendships between gay men were sheltered from the rampant self-interest exhibited by sex workers. Gaps had always existed between values and actions, but in post-Soviet Havana, personal desires were at odds with fundamental values to a new extent.

The criticisms of the sex trade articulated by Lisette, Osvaldo, and their friends, which I discussed in chapter 2, reflected mounting frustra-tions with the inversion of economic and cultural capital as sex work-ers gained financial mobility. Whereas some urban gays like Lisette and Osvaldo represented the rise of market relations in queer social circles as an invasion of relations *por interés* that threatened to contaminate authentic love and desire, Oscar and his friends disparaged the transformations brought about by capitalism but embraced the consequences. Complaints from urban gay men like Oscar, Ivan, and Ruben reflected emotional resentments, the result of personal disrespect and unrequited affection. In the next chapter, I turn to the lives of sex workers that frequented Havana's gay *ambiente* to explore how their perspectives about hard work and decency speak back to the criticisms leveled by urban gays. While young middle- and working-class urban gays represented hustlers as self-interested and seeking the "easy way out," I show how they also found their values at odds with their actions and felt stifled by the growing materialism and poverty in post-Soviet society.

CHAPTER 4

"Smarter Than You Think"

SEX, DESIRE, AND LABOR AMONG HUSTLERS

At almost noon one Sunday, I walked the seven blocks to Melba's apartment from my place. Centro Habana was bustling. I passed overcrowded apartment houses and hollowed out ruins where buildings had once stood. Trucks clattered through the uneven and dusty streets, narrowly missing old men pushing vegetable carts and singing out the names of fresh produce. Bicycle taxis blared reggaeton through jury-rigged Sony speakers and swerved to avoid a gaggle of children, who ran back and forth, using a plastic doll's head as a soccer ball. The smell of roasting coffee mixed with the salty sea air as the *vieja* on the corner stirred her black market coffee beans to sell from her kitchen window. Men sitting in doorways hissed and called out to me, the older ones offering flattery and the younger ones spitting crass sexual innuendos.

I arrived at Melba's place and knocked on the thin wooden door. "I'm in here," she shouted from her mother's living room next door. I removed the padlock and went in to find Melba under a thin floral polyester sheet, lying on the wooden bench that served as a couch, and watching *Billy Elliot,* that week's movie broadcast on state-run television. Melba, nearing thirty-five, was a corpulent and mocha-colored *mulata* with a plump face and freckles dotting her nose and cheeks. Although she occasionally took clients as a *jinetera*, Melba had established herself as an iconic figure in queer enclaves, not as a sex worker but as a go-between, or fixer, for hire. She looked exhausted. Her hair formed a messy nest on the top of her head, her mascara smeared under her eyes, and she was still wearing her shirt from the night before. Her slurred speech made me suspect that her hangover had been exacerbated by what she called her "blood pressure medication," an enduring Valium habit.

It was rare to find Melba alone, and I asked where everyone was. Her mother, a recently converted Evangelical Christian, had gone to church for the day. Melba's best friend and roommate, Domingo—a muscular, charismatic twenty-three-year-old *pinguero* with light cocoa skin, green deep-set eyes, and chiseled features—had spent the night in jail for starting a drunken brawl on the Malecón and had gone to his girlfriend's house to sleep it off. Melba's girlfriend, Yolanda, a thin twenty-one-year-old with doe eyes and light ochre skin, went to meet a stingy Spanish client who promised to take her shopping. "And Palio?" I asked of another roommate, a twenty-year-old *pinguero* with cinnamon-colored skin and light eyes. "I had enough of him," Melba said. "No me cae bien, lo voto por la calle (I don't like him, I kicked him out). He tried to fuck Yolanda." Then, changing the subject, she said, "I love this movie. This ballerina kid is a fag, right?" "Not sure," I said, and sat down at the end of the bench.

Melba had secured her own two-room apartment a month after I'd met her. With the help of the Cuban housing authority, Melba's mother, Sandra, had traded their studio apartment for a four-room place in a tenement around the corner. Sandra, a white, round woman with short coarse hair and tiny eyes, had become deeply religious with the reintroduction of evangelical Christianity to Cuba after the communist prohibition against religion lifted in the 1990s. Sandra doted on Melba, and Melba often reminded me that she was Sandra's favorite of her three children, "despite being the darkest." Now, instead of sleeping on a mat in the living room, Melba had a chance to build her own space. Sandra had paid for a cement division, which created two tiny, independent apartments, and Melba became determined to raise money for her renovations—building a bathroom and a kitchen.[1] Sandra babied Melba, but they often fought about the endless stream of young people living at Melba's and using Sandra's bathroom to "shower, shit, and brush their teeth," as Sandra put it.

Melba's apartment, without a kitchen or bathroom, had been especially crowded that summer. In addition to housing Yolanda and Domingo, this included Palio and his boyfriend, an attractive thirty-six-year-old African American novelist from Brooklyn. Melba had approached Terrance in

Parque Central during his first trip to Cuba three years earlier and they had become friends. He was affectionate, funny, and generous with the modest pile of cash he brought to Cuba. Melba and her roommates found Terrance to be an endless source of knowledge about African American urban culture, something that they prized and appropriated to craft their own identities. In a similar vein, Terrance preferred to stay with Melba because he didn't feel as if he was in the "authentic" Havana unless he was living in the poorest conditions, even by Cuban standards. Terrance's relationships with his male lovers resembled gay Cuban men's approach to hustlers. He would normally maintain a "boyfriend" for weeks at a time, supporting him and providing clothes, food, and shelter, rather than paying cash for discrete sexual acts. Terrance told me that his next novel, a tragic love story about a Cuban hustler and an American man, would explore what happens when "we are forced to use someone that we love."

It was Terrance who invited Palio to join him at Melba's apartment. When Terrance was about to return to the States, Palio told him that his mom had cancer and that he needed to return to Holguín to see her. Terrance gave him $50 for the trip. Instead of going home, Palio spent the cash on a new pair of Nike tennis shoes and a fake gold chain. When his money ran out, he started coming by my apartment four or five times a day. After I stopped answering the door, he started dropping by in the middle of the night and ringing the bell for hours at a time. He pestered me to e-mail Terrance and ask him to send money. In a note that he wanted me to send via e-mail, he downplayed his request for money, emphasized his attachment to Terrance, and kept up the lie that he'd gone home to see his mother. Given how aggressive Palio became after Terrance left, I was not surprised that he had tried to have sex with Melba's girlfriend even while living in her apartment. Melba generally allowed people to stay with her as long as they contributed small amounts of money or food to the household, but Palio had become greedy and crossed a line. The other hustlers in Melba's social circle agreed that Palio was untrustworthy, reckless, and a thief. Palio, Melba reassured me, was definitely gone for good.

Gay men and women in Havana often questioned the motives of sex workers in queer enclaves and suggested that the commodification of sex had spawned the decline of gay gatherings. According to their accounts, sex workers were homophobic and violent and pursued "easy money."

Lamenting how social status increasingly reflected the amount of money one possessed, regardless of how the money was earned, urban gays complained about how social standing was detached from educational attainment and work. For many urban gays, sex workers embodied this casual discarding of traditional values of decency and mutual respect. But Melba's reaction to Palio shows how participants in commodified sex also lived by a moral code that, while distinct from mainstream values, often led to conflicts among friends and acquaintances. While everyone in Melba's social circle used foreigners to secure a living, how people did so and whom they crossed in the process mattered immensely within Melba's social milieu. Out of the three households that I focus on in this book, Melba's was the most dependent on foreigners' cash and commodities to stay afloat and the only household where I encountered other non-Cuban foreigners on a regular basis. Yet Melba's household challenged Cuban stereotypes about *jineteras* securing lavish lifestyles through their foreign clients and defied academic understandings of the homoerotic sex trade in Cuba. While the male sex workers that lived with her more closely adhered to forms of masculine commodified sex that researchers have reported throughout Latin America and the Caribbean, Melba's social and sexual liminality reveals unique, unexplored aspects of female sexual desire and practice. Melba maintained a long-term girlfriend and male lovers but eschewed the label of "bisexual" and instead described her sexuality as "*moderna.*" She participated in queer gatherings but as a job, often describing the Malecón as "work."

In this chapter, I explore how Melba and her friends saw themselves as cleverly exploiting the economic crisis to ensure their survival and fashion fresh identities. Focusing on the relationship between their economic wants and sexual desires, I analyze how their participation in Havana's sex trade allowed Melba and her friends to challenge certain sexual, racial, and gender norms while reinforcing others. How did Melba and her friends and lovers make sense of their work, and how did sexual labor and bodily commodification influence their desires? To analyze their perspectives on intimacy, love, and sexual labor, I consider how economic restructuring had an impact on their romantic and emotional affective unions that was similar to the one that urban gays described. Hence, by illustrating the parallel experiences of urban gays and the sex workers they criticized, I hope to show how the everyday lives of Melba and her friends defy gay criticisms and to illuminate how one social circle of sex workers made sense of their involvement in emergent erotic economies.

GOING TO WORK

When I met Melba, in 2003, she had recently given up braiding. The police had begun to level fines against Cuban women who gathered outside the Cathedral in Havana Vieja and offered to plait the limp, straight hair of white European and Canadian tourists. Melba did not particularly enjoy the work. Lacking a legal permit, Melba had acquired two $20 fines and one trip to city jail for her business. In addition to the legal hassles, offering braids without a cart, photos, or a styrofoam mannequin covered with a braided wig made tourists skittish. Melba would timidly ask, "Braize, *amiga*, you like the braize?" as they hurried past her. Occasionally she threatened to get a "real job," and might mention openings sweeping a factory or working the counter in a perfume store that she had heard about through a neighbor or a cousin. But the meager $10-a-month state salary kept her navigating the informal economies of queer enclaves.

When underground economies and the sex trade exploded in Havana in the 1990s, Melba had been well positioned to profit. After her younger brother was killed by a car outside the apartment, Melba left home around her fifteenth birthday and became addicted to painkillers, which she procured from the public health care system. She spent a decade on the streets before returning home to her mother's apartment, and her intimate knowledge of Havana's marginal networks meant that she could create a career brokering information and keeping secrets in a tightly controlled state environment. For example, Melba relayed messages to hustlers who had no phones, sold used goods procured from tourists, placed hustlers with gay Cubans who accepted sex for rent, and protected her peers from arrest by holding their secrets. Melba and her friends interpreted their work as *jineterismo,* a collection of activities such as selling black market goods or working as an unofficial tour guide that included sex work.[2] This adaptability embodied Nadine Fernandez's description of *jineterismo* as an attempt to integrate oneself into the global market economy at "whatever level and through whatever means" (2010: 131).

Melba also developed new skills specifically related to dealing with foreigners. Contrary to her powerful and intimidating street reputation, she acted shy, even demure, and came across as infinitely helpful in the company of foreigners. Unlike Cubans working in the tourist industry, who were trained in the arts of hospitality, Melba had honed her unique form of "niceness" through trial and error on the street. She had had a keen intuition, lied effortlessly, and, over time, successfully refined her tourist façade. With new foreigners, she had perfected the art of making subtle, nonthreatening requests for modest gifts. Her performance often reminded me of what Zora Neale Hurston (1943) described as "the pet negro" act; Melba played down her power, her fierceness to inspire the patronage of wealthy foreigners. While Melba brokered a variety of deals and lived off networks of redistribution, Yolanda focused more decidedly on sex work. Yolanda explained that she had originally come to Havana because she could make $50 in one night and in her previous state job as an elevator operator, it would have taken her four months to earn the same pay. "It's risky," she explained, "but it's an easy way to make money. Young people work but don't see the fruits of their labor. That's why so many of us hit the street."

Among her peers, Melba acted tough and unafraid to speak her mind. Adding to her edge was her aspiration to become a rap star. After late nights of drinking, lazy conversations between Yolanda and Melba often turned to planning how to get a music video made and how to release their first album. Although Domingo only performed once, at a local community theater, Melba also described herself as the manager of Domingo's rap career. Melba brought her discerning attitude to bear on her haphazard involvement with the Cuban rap scene, and often criticized the beauty standards of the nascent industry. Melba wrote a rap that attacked the male-dominated culture in which she failed to fit. She and Yolanda often performed the song, titled "Solo Yo Confío en Mí" (I Only Trust Myself), as a kind of anthem to their defiance. "I may be a little ugly, but I'm worth something more / You think you know me, but I'm smarter than you think / I only trust myself, and no one else, I only trust myself / So get back."[3]

Since Melba and her friends prized certain elements of black American street culture, such as rap, hip-hop, and street fashion, they were all the more attracted to foreigners like Terrance and other African American tourists who could provide cultural knowledge and cachet alongside hard currency. The creative appropriation of U.S. blackness did not reflect skin color, however, as Melba and Domingo were the only ones in the household who would qualify as *mulato/a*, and even they were considered light skinned on the color spectrum.[4] Instead, the appropriation of U.S. black

Figure 4.1. Domingo and Palio wearing jerseys that Terrance brought from the United States.

urban youth culture symbolized a type of resistance to authority and linked them to transnational flows that signified status in the post-Soviet era. In her study of Cuban hip-hop, Sujatha Fernandes (2006) observes how hip-hop offered young black Cubans in slums and housing tenements a way to express their frustrations and aspirations during a moment of rising inequalities. The rise of hip-hop culture suggests how the opening to capitalist markets and foreigners following the loss of Soviet subsidies provided black Cubans, in particular, opportunities to inhabit new performative identities (Allen 2011: 40).

Melba also drew on networks of redistribution within hustling enclaves by demanding food and small payments from the rotating friends and lovers who stayed in her apartment. At any given time, between two and six people shared her bedroom, which boasted a thin mattress placed on the floor and a wire box spring covered with a sheet. Melba occasionally grew tired of sharing her tiny living quarters and demanded that Domingo move out. In particular, Domingo's girlfriends wore on her patience. "I'm not going to support (*mantener*) anyone," she said to me. "Especially Domingo's lazy girlfriends who don't do anything. They sleep at my house, eat my food. I'm not going to wash Domingo's clothes and take care of him anymore. That's their job." After suffering through another sleepless night listening to Domingo and his girlfriend having sex on the floor, she would kick him out. But, by the next month, Domingo was back sharing her box spring.

Domingo had left Holguín for Havana shortly after his eighteenth birthday and quickly discovered success in queer enclaves. He nostalgically reminisced about his first year. "I had such amazing outfits," he told me. "I was fresh meat from the provinces, so everyone wanted a piece. A hustler could dress nice and make a decent living from *multando nada más* (taking small amounts of money from tourists without having sex)." When a client wanted drinks at a club, for instance, Domingo would tell the tourist that the beer cost $3, when it was really $1, and then he would pocket the difference. The term *multa* had a particular resonance because it was most commonly used to describe the fine that sex workers paid police when they were arrested. By "fining" outsiders, hustlers taxed wealthy outsiders to support themselves. Domingo, however, identified as a *pinguero*, not a *jinetero*. Allen distinguishes between *jineteros* and *pingueros* in that *pingueros* offered sex, but *jineteros* were "unofficial market procurers" who most often did not provide sexual services, although sexual contact might occur (2011: 175).

Domingo's clients largely consisted of black clients from the United States and men from Latin America. After a couple of years in Havana, Domingo found a steady patron, a round-faced thirty-five-year-old gay white Puerto Rican man who visited twice a year. His patron had promised to take Domingo out of the country through Mexico and then smuggle him into the United States. Domingo felt that "it was only a matter of time" before he would leave Cuba. The hundred dollars he received monthly meant that Domingo didn't have to hustle, and he could spend his days lifting weights in the dusty neighborhood gym, having sex with his girlfriends, and hanging around the park. In 2004, however, his Puerto Rican *yuma* (foreigner) wasn't able to make the trip to Cuba after his mother had fallen seriously ill. The loss of physical contact, combined with new restrictions imposed by the U.S. government that mandated only relatives could receive money, meant that Domingo lost his financial support. He reluctantly returned to cruising the Malecón looking for clients.

Even as he successfully navigated a career hierarchy within Havana's queer enclaves, Domingo, like many sex workers, understood that his earnings were low within a transnational perspective. One handsome African American publisher from Chicago had paid Domingo $100 for sex. "Can you believe it?" Melba asked me. "The *yuma* told Domingo that he would have gone for $300 or $350 in the States. And here, he goes for $20," she said, raising her eyebrows. The knowledge that they were "cheap" by foreign standards added to sex workers' resentment and inspired a care-free attitude toward petty theft and minor cons of tourists.

For Melba and her friends, who legitimized their labor by describing it as "going to work," they insisted that there was nothing easy about the daily grind of patching together a living on the Malecón. Notably, they emphasized feelings of boredom and monotony in their descriptions—feelings often linked to a dead-end job—rather than victimization or vulnerability at the hands of foreign tourists or gay clients. Hence, sex workers identified their struggle as "hard work," on par with any form of labor. For instance, Melba often seemed annoyed with me when I asked her if she was going out to the Malecón on any particular night (a common question among urban gays). "I go every night," she said to me. "It's not social, it's work. I can't afford to miss a day, even if I get sick." Her frustration seemed to stem from my inability to recognize the differences between gays who frequented queer enclaves for social and sexual reasons, and her own financial motives. In addition to challenging gay criticism, Melba often offered me proof of her strong work ethic, presenting herself as a diligent laborer who was so dedicated that she never missed a day of work. Her description of her single-minded focus on earning a living echoed socialist rhetoric of industriousness, typically associated with the flat hierarchy of jobs under socialism. Framing her participation on the Malecón as "working" she challenged urban gays who accused them of taking the "easy way out," as if suggesting that hustling was not labor at all.

Rather than become victims to economic restructuring, Melba and her friends and lovers relied heavily on the minimal safety nets provided by the state and found ways to exploit the new black market niches that grew where state socialism collided with market capitalism. The tempered introduction of tourism allowed some Cubans to make a legitimate living, but for those without access to dollar economies it was the *coexistence* of pockets of capitalism and state centralized socialism that sustained them. For instance, the segregation of foreign tourists from Cubans created an opportunity for enterprising go-betweens to help visitors negotiate an urban landscape crisscrossed with opaque illegalities. Melba could survive within the dual system because what she managed to glean from the dollar economy held so much value in local peso economies. For instance, if Melba could earn $10 a month taking $1 for each foreign tourist she introduced to a male hustler, she could live a standard working-class lifestyle without suffering long hours in a state job. If Cuba were to transition to a free market system, Melba and her peers would lose the social benefits that allowed them to live so modestly. Rather than advancing or promoting a capitalist, free market system, many young Cubans in black markets took advantage of the excesses that arose from the dollarization of the economy. By exploiting the fissures between systems, Melba and her peers could act as dealers, combining black market earnings with state rations to survive.

GENDER AND SEXUAL TRANSGRESSIONS: *LAS MODERNAS*

One sleepy Sunday afternoon, we sat on three lawn chairs pulled up to Melba's round wooden table in her otherwise empty apartment. Melba and Yolanda shared a cigarette as Yolanda stared at her reflection in a shard of broken mirror and applied blue eyeliner. Yolanda wore her habitual outfit—tight white jeans rolled up to the knees, a red surfer shirt, leather sandals laced up to the knee, hair gel that she swiped from my bathroom, and dark lip liner.

They told me how they'd met. During Yolanda's first trip to Havana from Sancti Spiritus, a tiny colonial town on the banks of the Yayabo River, Yolanda's boyfriend had introduced her to Melba with the hope of finding her work in the sex trade. Yolanda had never had a girlfriend and Melba, nearly ten years her senior, quickly seduced her. "She attacked me while we were sleeping," Yolanda told me, "You can imagine, she's so big—she pretty much raped me," she said, laughing. Immediately, the pair became inseparable. "We went everywhere together," Melba told me. "We slept in the same bed, showered together, spent all our time around each other. I would even go with her to turn tricks."

During the countless days that I spent with Melba and Yolanda, they each had a number of boyfriends and male lovers. They never vocalized any resentment over their relationships with men but often fought over suspicious liaisons with other women. I asked about their relationship.

"We are very *modernas*," Melba said, "Really, really modern. No one in Cuba has a relationship like ours, a modern one."

"No one in Cuba has seen anything like this," Yolanda added.

"The two relationships that I had with women before, have been like me," Melba said, interrupting Yolanda and pausing to ash her cigarette into an empty glass. "It's better because you can't marry a woman, and sometimes you need a cock." She held her hands a foot apart as if she was measuring.

Yolanda laughed.

"It's true," Melba said.

"I know, it *is* the truth," Yolanda conceded, smiling.

"I tell Yolanda to find a cock that she likes," said Melba. "Men don't matter, women do matter, because I'm a woman and she's a woman."

"And the men don't know anything. We say that we're best friends, or sisters, or in-laws."

"And you don't get jealous when you see your girlfriend with a boy-friend?" I asked.

"No, I don't," Yolanda answered, deliberately shaking her head.

"Men don't have anything to do with it," Melba said, shrugging her shoulders.

"We're really modern, really unique."

Melba and Yolanda blurred the boundaries of sexual practice and identity by characterizing their intimate bond as outside of homo- and heterosexual binaries. Rather than refer to themselves as *bisexual*, as other Cubans might, they preferred to eschew labels and position themselves beyond the confines of conventional language, calling themselves *modernas* and cleverly manipulating gender and sexual codes. Many male sex workers also suggested that their contact with foreigners and the "gay scene" (*ambiente homoerótico*) led them to view their sexuality as more open and "modern" (Sierra Madero 2012).[5] Traditionally, many analysts might exclude Melba and Yolanda from transcultural studies of homosexuality because their relationship did not result in a homosexual or bisexual identity. Gloria Wekker (2006), however, presents a similar case in Suriname in which women maintained sexual and emotional relationships with other women, yet also frequently had male partners. Just as Melba and Yolanda articulated a critique of same-sex identities that suggested the terms available would trap them in rigid roles, Wekker discusses how the women who engaged in "*mati* work" challenged the tidy links between homoerotic practice and homosexual identity. Growing out of post-Soviet mixed market economies, new sexual and emotional intimacies subverted standard models of sexuality and reflected how affective intimacy embodied political, economic, and historical forces (Giddens 1992).

The majority of Cubans, gay and straight alike, tended to be endogamous, establishing partnerships with people who were close to their color and ethnic identities. Yet, Melba, Domingo, and their friends contradicted this trend and engaged in erotic relationships, both short and long term, that crossed color lines more than any other household that I studied. While they did not emphasize color blindness as an aspect of their "modern" desires and practices, I interpreted their openness to interracial relationships as part of the sexual "freedom" that they described. Unlike other Cubans, they did not start conversations about sexual desire with questions about racial preferences. In a Cuban study conducted by Pablo Rodríguez Ruiz, he found that Cubans living in shantytowns outside of Havana tended to have interracial partners much more than the national average (2008: 91). The more marginal the community in Cuba, the more integrated white Cubans, and the less significant racial differences became. Melba and her friends reflected this pattern, as their marginal social class tended to minimize other racial differences that often arose within the romantic couplings of the urban gays I knew.

Sex workers described nascent queer enclaves as both important opportunities for employment and an environment that allowed for a certain amount of sexual freedom. Melba and Yolanda understood their ability to exercise sexual and emotional openness as a sign of sophistication that distinguished them from Cubans stuck in the mire of traditional relationships and gender performances. For instance, Yolanda preferred Havana to her rural hometown because she could enjoy multiple lovers while escaping the judgmental gossip of her narrow-minded neighbors and parents, who encouraged her to settle down with a husband. For many sex workers with whom I worked, sexual adventures offered relief from the widespread ennui endemic among Havana's youth. They described sex as a popular pastime, fostering a climate of permissiveness and sexual experimentation. For example, Melba and Yolanda showed me two well-organized lists of their past lovers. Yolanda's list boasted ninety-three boyfriends in five years, with many of the names highlighted in pink. "My girlfriend is a slut," Melba said wryly, handing me a plastic cup of rum. "The highlighted names are the ones that lasted," Melba said, preempting my question. Yolanda reminded her that Melba had earned forty-nine names, counting both women and men. For both Melba and Yolanda, a significant majority of their lovers had been involved in the sex trade, reflecting a general trend in which sex workers frequenting queer enclaves tended to maintain romantic relationships with fellow sex workers.

Comfort with transactional sexual relationships and flexibility around personal sexual practices was not unique to Cuba but reflected trends within the Caribbean in which women viewed sex work as a legitimate way to secure a living for their families and often rebelled against confining systems of traditional gender and sexuality (Kempadoo 1999; Brennan 2004). For Melba and Yolanda, the hint of superiority implicit within their declaration of being *modernas* reflected a confidence borne from their ties to Havana's black markets, which linked them to global flows of people, ideas, and commodities otherwise prohibited by the Cuban government.[6] The sex trade cultivated camaraderie and tolerance for sexual transgressions. For instance, Melba once described a powerful image of waiting for Yolanda under a stairwell while Yolanda had sex with a client—they had become partners in crime, and tenderness blossomed from feelings of mutual protection. Similarly, the women nurtured their intimacy by poking fun at clients, hiding their relationship from unsuspecting boyfriends, and using slang and sign language to demean foreigners in their presence.[7] Similar to Roger Lancaster's discovery that sexuality in Latin America could emerge contextually rather than as an essential nature, sex workers often described their desires as something that had emerged *between* them in the context of the sex trade, not as a matter of essential identity *within* them (1992: 270).

The women's romantic attachments made sense within the context of a homoerotic sex industry, which had spawned a social world built on nonconforming gender and sexual performativity. Yet the sexual and emotional bonds between people making a living from the sex trade also led to jealousy, as financial support intersected with emotional attachments. As anthropologist Gisela Fosado (2004) observed in her research with Cuban *pingueros*, *la mecánica* (the hustle) and the professional performances of hustlers bled outside of their work as they started to see their own relationships with lovers and friends as motivated by self-interest. While most female sex workers in Havana did not maintain pimps, some in Havana's queer enclaves had longer-term relationships with more masculine female partners who expected to split their earnings. At times, the relationship between Melba and Yolanda seemed to fit this mold. For example, if Yolanda bought new earrings or a skirt, Melba would demand to know how much it all cost, with the tacit accusation that their money should be shared. Although she tolerated Melba's nagging, Yolanda often lied about her earnings in order to appease Melba.

Gender and sexual nonconformity with its potential for rebelliousness should not be conflated with an unfettered freedom or political resistance. For example, Yolanda often told me how, every six months, she alternated between dressing as a man and a woman. Her conscious gender performance revealed how both masculine and feminine personas were forms of drag (Butler 1990, 1993). Nevertheless, she could not always command her gender performances. One evening, Yolanda had donned a masculine aesthetic to attend a lesbian party, but when the police shut down the party, she decided to go to the Malecón to look for foreign clients. She had to rearrange her outfit on the spot—shortening her shorts, tying her men's T-shirt into a tight half-shirt, removing her baseball cap, and applying makeup—in order to attract male tourists. Moreover, Yolanda preferred Havana to her small town, but Yolanda's father, a prominent judge, once came to Havana looking for her. Scared that she would be in trouble with the law, Yolanda returned to her hometown for a year to "attend church, gossip, watch soap operas, go to CDR (Committee for the Defense of the Revolution) meetings, clean house, and have boyfriends." In other words, there were concrete limits to the extent to which Yolanda could undermine or escape patriarchal control by experimenting with various gendered identities and refusing the values of her parents.

At the same time that Melba and Yolanda challenged sexual categories and racial norms, however, they reinforced gendered standards. Melba and Yolanda described women with short hair and men's clothing as too *fuerte* (strong), and I suspected this had something to do with their rejection of a homosexual identity. They found many foreign lesbians unattractive because they were too *macho*. Similarly, if a male lover was too passive sexually, Melba would describe him as "a woman in bed," which was not a compliment. Likewise, when a male lover stood up Yolanda for his foreign male client, she angrily declared that her new boyfriend was a "fag." Hence, while their erotic desires and practices challenged many mainstream norms, Melba and Yolanda expected a certain degree of gender conformity and found deviations from these norms repellent. Their seeming flexibility actually harbored definitive notions about gender and sexual conformity.

Melba and Yolanda challenged certain traditional gender roles by fostering homoerotic relationships, engaging in transactional sex, enjoying multiple partners, and questioning dominant standards of beauty and femininity. Yet, at times, they conformed to feminine gender roles by acting as good daughters and caretakers to male friends and lovers. Likewise, in order to attract foreign clients they had to dress in more revealing, feminine attire and complained that certain lesbians were too *fuerte* or butch. While they bantered about sex with foreigners, often making fun of clients, their involvement in commodified sex and homoerotic relationships challenged their ability to fulfill their designated roles as women. In contrast, male sex workers could reinforce their masculinity and sexual prowess through their involvement in the sex trade, as the *pinguero* represented mastery over one's body and control over the male client. Women still described themselves as daughters and mothers, whereas men emphasized their role as workers and providers. Melba and Yolanda hid their romantic attachment in a way that unwittingly reified heterosexuality, just as male sex workers often reinforced traditional heterosexual masculinity to counteract their constant presence in Havana's queer enclaves and relationships with foreign men.

HYPERMASCULINITY AND POWER

Keeping with our routine, I walked with Domingo down the dim streets of Centro Habana, past the stench of steaming garbage heaps, to the back of the capitol building, where we waited to catch the bus to Vedado's tourist district. In line, he greeted everyone and caught up on gossip, "Giovanni's not coming?" "He'll meet us there," "Where's Yolanda?" "Already found a *yuma* (foreigner)," "Have you seen the twins?" "They haven't been out all week." Normally, Domingo sported an urban, hip-hop aesthetic—chains, visors, Yankee jerseys, Adidas wear—but that night, he had donned the clothes of his last client, a forty-two-year-old Afro-Canadian filmmaker. Relishing his high-fashion, bad-boy look, Domingo had freed his thick hair from orderly cornrows into a bun at the nape of his neck. His baggy tracksuit had been replaced with a fitted Armani T-shirt and dark washed Tommy Hilfiger jeans, which hung low to expose Calvin Klein briefs. A chain hung from his pocket, and he wore brand-new burnt rust Timberlands. His outfit possessed the sheen of foreign exclusivity, since none of the items were available for purchase on the island.

Domingo fidgeted with an ivory-handled knife and told me that he had just finished watching a pirated copy of *Finding Nemo*. He concluded that the film would never measure up to *Shrek*, which he had seen "at least forty-two times." As always, with the mention of *Shrek*, Domingo began to reenact his favorite scenes until he doubled over laughing. Domingo's *Shrek* performance bled into a discussion of his favorite Hollywood movie stars. "The top three are Antonio Banderas, Tom Cruise, and Brad Pitt," he said, adding that Denzel Washington was "*el maximo* (the best) and *que bonito*" (how handsome). "You like him?" I teased. "Come on, you know I don't like men," he assured me and went on to describe Antonio Banderas in different roles. "Remember when he played a fag, and there was one when he wore a mariachi outfit. I loved *The Godfather*, the first one was amazing, and *Gangs of New York*, I loved the butcher, and *Training Day*, and Cuban movies," he added. "Like *Fresa y Chocolate* was incredible."

Finally when the bus pulled to the curb, everyone cut in line, rushing to board. A few people inevitably slid by without paying, but by the time the fare collector noticed, they were sprawled in the back seat, laughing and smoking cigarettes. I hadn't yet perfected my technique of pushing through the raucous crowd, so Domingo always saved me a seat, defending it by yelling and waving his arms. The bus made its rounds through Centro Habana, collecting young sex workers wearing inventive variations of Havana's latest trends—pleather jackets, baggy jeans, thigh high boots, sheer tank tops. People would shout to one another from the front to the back of the bus, ashing their cigarettes on the floor and passing shared aluminum cans of Crystal beer. Three hustlers with gel-drenched hair and wrinkled button-down shirts beat a rhythm on the ceiling of the bus. Starting a sing-along with revised lyrics to "Under the Sea" from the Little Mermaid, the hustlers initiated a call and response with the passengers: "Under the sea, way under the sea. A *jinetero* under the sea, a *pinguero* from the Oriente under the sea, he came to find a *yuma* under the sea." The handful of passengers who were not part of the nightly migration to Vedado pretended to ignore the ruckus as mothers pulled their babies closer and men checked their watches.

His nightly bus ride to Vedado signaled Domingo's place as one of the Malecón's more successful hustlers. More than his rugged handsome exterior, what made Domingo irresistible to both foreign tourists and gay Cuban men—who often lent him money without receiving sex or the hope of a payback—was his ability to embody a bad-boy irreverence that bordered on violence, while holding onto a tender, honest vulnerability. The contrast of prowess and gentleness combined with an uncanny ability to read people and an unabashed command over his sexuality fostered an endearing charm. The type of black masculine fashioning that Domingo embraced was unique to young Cubans seeking to project a sense of defiance, which challenged the respectable masculinity promoted by older generations of black Cuban men (Allen 2011: 117).[8]

The womanizing bravado that many *pingueros* projected often differed slightly from their actual lives. For instance, despite being notoriously flirtatious, over the course of a year, Domingo maintained intensive long-term ties with two different women and rarely, if ever, strayed from those relationships. Domingo appeared loyal, even in his infidelities. His primary girlfriend of four years was a white, delicate, twenty-year-old deaf woman known as *la Muda* (the deaf woman). Although Muda also had sex with tourists for money, she did not frequent the rougher hustling areas with Domingo, and he continually tried to convince her to stop working in the sex trade altogether. He had been living in her apartment for six months with his pit bull when Muda's mother kicked him out for having another girlfriend. She forbade Muda from seeing Domingo. She felt Domingo took advantage of Muda and explained that he lacked respect for her and for her daughter. "He called me a *puta* (whore) and a *pinga* (dick) to my face. After I sell clothes so he can have food, and I clean and cook for him. He never brings home money or food, and he disrespects my daughter in the street. So, that's it, I threw him out!"

At that point Domingo moved in with his other girlfriend, nicknamed *la Negra* (the black woman), a tall, striking, dark-skinned twenty-one-year-old who worked the Malecón alongside Domingo. She and Domingo were notorious for their public fights and zealous sex life. The relationship was volatile, especially because Negra knew that Domingo had another girlfriend and would occasionally lash out to assert her independence. One Saturday night, after spending all day having sex and fighting with Negra, Domingo took Muda out on a date to the Bim Bom ice cream parlor. He broke away from Muda to come talk to me. "If you see Negra, can you tell her I love her?" he asked me, anticipating a fight. "I hate him, but he's in my heart," Negra said, putting her hand over her chest when I delivered the message. Domingo's double standard for his two girlfriends, the white "virgin" and the black "whore," seemed almost too predictable. Unlike his protective stance toward Muda, which was intensified by her disability, he encouraged Negra's hustling and even reaped the benefits. When they had been together for three months, Domingo was arrested for fighting. The judge ordered him to pay a fine, and Negra had sex with a tourist to pay his bail.

The fears of some urban gay men and women who accused *pingueros* of bringing violence to gay enclaves were reflected in Domingo's penchant for fighting. On occasion, masculine performativity among *pingueros* resulted in violence against women and effeminate gay men. For instance, Domingo was once arrested for punching a gay man in the nose because the man had stared at Domingo's crotch while he urinated off the Malecón. Barefaced sexual innuendos were typical in queer enclaves, and many bystanders felt Domingo had overreacted. A certain degree of homophobic impulse was expected, but he had crossed the line. As one older gay Cuban friend of Domingo's described, "Domingo is the most genuine man. He would do anything for any of us, including you, but he has a rage inside of him that scares me."

While certain aspects of their homoerotic performances threatened traditional standards of respectable masculinity, young *pingueros* reinforced traditional masculine roles by emphasizing their status as fathers and providers—often explaining how their work with gay men offered a means to support their wives and children in the provinces. Jorge, a nineteen-year-old *pinguero* who lived with Melba for four months, had three young children by three different women, one of whom was expecting another child. We sat together on the Malecón as he strategized how he might sell clothes from his last client to buy the bus ticket home for the birth. "I have three kids and another on the way," he told me, "What am I expected to do? If I can just earn enough cash, just a couple more clients, that money stretches so far in *el campo*. I already bought a few things for the new baby and a nightgown for his mom. With $40 more, I'll be set for months." Jorge was now experiencing the consequences of his womanizing, and he talked about his work with gay clients as a viable strategy to fulfill his duties as a father. Rather than seeking to experiment sexually while obscuring homoerotic identity, same-sex sex work offered a means to solidify his role as the traditional masculine provider.

To highlight their heteromasculinity, many *pingueros* with whom I spoke characterized themselves as womanizers, emphasizing hypersexual drives. The lengths to which *pingueros* went to display a hypermasculine, at times homophobic, heterosexuality suggested anxieties around their presence in queer enclaves. *Choteo*, informal teasing and jokes in the form of stories, provided a powerful way to manage the anxiety produced by participating in homoerotic relationships. One joke in particular portrayed circumstances in which necessity gave way to same-sex encounters:

A guy walks into his house and finds his wife cheating on him with another man. He takes a machete and goes into the bedroom and tells the guy to get off his wife and get onto his knees. The husband demands that the guy unzip the husband's pants and take out his dick. "No, no, I'm a man, what the hell are you talking about? Come on!" But the husband puts the machete to the guy's throat so he does it. "Now suck it," says the husband. "What are you talking about, I'm a man," responds the guy, but he does it. After the husband comes he says, "Now if you tell anyone that I'm a *cabrón* (bastard), I'll tell them you're a *maricón* (fag)."

The husband uses sexual acts with another man to reaffirm his threatened masculinity. It is important because both men are "forced" into same-sex practices despite their secured heterosexuality through the desire for the wife, thus highlighting how survival can justify same-sex practices. The story also relies on homophobia as a way to secure masculine status, because the husband threatens to tell the world that his wife's lover is a fag because the lover was the receptive partner. The husband's masculinity would not be threatened because he was the active partner, and thus he can engage in homophobic discourses as a means to secure his masculine privilege.

Like Domingo, many male sex workers did not want to sacrifice their heteromasculinist privilege and maintaining the image of an *activo* could prevent people from accusing them of homosexuality. Keeping with cultural tropes, a man who anally penetrates another man is not considered homosexual, but rather in various local idioms across Latin America, he is considered a "man" (Kulick 1997a: 574). Indeed, scholars who have studied the masculinities of male sex workers in Cuba have often noted similar recourse to masculine posturing among *pingueros* (Allen 2007, 2011; Cabezas 2009; Fosado 2005; Hodge 2001; Sierra Madero 2013). Yet analysts have also shown that the sexual subjectivities of young men engaging in homoerotic sex work were both more complex and diverse than these categories might allow. *Pingueros'* appeals to hypermasculinity, as Allen points out, offered more of a rhetorical performance than a social fact or experience (2011: 126). In other words, an *activo* position delineated a persona more than an actual sexual practice. In a similar vein, Sierra draws on interviews with *pingueros* to suggest that the experience of homoerotic sexual labor often held the potential to challenge traditional stereotypes about rigidly defined sexual roles for male sex workers (Sierra Madero 2013: 182).

Domingo's self-representations as virile and hypersexual also exaggerated a common, mainstream cultural trope that linked sexual prowess to national pride.[9] In a study of Cuban nationalism, David Forrest (1999) points out that Cubans prided themselves on their mythical sexual prowess. Similarly, an unpublished study at the University of Havana on sexual self-perceptions found that Cubans believed themselves to be "the hottest (*más caliente*) sexually in the world," and enjoyed their international fame for being sexually "uninhibited" (1997: 88).[10] Likewise, Cuban jokes often referred to uncontrollable sexual appetites and commented on how Cubans would pursue sexual satisfaction even to the point of transgressing their sexual identities. Cubans might have boasted of their sexual prowess, but this did not predict how people actually acted in their sexual relationships. Instead, sexuality had become a powerful idiom of self-expression that reflected a colonial history in which sexual stereotypes demoralized Cubans, and were reclaimed and appropriated in creative ways.[11] In a more recent example, the Cuban tourist industry has utilized the transnational circulation of stereotypical depictions of Cuba as sexually *caliente* to inspire visitors.[12]

COMMODITIES, CONSUMPTION, AND LABOR

Critics of the sex trade fixated on the material aspirations of sex workers, often emphasizing how commodity desires chafed against socialist ideals. Accusations from urban gays that hustlers caved to materialism and sought "easy money" resonated with wider public discourse. In a series for a Cuban newspaper, journalist Miriam Elizalde (1999) conducted interviews with female sex workers and offered the standard conclusion that poverty was not their motivation, but rather *jineteras* sought to support their consumeristic lifestyles. Similarly, Cuban scholars Celia Sarduy Sánchez and Ada C. Alfonso described a moral crisis that encouraged a philosophy of consumerism "without worrying about the methods of acquiring the goods" (2000: 65).[13] Yet rather than deny how consumptive desires inspired forays into sexual labor, many *pingueros* readily acknowledged that they journeyed to the capital to earn enough hard currency to buy designer tennis shoes or clothes and then planned on returning home. These motives, however, cannot be reduced to superficial materialism.[14]

Critics accurately represented the commodity desires of young sex workers but underestimated the importance of consumer goods in defining one's status in the post-Soviet urban landscape. The desire among young Cubans to consume and fashion their identities, as Jafari Allen aptly observes, offered critical forms of personhood in a situation where people all suffer from poverty and, therefore, what one "*has on* and how one looks" determines social class (2011: 165, 38). Imported shoes, clothing, jewelry, and accessories signaled a type of agency on the part of the consumer that transformed things into symbols of status and access. More specifically, homoerotic sex workers described commodity culture as intrinsic to maintaining heteromasculine status, linking their consumer drives to their ability to attract women. For example, Mateo, an eighteen-year-old *pinguero* from Bayamo, told me that women in Havana were increasingly materialistic. "You can start talking," he said, "and they might even think that you're attractive, but if you can't invite them to a beer, or on a date, forget about it. You have to have something to offer." He argued that Cubans in Havana were obsessed with brand name clothing, but he felt differently. "I don't really care about the clothing so much," he said. "If it's this brand or that brand I'll put on any shirt."

In order to "be a man"—attract the attention of women in Havana and compete with other Cuban men—Mateo, like many of my respondents, felt forced into nascent dollar economies. The transition to a post-Soviet service economy, in particular the rise of tourism and the introduction of black market consumerism, fostered new standards of manhood among urban youth. As Kevin Floyd (2009) highlights, certain types of masculine performance correspond to moments of economic development. As the market necessitates new forms of labor, production, and consumption, gender and sexual performativity change in relation to these shifts. Whereas manhood was once defined by sacrifice in fields of battle and sugarcane, after the 1990s, urban youth fashioned masculinity through modes of individual dress and style.

Finding and consuming the right fashion to craft a personal aura of flash and power in an environment largely devoid of advertising, fashion magazines, malls, and consumer culture took great dedication. Through inquisitive inspection of foreigners and the advice of diasporic family visiting from abroad, young urban Cubans could piece together the symbolism of certain items.[15] Many in Melba's social circle were fixated with

Figure 4.2. A *pinguero* window shops in the lobby of the Hotel Habana Libre.

la marca, or the brands, of all the items I wore and carried to Cuba. "Is this," people often asked, "a good *marca*?" One of Melba's lovers sported an Adidas tattoo, another asked if I could bring Dolce and Gabbana sunglasses back from the United States. Because consumer culture was largely underground and ad hoc, brands were easily misrecognized and appropriated in unexpected ways.[16] Occasionally, cheap brands gained an air of exclusivity. Melba, for instance, was obsessed with Pantene hair products, considered high end in Cuba, and requested jumbo containers of shampoo and conditioner on each of my return trips to Havana. In an attempt to become fluent in the symbolic meaning of objects, their multiple meanings emerged in a way that reflected Marx's (1978) understanding of the enigmatic aura of commodities.[17]

For Melba and members of her household, consuming certain brands associated with the black diaspora and African American urban culture was especially important. Scholars of Latin America and the Caribbean have discovered similar trends in other contexts in which signs and commodities associated with U.S. blackness have served as cultural resources to craft specific forms of personhood and politics (Anderson 2005, 2009; Brown 1998; Fernandes 2003; Sansone 2003; Thomas 2004). Rather than assume that capitalist consumption oppresses those invested in brand names, Deborah Thomas found that young Jamaican men often used consumption to empower, through a type of "radical consumerism," a creative and potentially liberatory process in which they appropriate U.S. black urban culture to resist "middle-class models of progress" (2004: 250). Mark Anderson (2005, 2009) similarly found that Garifuna men in Honduras utilized commodities associated with Black Americans to construct an emergent "black" identity that projected power and resistance.[18] In Cuba, the appropriation of U.S. street culture and commodities similarly indicated a desire to question state and social standards of respectability.

While consumer drives inspired some sex workers, hustlers also detailed the impossible realities of post-Soviet poverty as motivating their experience in the sex trade. Many from rural provinces often justified their decision to pursue sex work by relaying stories about the profound impact of the economic crisis on rural life. Domingo and his best friend Esteban, a twenty-one-year-old with cream colored skin and black curly hair, lounged on Melba's box spring and, after smoking a thin joint, laughed over stories about the Special Period. "I came to Havana from the Oriente provinces when I was sixteen," Esteban explained, "I didn't know anyone. I ended up driving a bicycle-taxi for four months. A guy picked me up, a *yuma*, and offered me money to sleep with him. I freaked out, punched him and called him a fag." Esteban laughed as he told the story, "Can you imagine?" he asked shaking his head at his naïveté. "Then, every time a guy would look at me, I would tell him off." "What changed your mind?" I asked. "Hunger," he replied, smiling. "Hunger gave me a new perspective, so I went back and said I was ready and that was it." Domingo chimed in with stories about the Special Period. "There was *nada, nada, nada,*" he said. "Like this," he said holding up his pinky finger to mean that he was just skin and bones.

> After the Soviet Bloc fell prices went sky high. There was never electricity. Everyone wore plastic shoes that gave them blisters, but it didn't matter, they only had that one pair. When things started to get better, we threw them to the dogs to chew on, that's how useless they were. Then people left. So many people died. Body parts would wash up on the Malecón. We were twelve and thirteen and hungry, when everyone started trying to leave.

Not only did the Special Period bring about widespread poverty, but hustlers expressed a crisis within traditional socialist value systems as well. Domingo explained that when Cubans fled the island in the 1980s during the Mariel exodus, in which the Cuban government opened the port at Mariel to allow the "scum" of Cuban society to leave for the United States,

"Their neighbors threw eggs at them and called them *gusanos* (worms). In the nineties, the Marielitos came back to the island to vacation and their starving neighbors begged to eat the eggs they brought from the U.S."

Rather than become prey to the nascent capitalist system and the dollarization of the economy, which funneled currency to tourist zones and away from the provinces, young hustlers accustomed to egalitarian policies would master the new system. My neighbor in Havana, Digna, a fifty-nine-year-old poet and fervent supporter of Fidel Castro, recast sex workers as using illicit methods to uphold ingrained ideas about equality:

> These kids grew up in a society where everyone was equal. . . .
> If a person in the city received ten yards of cloth, everyone in the country received ten yards of cloth. If someone in the provinces got a pound of rice, we all got a pound of rice. Then, in the 1990s, tourists started coming to Havana. You bring your tennis shoes and fancy bags [she points to my backpack] and the kids see this and want the same things, they expect the same things. They have never known a world in which some people had things that others could not. So, they do whatever it takes to even the score. These are generations that have no concept of inequity; they cannot accept it.

Digna suggested how histories of socialist equity could lead young people to "even the score." Whereas urban gays criticized *pingueros'* use of *matando la jugada* ["killing the game"] to describe sex work, claiming that gay clients were "the game," an alternative reading highlights how "the game" itself could also be the new neoliberal inroads into Cuban society.[19] Within the mixed market economy, the phallus could represent the *pingueros'* tool to transform inequality into an act of control.[20] Likewise, Melba and her friends, like most hustlers, referred to their work as *luchando* (struggling or fighting). Hustlers cruising the Malecón for tourists often addressed one another by saying, "What's happening?" and responding, "*Aquí en la lucha*," or "Here in the struggle." In Cuba, *la lucha* historically meant the ongoing battle to achieve the goals of revolutionary society (Roland 2011). Tying hustling to Cuban revolutionary survival, Melba and her friends appropriated and deployed socialist rhetoric both with and against the new mixed market economy.[21]

A central aspect of the work Domingo and his friends performed was coming to understand their own bodily performances and affective labor as potential commodities. Separating one's self from one's body marked the body as an item with a market value, distinct from the person. Every commodity system, as Igor Kopytoff (1986) suggests, represents a moral economy because commoditization is a cultural process through which a commodity is recognized as a marketable object. The body can at times become a commodity, and at others go through a process of "singularization," in which it is no longer socially acceptable for bodies to be commodified. Commodity desire supplanted sexual desire in a way that guaranteed virile sexual performance, as the body became at once an item on the market and a vehicle to extract cash and commodities circulating in black markets.

Many male sex workers explained that their bodies responded to the fantasy of cash. They told me that they focused on the money to maintain an erection. Domingo would often simulate taking a tourist from behind, and pretending that his arm was a swelling erection, he would strain out the words, "Ten dollars, twenty, thirty, forty!" as he shot his fist into the air. Young urban men and women increasingly found commodity drives and sexual desires becoming isomorphic, as is often the case under capitalism (Parker and Gagnon 1995: 13).[22] The post-Soviet cultural context at once enabled hustlers and *jineteras* to commodify their bodies while many Cubans denounced the process, suggesting how multiple moral economies can coexist and compete.

Crafting selfhood from brand names and imported goods shaped how *pingueros* honed their bodies as commodities in the post-Soviet economy. Even as sex workers utilized sexual labor to "even the score" or "kill the game," they engaged in a hierarchy that marked only some bodies as exclusive. Their sexual labor circulated in the same black markets as the clothing, shoes, and jewelry that they sought. In the absence of strip clubs, a red light district, or brothels, all sex workers worked on the "street" to one extent or another. Yet a racial topography informed the status of certain zones where hustlers worked. The hustlers in the whiter, middle-class tourist district of Vedado launched their careers in front of the Payret movie theater in the working class, predominantly black and brown neighborhood of Centro Habana. New arrivals would stand awkwardly in front of the theater, wearing worn-out T-shirts and ill-fitting jeans that still held the earthy smell of the provinces. They spoke to one another in thick country accents and wore tennis shoes without socks, an unavoidable habit that led to a putrid stench in a matter of days. They would stand with their hands in their pockets, asking for cigarettes, practicing English phrases such as "Would you like to make love to me?" and "Excuse me sir, where are you going, may I help you?" Eventually the most attractive and charismatic young migrants would make enough money to purchase a new trendier image—tight jeans that flared at the bottom, a fitted lycra top, and designer tennis shoes—so they could take the 11:30 PM bus to Vedado, where they expected to find a higher-paying clientele.

Critics of the sex trade often overestimated the extent to which young people like Domingo could gain class mobility through their success within Havana's sex trade. Many suggested that male and female sex workers were living the *hi-life* through their access to hard currency without toiling away at low-paying jobs. While it is possible that some sex workers benefited financially, those in Melba's social circle barely secured a lifestyle equal to Cubans who received modest remittances from family abroad or earned tips in the tourist industry. If anything, incursions into transactional sex counteracted the severe financial losses that younger generations had experienced since the post-Soviet crisis and allowed them to rectify growing inequalities of wealth. Similarly, consumption played a significant role as commodities enabled young people to fashion new forms of personhood and masculinity. Yet, sex workers' embrace of commodity culture as a means to "kill the game" also meant the commodification of their bodies in ways that perpetuated new hierarchies between them.

DANGER AND THE STATE

The power went out again. No lights, no fans, no air conditioning. We left Melba's apartment and maneuvered down the dark stairwell. As had been our routine for months, we headed to the Malecón. Melba had swept her freshly straightened hair into two side ponytails and was wearing a low-cut spandex dress from a gay male Aruban flight attendant. She wore a pair of army pants from Terrance under the dress, and a new pair of Nike trainers that I had requested from a Canadian lesbian couple. "I look like a rapper, right?" she asked me, proud of her inventiveness.

Melba used the diffuse yellow light from the street lamp to read our horoscopes from a tattered pamphlet a Mexican tourist had given her. As Melba started to read, Yolanda sauntered over, complaining about a cheap Italian who tried to pay $5 for sex. Melba shook her head, and Yolanda lit a cigarette. Suddenly, Melba seemed agitated, raising her voice to tell Yolanda about something that had happened. I could barely make out what she was saying. "Two men from the government came to my house . . . *pinga* . . . who the fuck had given them my new address . . . Domingo only stayed with me three weeks . . . never again," she told her. "It isn't over?" Yolanda asked, looking at the sea. "No, not yet," Melba said.

I waited for Melba to calm down. "Don't you know about the girl who was cut up into little pieces?" Melba asked me impatiently, taking a drag off Yolanda's cigarette. "A couple of years ago, she hung out with us (*andaba con nosotros*). So when she came up, chopped into little pieces and thrown around Havana, Domingo and I went to prison for her murder. She was *jovencita*—seventeen years old."

"Domingo's girlfriend?" I asked, remembering that he had told me about his girlfriend being murdered the first week we had met. I never knew that he and Melba had been accused of killing her.

"Yeah, you remember now. Two months and four days I was in for. I lost seventeen pounds. I can't take that place. It makes me crazy." Just being associated with the girl had been enough to send Domingo and Melba to prison, even though they weren't found guilty of the actual crime.

"But why were they at your house?" I asked.

"The case is still open, they never figured it out. I already served time because I was the last one with her. It was raining, we were at the Yara and it was full of people. I saw her from a distance and told her to come over to me. She said she'd be right back. I told her to come over again; she said that she would come in a little while. I waited; she never came back. I checked at her house, but she wasn't there. Why wasn't I worried?" Melba asked, repeating the question that everyone had burned into her. "I don't worry about anyone but myself. You see me with Yolanda. She goes off, and I don't follow her; she doesn't tell me everything that is going on. I thought the girl had gone with a *yuma*, but I didn't know who she was seeing."

"The girl worked the streets?" I asked.

Melba nodded her head and averted her eyes, "But how was I supposed to know what was happening?" she defended herself against an invisible accuser.

"They never found the murderer?" I asked, wanting Melba to be innocent. Her story sounded so rehearsed that it made me think of all the times she had repeated it for the police, strangers, friends on the hustling scene, and to herself. It came across as a lie, but her story could have simply grown stale from repetition. I wondered if Domingo had been with the girl the night she disappeared but didn't want to risk sounding accusatory.

"It was *profesional*," she said. "The perfect crime, they never figured it out."

"It was a *yuma*," Yolanda said. "Whoever did it, did it fast, and left the country, that's all there is to it."

"I didn't kill anyone," Melba said, looking away from me, balling up the clear plastic wrapper to her cigarette pack and stuffing it between the gaps in her teeth, pressing it into her gums. She threw the wrapper onto the street and lit a cigarette from a new pack. If they arrested her again the day before her birthday she was going to kill someone, she added without a hint of irony.[23]

The most important marker that distinguished Melba's social network from the urban gay households, which also suffered from poverty, was dependence on and vulnerability to the state. Guilty by association, young Cubans involved in the sex trade would eventually be caught in the wrong place at the wrong time—arrest seemed an inevitable consequence. Melba's story of serving time for the murder of the young *jinetera* she knew offered an extreme case, because violent crime was unusual, but the general trend of detention and criminality held true for much lesser acts. Participation in black market economies related to sex tourism frequently resulted in arrest, detention, and deportation back to the provinces. Darker-skinned Cubans were more likely to be assumed criminals, and therefore harassed by police and asked for their identification cards more frequently. Yet, in Melba's social circle, everyone lacking a Havana-based address was detained at one point or another regardless of skin color. The majority of the sex workers in queer enclaves with whom I worked had been detained for illegalities related to the sex trade, including migration from the provinces, theft, and minor assault. Most often they were detained under the law of "social dangerousness" (*un estado peligroso*), or crimes against "the norms of the socialist morality" (Ley no. 62, Código Penal). Sentences ranged from one night in Havana's city jail to one year at a "reeducation camp." Whereas gay Cubans were *mistakenly* detained in round-ups of sex workers in queer enclaves, Melba and her peers constantly negotiated detentions as part of daily life as the government sought to control the influx of foreigners and the rise of illicit markets related to sex tourism.

Police had established a consistent presence in queer enclaves, often moving the crowd from one place to another or demanding to see identification cards to verify that no one was staying in Havana without the proper permits. In the most common interaction, police would detain sex workers for a few hours and then release them after they paid a fine. Rather than arrest someone for sex work, police would detain anyone without a Havana-based address. Esteban explained the *multa* system:

> There are different fines for different things, but being illegal is a 300 peso fine. If you don't pay after two weeks, it goes to 600, then 900; then they arrest you. After you get a fine, you can't get another fine for three more days. So you have three days in Havana before you have to leave.

For instance, one Friday night, Esteban and I were walking toward the Yara when an officer asked for Esteban's identification. As the officer called in his information, Esteban spoke to me in quick hushed tones. "*Mira*, tell the officer that you're my girlfriend. You came from the United States to see me. You called me a week ago and asked me to meet you. We met three years ago, and we're getting married. Got it?" he asked. The police officer told Esteban that he was taking him in for *molestando un turista* (bothering a tourist). I explained that we had been together for years with plans to marry, and the officer told me that I could pick up Esteban at the police station later that night. "Come to the station," Esteban said. "If they see you there they have to let me out because you're a foreigner," as he ducked into the tiny Lada police car. But, at the station, the officers refused to let me in the door. I waited with Domingo outside in the parking lot. Four hours later, Esteban emerged from the station with a 300-peso fine and cursing the police. "In my own country, they say I'm illegal. How can that be?" he waved his hands. "A Mexican can come here on vacation, but me, a Cuban, can't come to Havana?!" He took off his Adidas tennis shoes, a gift from a client but a size too small, and walked in his socks to the nearest major street.

Urban gays described emotional, psychological, and occasionally physical risks that relationships with sex workers presented. In contrast, economically motivated participants weighed the benefits of financial gain against the threat of arrest. Police cited Yolanda twice for being in Havana illegally, and after she stole a piece of chicken from a tourist's plate in Chinatown, they arrested her and sentenced her to a mandatory reeducation camp in the provinces for one year. Similarly, Domingo was eventually arrested for "social dangerousness" after he assaulted a young hustler and, after numerous smaller detentions, was sentenced to nine months.

As much as Melba navigated police harassment and detentions, her vulnerability to poverty intensified her reliance on government subsidies in a way that fortified her faith in the Cuban government. Like Melba, many poorer Cubans chafed at the new class divisions that emerged in post-Soviet society, but their participation in black markets did not predetermine political opinions about the Cuban state. Poor by the strictest official Cuban government standards, Melba relied heavily on diminishing state rations. She often defended the Cuban government and worried about her future should the socialist government fall. When she did blame the government for her daily frustrations, Melba fingered the men surrounding Fidel Castro for "lying to him about the realities of life." She believed that if President Castro knew what was really happening he would make things better. "He is a brilliant man," Melba often told me, "But he is only one man, the people under him don't know what they're doing, and that's what messes the country up. There is no middle class, only two classes in Cuba." While the most marginal communities suffered the greatest impact of economic crisis, they also became the most reliant on socialist safety nets such as food rations, health care, and government housing. Their vulnerability to abject poverty raised their stakes in the success and maintenance of government programs. Melba came to imagine the state as an overly restrictive paternal force that both protected her from destitution and forbade her from accessing hard currency in ways that forced her to be brave, clever, and creative.

PARTING WAYS

Many sex workers took a defensive stance against foreigners—an approach that was fundamental to their success but made it more difficult to feel confident that I had ever completely gained their trust. For instance, when Yolanda arrived unannounced from her hometown in the provinces just weeks after I had met Melba, she refused to talk to me. She simply referred to me as "the *yuma*." When forced to make conversation, she stuck to the classic hustler script—asking where I was from (California), how long I'd been in Cuba (three months), if I liked it (yes), and if I'd slept with anyone (no). By her third week in Havana, perhaps realizing that I was going to be a more long-term problem, she warmed up to me. But I could never shake that initial feeling of distance. I learned the most common tricks that *jineteros* played on foreigners but never felt like an insider—I was always part friend, part mark. One time, Melba and Yolanda recounted a story about a Mexican-American anthropologist whom they had told that they were sisters. They told me the story to inspire confidence, hoping that I might feel welcomed into a private inner circle. Instead, I felt just as naïve and out of place as the anthropologist, who most likely went home to write a chapter about "sisters in the sex trade." I wondered how much Melba and Yolanda were acting to inspire my generosity as a long-term patron—a role that I actually embraced because it assuaged some of my guilt about mining their personal lives for academic research. I often found the open-handed way that they used me for money, connections to other foreigners, and commodities somewhat comforting.

As much as I sympathized with their difficult economic situations and criticized the ways that she and her peers had been criminalized, the possibilities of theft and violence impacted my ability to remain in Melba's social network. Although the infractions were minuscule compared to the guns and drug trade that comprised typical street violence in comparable poor communities in the United States, the possibility of becoming a target for Melba or her friends kept me on guard. Not to say that my friendships with urban gays were immune from economic motivations—my privilege made me an attractive friend and contact—but urban gays did not ask for money on a regular basis and, despite my best efforts, often gave more than they received.

Rumors and accusations from Melba's acquaintances heightened my concerns. For instance, one afternoon Melba's friend Silvio dropped by my apartment. Brushing his shoulder-length, black curly hair away from his face, he pulled out a CD of Cuban love songs that he had brought me as a gift. I waited for him to ask for money, but instead, he warned me to be careful of Melba.

"I don't know if you've heard, but she killed someone and is under police investigation for it. Only she knows what really happened, but she is supposed to maintain contact with the police and hasn't done so for two months." He told me that she might set me up, because one time she had arranged for him to get robbed. "She doesn't do it," he told me, "but she sends people to do it. She might even be with you so it looks like she's not involved. You shouldn't go anywhere alone, and be careful with your camera, because she could send someone to steal it if she knows you're going to be at this spot at this time, like waiting for the bus with the camera."

He left after inviting me to a more "upscale" place than the Malecón to hang out. My first instinct was to distrust this man, whom I had only met a few times, and although he seemed much more self-sufficient than the hustlers I knew, it was clear that he wanted something from me. There was always competition for foreigners, but this seemed extreme. Even though I didn't trust Silvio, I became more suspicious. I told Melba that he had visited me without her, and that I thought it was strange, but I never told her what he had said. I became paranoid and began to wonder if she had sent him to test me. A few nights after his visit, I began having a recurring nightmare that Melba was feeding me dinner, and I realized that she had set me up. In the dream, she was keeping me in the restaurant so that I would be killed. The dream always ended the same way—I realized the danger, started running, and she came after me.

The unspoken tensions I felt with Melba climaxed of their own volition. It was a calm Tuesday night on the Malecón when Melba ran up to me with wide, blood-shot eyes from drinking. I went to kiss her cheek, and she held me back with a strong hand. "You betrayed me," she shouted pointing a stubby index finger at my face, "You're a *traicionera* (backstabber), I should have known." Stunned and embarrassed, I walked away with Melba's shouts trailing off behind me. Silvio's visit could have sparked the confrontation, but the conflict also arose after I had spent a week with a group of wealthy gay tourists from Los Angeles. From Melba's perspective, I had shifted my affinities on the Malecón and excluded her, abandoning my usual role as a go-between for her and foreign patrons. Foreigners who knew Melba assured me that her anger was routine.[24] Many of my gay Cuban friends interpreted Melba's behavior as a result of jealousy and frustrated romantic desires. "It's obvious," one lesbian friend explained, "that she was in love with you. She understood you would never be with her, but when you stopped paying attention to her, she felt betrayed."

For me, our falling-out suggested how resentments and failures to maintain intimacy play a critical role in the construction of ethnographic knowledge.[25] Although my conflict with Melba seemed to resolve itself— we never spoke of it again and months later I would return to her house for brief visits—our friendship never returned to the initial intimacy that I had enjoyed those first few months. I often thought about her accusations of "betrayal" as an attack on the two-faced nature of ethnographic fieldwork, what Zora Neale Hurston described as "the spyglass of Anthropology" (Hurston 1990: 1), which enables us to observe but also implicates us in acts of surveillance. I took comfort in Aihwa Ong's notion, however, that anthropologists can also betray their collaborators if we refuse to represent their voices, which often "insist on being heard" (1995: 354).[26] Most important, my own inability to maintain the same level of integration with Melba that I created with urban gay households suggested that my movements and relationships, and hence perspective, were subject to very real social boundaries. Rather than signifying failure, my tension with Melba taught me an invaluable lesson about my own place in the emergent social hierarchies cutting through Havana's contemporary queer enclaves.

While my insight into the lives of Melba and her friends might have been partial, from my perspective it seemed that she and her peers did not see their behavior as morally corrupt, which reflected trends among *jineteras*.[27] Undeterred by accusations that they were "low-class" or "marginal," many young people working in Havana's queer enclaves cast themselves as smarter than the rest for taking advantage of new prospects while creating solidarity with others in similar situations. Hence, instead of narrating their life stories as victims of poverty, they alluded to the structural disadvantages that shaped their lives while honoring the ways in which they creatively navigated the changing social-sexual landscape of post-Soviet Havana.[28] They challenged some entrenched values but held tight to traditional beliefs about gender and hard work. Melba and her friends survived by using informal systems of redistribution—customary Caribbean values of sharing intensified by years of socialism— but these ideals chafed against enduring poverty. From Melba's perspective, the measured introduction of foreign capitalists and dual economies had split Cuba into two classes—rich and poor.

CHAPTER 5

"Get Off the Bus"

SEX TOURISM, PATRONAGE, AND
QUEER COMMODITIES

Beginning in 1997, Boyd and Karl traveled twice a year from Scotland to vacation in Havana, where they would hunt for black market antiques, drink rum on the Malecón, and pay *pingueros* for sexual favors. Boyd, a wiry white schoolteacher in his sixties, wore large oval eyeglasses and crossed his legs at the knee. Upon meeting me, he laughed and declared through a thick Scottish accent, "We've had so much cock I'm about to be bloody sick!" The couple, both nearing retirement, had been together for twenty-eight years. Boyd and Karl had never told anyone in their provincial village about their relationship for fear that Boyd would have lost his position at the local middle school. They lived in separate houses and limited the number of nights they slept over. Karl, a mailman with red hair, a freckled face, stocky build, and Scottish pluck, joked that the distance was the secret to the longevity of their relationship. Boyd, unamused by Karl's antics, lamented the absence of even an underground gay community.

Discussions of their oppressive hometown bled into a broader conversation about the political tensions between Scotland and Britain. Pointing out that Scotland had only recently won its independence, they recognized similarities between their country's strained relations with England and Cuba's ongoing struggles with the United States. Boyd worried that once Cuba lost Fidel Castro, the government would cease to resist U.S. military aggression. "It's all going to change when Castro dies," he said, pouring rum into a plastic cup, "Raúl doesn't have the following. He's an alcoholic and everyone thinks he's gay. Then you all [the United States] are going to invade and it won't be the same. It's bound to happen."

The couple claimed that they were addicted to Cuba even though Cubans "always tried to rip off tourists." Karl explained, "Even our tour guide, who we use every time, rips us off. Everyone does, you get savvy after a couple of trips. We get home and complain and swear we'll never be back, and then a week later we look at each other and ask if it's time to make the flight reservation." They stayed at the four-star Hotel Nacional overlooking the Malecón, but lied to Cubans and said that they were guests at the Habana Libre Hotel, the former Hilton, so Cubans wouldn't realize how wealthy they were. (For most Cubans, however, the Habana Libre reeked of the same level of foreign affluence as the high-end Hotel Nacional.) The state-imposed segregation between foreigners and Cubans bothered them, "The Cubans can't even get into the hotels!" Karl said. "Not even our tour guide. He has to wait in the lobby. It's absurd." The laws prohibiting Cubans from entering hotels prevented Boyd and Karl from entertaining *pingueros* in their room, so they rented an additional bedroom in a *casa particular* (private house).[1] They normally paid between $15 and $20 for an evening of sex, gave *pingueros* a few dollars extra for the cab ride home, and offered presents such as Calvin Klein underwear. "They love the brand names," Boyd remarked. The couple imagined themselves as a neutral, if not positive, presence in Havana and felt they could do more to further national development if the government would lessen the restrictions on their participation. "It's really too bad they won't let us buy houses. We'd keep them up. We could help and buy paint and make the city look nice," they said.

Havana provided Boyd and Karl with a space outside of their homophobic hometown where they could be open about their relationship and pursue same-sex encounters. As Jon Binnie points out, tourism often offers gay travelers an opportunity to belong (Binnie 2004: 88). Ironically, the freedom Boyd and Karl described had little to do with the leniency of Cuban social mores regarding homosexuality but rather reflected the privileged status afforded to foreign tourists. These privileges, combined with their feelings of political solidarity toward Cuba, sheltered Boyd and Karl from discerning how foreign tourism contrasted with Cuba's traditional socialist value system and compromised the defiant nationalist politics they lauded. Ignoring the dissolution of private property as a key tenet to building Cuba's revolutionary society, Boyd and Karl were unaware of how tourists contributed to the rise in commodity desires and materialistic values in Havana. For instance, they noted that *pingueros* loved Calvin Klein underwear but did not connect this brand loyalty with recent social transformations and the tireless efforts of the Cuban Ministry of Culture to discourage consumer culture. Similarly, Boyd and Karl argued that segregation of tourists was unjust but failed to recognize how government leaders had created the laws to prevent sex tourism, the very thing that brought Boyd and Karl to Cuba.

In this chapter, I explore the stories of gay men who made repeated trips to Cuba. I argue that multiple layers of mistranslation and misunderstanding distorted the perspectives of gay foreigners on holiday in Havana. Scholarship on queer tourism has often divided gay travelers into two groups—activists invested in political travel and pleasure tourists seeking sun, sand, and sex (Puar 2002).[2] This perceived binary between the political gay activist and the hedonistic sex tourist is false; in Havana politics and sex worked in conjunction to structure tourist experiences. Cuban revolutionary history played a key role in attracting gay tourists to Havana, yet in order for tourists to view sex workers as commodities, they had to ignore socialist collapse and embargo politics and discount the sexual identities of the straight hustlers they hired. In a classic case of "imperialist nostalgia" (Rosaldo 1993) or longing for that which they had destroyed, queer tourists remained blind to the impact they had on local, informal economies. Rather than fault the travelers for cultural insensitivity or ignorance, however, I examine how their perspectives were influenced by tourist segregation policies and international media representations of Cuba, which were at an all-time high during the first decade of the twenty-first century.

Numerous scholars have documented the neocolonial and heterosexist underpinnings of the tourist sex trade around the globe, with a particular wealth of research on Cuba.[3] Sex tourists are typically imagined to be middle-aged, single, heterosexual white men who travel to Third World countries to take advantage of bargain prices for sexual services.[4] Scholars have more recently highlighted, however, that sex tourist encounters between foreigners and local sex workers exhibit a range of entanglements that blur the lines between transactional sex and noncommodified forms of intimacy.[5] Yet, scholars often imagine sex tourism as a fundamentally heterosexual enterprise, so little attention has been paid to the experiences and perspectives of gay tourists who purchase sex on holiday. This analytical vacuum makes it easier for depictions of gay foreigners to border on stereotype and to perpetuate the notion that sex tourists are motivated by sex alone.[6] In an effort to nuance our understanding of tourists' roles in post-Soviet Havana, I do not assume that all relationships between foreigners and Cubans were exploitative simply because they crossed uneven racial, national, and sexual boundaries (Binnie 2004: 106). I show how relationships between foreign gay patrons and young male hustlers inspired multiple forms of intimacy and reciprocity that at times obscured unequal socioeconomic positions, and at others drew foreigners into reciprocal ties with hustlers and their families. Even as gay travelers in Havana embodied forms of racial and gender privilege that underlie sex tourism, they also challenged the heterosexism at the heart of the global sex industry.[7]

Anthropologists often go to great lengths to distinguish themselves from tourists, citing the duration of their trips and our erudite approach to the politics, history, and culture of the fieldsite. During my time in Cuba, however, I often found myself in a similar role to that of foreign gay tourists. Although my relationships with sex workers were platonic, the long-term patronage ties I established mirrored the bonds between hustlers and foreign gay clients. In place of sexual intimacy, hustlers offered me access to their daily lives. My exchange of gifts and money for friendship reflected common practices of ethnographic fieldwork, but, surprisingly, this dynamic was often reversed in my relationships with older, wealthy gay male tourists.

As a young female graduate student from a working-class background I enjoyed privileges denied to Cubans but ranked in a lower socioeconomic standing than the majority of gay male tourists with whom I spent time. Ironically, as the recipient of the friendship, gifts, and social connections of wealthy foreigners, I was often aligned with Cubans. One experience stands out in my mind as emblematic of this dynamic. I had met Cole on the Malecón. He was a fifty-one-year-old, handsome white Jewish fashion designer originally from South Africa who was now living in Beverly Hills. After spending two weeks as part of his entourage, we had become "best girlfriends," as he described it. After months suffering through power outages, food shortages, and homesickness, I accepted his invitation to share his room at the Hotel Nacional. He invited me to take a bath, relax in his fluffy bathrobe and Prada slippers, and gossip about his Cuban boyfriends as we drifted off to sleep. The line between research and friendship had collapsed.

The next morning Cole and I met with his four gay male travel bud-
dies in the lobby as the porter loaded their Louis Vuitton luggage into a
black Mercedes to head to the airport. I stood awkwardly by the side of
the car, about to be left behind, after having spent two weeks squished
beside Cole's friends and handsome young Cuban hustlers as we were
chauffeured from the beach to salsa competitions and high-end restaurants around Havana. As the car sped down the long palm-lined driveway
of the Hotel Nacional, the four Cuban "boyfriends" began walking down
the driveway without me. As I called to them, they turned and laughed.
"We thought you were leaving with them!" one young hustler said. "No
more Mercedes, right?" Alongside the young men, I carried my plastic
bag of clothing, gifts, and designer toiletries as we walked back to Centro
Habana.

If I had met Cole under different circumstances, we would have established a friendship without an undertone of patronage. But he became
my patron as well as my friend and sent me his clothing designs, called
me regularly despite the inordinate cost of calls to Cuba, and invited me
on his adventures during return trips to the island. I positioned myself
as both a fellow foreigner and a beneficiary of wealthy tourists; I found
myself playing both sides, both hustler and hustled.[8] These experiences
helped me to understand the complexity of Cubans' relationships with
tourists, many of whom Cubans might genuinely like, even if their encounters were motivated by money. I adored Cole and would have established a friendship without his generosity. Yet, at the same time, it was
impossible to imagine an alternative version of our friendship because
his glamorous embrace of the high life so thoroughly defined him. So
while my affection was authentic, it was inextricably shaped by his material generosity and my ethnographic need for access and information.

Being on the receiving end of this patronage relationship illuminated
how Cubans' ties with foreigners, including me, did not have to be based
entirely upon strategic instrumentality, but at the same time, part of the
appeal of and attraction to foreigners was undeniably the privilege and
potential for opportunities that they embodied. The visits of wealthy
tourists broke the monotony of daily life and offered a feeling of exces-
sive luxury and leisure in a world dominated by scarcity. It was a rush
just to have something glamorous to do to counteract the boredom. I
also came to appreciate the rescue fantasies of Cubans who worked the
Malécon tirelessly in search of the right connection that could alter their

lives indefinitely. With wealthy tourists as the ambassadors from abroad, even I was seduced by the impression that riches could be easily accessed beyond the island's shores, that fortune could come without effort, and I began to imagine the world outside Cuba as a land of endless opportunity. I began to wonder how my own family had managed to remain working-class in such unfettered abundance. The tourists brought with them a charged aura of boundless potential that stretched beyond the scope of the imagination. Yet, eventually, foreigners—including me—always departed the island and left Cubans behind to make the long, hot walk back to their normal lives.

CRAFTING KINSHIP TIES

Orlando was a single, white, forty-four-year-old lawyer from Spain who made month-long visits to Cuba every three months. Tan with salt and pepper hair, Orlando had a soft, relaxed demeanor. We met at a birthday party for Melba, and he immediately corrected my Cuban accent with a warm air of familiarity, as he fondled the biceps of a shirtless twenty-one-year-old hustler. Orlando's Cuban boyfriend, twenty-three-year-old Juan, also attended the party, and Orlando explained that he supported Juan when he was away and always included him on his visits, but also hired other hustlers for sex. During a few of Orlando's visits to Havana, he traveled with his ex-boyfriend, a British photographer with closely cropped red hair and pale skin. They always rented the same apartment in Vedado, where they had three or four young hustlers who would cook, clean, pose for nude photo shoots, host parties, and have sex. Juan was always welcome, but only stayed with Orlando a little more than half the time.

Within a month after they met, Orlando became involved in Juan's family affairs. Orlando described his first visit to Juan's house, where he was shocked at the miserable living conditions. "Five people in one room, with no bathroom and hardly a kitchen," he said, shaking his head. "It was incredible. So I moved his family into a rental with furniture and everything, and I paid the rent for six months." Orlando "adopted" his boyfriend's three-year-old nephew, who learned to call Orlando "papa." Orlando's integration into Juan's family and his long-term commitment to Juan's nephew suggest how hustlers and gay Cubans forge alternative kinship links with foreign tourists. The fact that Orlando sent money during his time in Spain mirrored the kinship ties of Cuban émigrés who sent remittances to their families on the island.

Same-sex hustlers in Havana often had no access to hard currency and received no money from family abroad. Hustlers who crafted ongoing kinship ties with foreign gay tourists ensured that they and their families would receive some form of support for an extended period of time. According to Cuban reports, in 2002 remittances were around $820 million, and 60 percent of the population was receiving money, with Cuban individuals on average receiving more from foreigners and Cubans living abroad than the average annual earnings of state workers (Mesa-Lago and Pérez-López 2005: 78). The distribution of remittances is hard to measure, but Cuban analysts estimate that although 35 percent of total households received them in 2001, only 5 percent went to the lowest income bracket (Iniguez et al. 2001). The reliability of gay patrons' remittances as a source of income is impossible to determine. It is not clear if gay remittance relations were any less reliable than those of blood relatives, who would often cease support due to personal circumstances and a growing distance from their responsibilities on the island.

Transnational systems of queer kinship would appeal to gays from the United States and Europe, where kinship discourses were often used to create alternative families. As Kath Weston (1991) highlights, gay men and women in San Francisco used discourses of "family" and "kinship" to mold bonds of affection, intimacy, and secure financial support. Weston argues that rather than displace or deconstruct the links between procreation and kinship, urban gays challenged the idea that "blood" was the only way a family could be made. Similar to urban gays in the United States, queer tourists who adopted the role of family members with male sex workers saw families they chose as acts of self-determination and creativity. Although some foreign gay tourists were able to invite Cuban boyfriends or hustlers out of the country, the state-sanctioned option of marriage was not available to most gay foreigners in Cuba at the time of my research.

Yet, the patronage relationship functioned only as long as the foreigner could dictate the terms of distribution of goods and cash. Despite Orlando's financial assistance, Juan's mother was adamant about receiving more money. "After I rented them the house she said I should buy her a house instead," Orlando told me. "And then, she paid me a visit yesterday morning, I wasn't even out of bed. There was no 'How are you, sorry to wake you up.' I opened the door and she said that she had received a $100 fine and she needed the money." Orlando took a drag off his cigarette. "Of course, I said, I'll take care of it, don't worry about it." He proceeded to tell Juan's mom:

> And if it's a legal fine, then we can appeal it or I can go to this place and pay it for you. However, if it is an illegal fine then I will give you the $100 right now, and never give you anything else and it will be good-bye, you'll never come here again. Oh, she said, I think I have someone who can help me take care of it. And sure enough, that afternoon, she calls me and says that her friend pulled some strings and miraculously the fine disappeared. I do everything for the family. I got them a house. I give them money for food. I buy the kids clothes. After all that she comes to my house with a fine. Juan was crying in bed last night because he can't stand his mother. She's always telling him to ask for money and things from me so she can have them. He can't take it.

Cubans would often apply the same pressure to foreign patrons as they might to family members. While Cubans abroad assumed familial obligations, gay tourists did not see themselves as responsible for Cubans on a permanent basis. From their perspective, they were being charitable, and charity had limits. Rather than depart from dominant blood kinship, however, this bounded intimacy actually reflected the dynamics of many family relationships in which migrants would abandon family obligations once they moved off the island. While Cubans might contrast the relationships of choice and blood, the similarities between them highlight how both types of kin bonds were socially imbued.

In Cuba, many foreign gay tourists, like Orlando, were inspired by the performances of same-sex hustlers to create alternative kinship and marriage systems through which remittances solidified the bonds between them. Analysts have shown how sex tourism is unique because, unlike prostitution, direct monetary exchange for sexual services is often absent and tourists spend extended lengths of time with sex workers.[9] A number of studies show how a relationship between a tourist and a sex worker can evolve and change over time. The interaction may start with sexual service for cash, and then the tourist and sex worker may become "travel companions" or marry (Cohen 1993). Gay sex tourism similarly fit these models, with the added dimension of creating transnational networks and sharing notions of political solidarity and mutual transgression of social norms that made gay tourists feel even more at home in Havana. At the same time, the patronage dynamics between foreigners and Cubans often led tourists to underestimate the extent to which they dictated the terms of the agreement.

In order to understand these varied relationships, I draw on enduring anthropological inquiries into gift giving and reciprocity. This analytical tradition builds on the work of Marcel Mauss (1967 [1923]), a French sociologist who suggested that even within capitalism, forms of exchange still fostered social solidarity. Mauss was writing in the 1920s, a moment when people had heightened concerns about the deleterious effects of capitalism. His perspective is often read as a counter to Marx's (1978) notion that capitalism fosters widespread alienation because commodity exchanges obscure the relationship between the consumer and the producer. For Marx, capitalism destroyed social bonds, but for Mauss a market economy could forge connections of reciprocity between people.[10]

What I discovered in post-Soviet Cuba, however, was the coexistence of systems of solidarity and alienation. Sometimes, Cubans viewed foreigners' gifts as initiating them into a network of reciprocity that was distinctly socialist, whereas foreigners approached the transaction as bounded from the start. At other times, gay tourists initiated kin-like relationships with sex workers that reflected gay kinship structures in their home countries, and sex workers sought to limit the interaction to sex for cash. In both cases, the commodities, cash, and affect traded between gay foreigners and sex workers suggested how the collision of economic systems in a post-Cold War world was profoundly shaped by competing cultural understandings about intimacy and obligation.

DIFFERENT APPROACHES AMONG SEX TOURISTS

Marc and his partner of twenty years, Paul, had been traveling from Beverly Hills, California, to Havana three or four times a year for six years. Marc was a strapping, six-foot-four advertising executive in his late forties with clear gray eyes, a thick mane of graying hair, and an unassuming, pink-cheeked countenance. Slightly shorter, with a shock of thick blond hair, Paul was in his late fifties and had a pockmarked face that seemed to disappear behind the wide rectangles of his tangelo-colored, plastic-rimmed glasses. The son of a billionaire California real estate baron, Paul enjoyed a successful career as a high-end interior designer. Marc and Paul's first trip to Cuba was with a Latin American art dealer who brought them to galleries in Havana to shop for up-and-coming talent. "We have so much Cuban art, it's like cocaine," Marc told me the night we met, "We have an entire storage locker full, but I can't stop buying it."

The goal for many gay tourists was to have sexual adventures with attractive young men, but the context of Cuba was central to the fantasy. Especially for U.S.-based tourists, the allure of an illicit island fostered the aura of an elite, queer cosmopolitan subjectivity. I had introduced myself to the couple on the Malecón when I overheard Marc explaining to a *pinguero* what DKNY meant in English. "Don't you just love the Malecón?" he said when he found out I was from the United States. "We always get the party started. We show up and suddenly there's music, and everyone wants to talk to us because they can see that we're having such a great time. I just love to come out here and really get things rolling." Paul added, "I've worked for a lot of really rich people, and they are all miserable. These people have nothing, and they find such joy in life. It's amazing. Totally divine."

Marc and Paul had a reputation for wealth and generosity. They had invited one of their Cuban boyfriends, Junior, to move in with them for a year while he established himself in the United States. Junior eventually became a high-paid masseur who offered sexual services in Southern California. When Marc and Paul vacationed in Havana they always visited Junior's mother, taking gifts and cash along with news of her son. I accompanied them on one of the visits and watched as Junior's mother cried and thanked them for their help. The couple sent money every month to the hustlers that they had been visiting for years, and although the group had expanded, they always showed financial loyalty to their original contacts. Marc tried to establish relationships that would last even if he moved on to hiring others for sex. During one visit, Marc developed a crush on a blond, gay-identified hustler who spoke good English, which allowed a deeper level of trust and connection between them. "I just gave him a hundred dollar bill," Marc said to me, a little drunk. "I told him that he needs it more than me, and that's no bullshit, I hope that we can be lifelong friends."

One night while Marc was waiting for his date, he told me about his latest love interest. "He called me and said, 'I like you and I want to see you tonight,' and I thought, '*You do*?'" Marc stared up the sea wall for his new lover. "So, we've worked it out for tonight. Paul has a boyfriend and they're going to go off so I can have my date," Marc said. "I mean, really, what's the big deal? We've had sex every night since we got here. It's really nothing to go off with some young kid and jack off together; it's just about the fantasy of it." I understood this to mean that transactional sexual encounters freed Marc to position his relationships in a realm of fantasy, outside the world of domesticated sex that he shared with his partner. His perspective embodied a trend in the United States in which sexual consumption among male buyers had shifted to a recreational model of sexual behavior, in which the commodification of sex did not hinder, but rather facilitated, erotic pleasure (Bernstein 2007: 108).

Youth and beauty were especially important to Marc and Paul. They told me in great detail about an anti-aging clinic they visited regularly where they received Botox injections and vitamin IV drips. Their obsession with staying youthful inspired Marc's comments on the bodies of younger hustlers and nurtured the feeling that they were keeping up with the young, gay boys in Havana. Attesting to the rejuvenating qualities of Havana, Marc and Paul had brought along James, a seventy-five-year-old self-identified "queen" with a wide smile to infuse him with vitality. James put his hand on my knee while he talked openly about sex, love, and growing up gay "before it was trendy." Formerly a nurse, James now worked as a hairstylist for major Hollywood film productions. He rattled off a list of impressive celebrities that he had styled. Marc chimed in, "James recently bought a white Rolls Royce, you'd think she was rich, not crazy!" "I've barely put a mile on it," James admitted, "We just drive it twelve miles a week. But I have a guy who polishes it inside and out every day. We go two blocks and turn around, and I feel absolutely glamorous."

James told me that he had taken Viagra an hour before because, as he said, "at seventy-five I don't get it up anymore." The pill started to kick in and he excused himself as he hurried away to a *casa particular* to have sex with Eugenio, a young muscular hustler with a deep golden tan, spiky hair dyed blond, and deep dark brown eyes. Later James explained:

I've been going to the same gay bar for twenty-five years and the difference is that in LA, a kid this young and this good looking would never put his arm around me. I mean never, not in a hundred years. So what if he needs a little money. It's worth it, to feel wanted, and by someone so young and good looking. Sister, it's fantastic!

He expressed relief that someone so young and attractive would be openly affectionate with him, something that he felt he could never get at the gay clubs at home. James had met Eugenio on the beach three days earlier. "Can you believe it, this one approached *me!*" he exclaimed.

Eugenio was deaf and accompanied by his friend Vicente, who served as an informal sign language interpreter. Vicente explained that Eugenio had traveled to six different countries, including Russia and Italy, through the invitations of foreign tourists. Despite his disability, Eugenio did not see himself as a victim to the sex trade. James felt Eugenio's hearing impairment made theirs a perfect match, "We can't even pretend to talk. I have no idea what the fuck he's saying, and you should see his cock! My god!" James admitted that Eugenio needed financial support but still felt flattered that he would "choose" James as a source of assistance. He described a genuine affection for Eugenio and wanted to help him buy his hearing aid. But James did not want the same type of long-term patronage relationship that Marc and Paul sought. In fact, he often criticized Marc and Paul for being naïve and getting too involved with the Cubans they met, who were just looking for a "Mr. Goodbar." James's attitude reflected the broad range of involvement that could exist among tourists—even friends who frequently traveled together—and illuminates the diversity of the "sex tourist" experience among gay travelers.

While Marc and Paul often exceeded the norms of payment and were understood as generous by Cuban hustlers in their social circle, for the wealthy tourists from L.A., their relationship to Havana served them professionally back home. For instance, Marc and his friends were high-end producers in the culture and fashion industries. Marc worked in an innovative marketing firm that designed advertising campaigns for companies like Guess clothing, which was considering an entire series called the "Havana line." They took Cuban fashions to be authentic and "more hip than anything you'd see in the United States," and used what they saw in Havana as inspiration for their own creative designs. Likewise, Marc and Paul attended meetings with the "Havana Company," a Cuban and Canadian cofinanced corporation. The Havana Company was looking for foreign investors to support their fledgling efforts to market Cuba's culture industries—music, fashion design, and models—and planned to sell the rights to U.S.-based conglomerates once the island opened to capitalist markets. As Ana Dopico suggests, the United States was flooded with Cuban images but lagged behind in economic investments in a way that inspired market appetites (2002: 452).

Marc and Paul assumed the styles Cubans wore on the Malecón were original, local creations and then refashioned the looks into commodities that could be sold on a global market. Unaware of how the clothing and combinations were gifts brought from tourists and families in Europe, Latin America, and Canada, Marc and Paul described them as authentically Cuban. In a queer transnational feedback loop, commodities from abroad would come to Havana and gay tourists would refashion the designs. The gay enclaves in Havana provided gays an opportunity to discover the familiar in an exotic context, and therefore to feel as if their tastes were validated by their universal appeal. The tourists from Beverly Hills traversed cultural differences, language barriers, and border patrols to find that the natives, like them, were wearing Gucci.[11]

RULES OF PATRONAGE

Many gay travelers like James and the couple from Scotland returned to Cuba on a regular basis and brought gifts for hustlers whom they paid for sex. Their embrace of the "boyfriend" experience reflected similar trends that scholars have noted among heterosexual male tourists. For instance, Julia O'Connell Davidson (1995) describes how tourists would stay with one woman for several days or weeks, paying her expenses and offering financial help, which enhanced the illusion that the attraction was mutual.[12] Other gay tourists like Marc, Paul, and Orlando were sincere in their concern and affection for the hustlers they came to know. They established continuing patronage relationships with Cuban hustlers, arrangements that might involve very few sexual interactions as the foreigners found new lovers. Yet, even these more intimate encounters with hustlers and their families could be tested when the Cubans refused to play by the rules of patronage, showing the limits of tourists' generosity. On many occasions, I heard tourists complain that their "boyfriends" were never satisfied with the gifts they brought for them, no matter how extravagant. For instance, Paul told me that he was annoyed with Humberto, who had requested a pair of red Puma tennis shoes, which Paul had bought. The next day, Humberto asked for $30 to buy a pair of tennis shoes from a friend. "It wasn't the money," he explained, "but I just felt like he was getting a little greedy when I had just bought him some shoes." What Paul didn't realize was that Humberto needed money, but asking for shoes or "gifts" instead of cash helped to soften the financial motivation of their encounters. It was easier to ask for commodities that he could sell on the black market after Paul had left the country. I believed Paul when he said that it wasn't about the money; he continued to spend hundreds of dollars a day on Humberto. Rather, his discomfort came from the notion that Humberto controlled the terms of exchange. This forced Paul to consider economic realities on Humberto's terms. Consequently, tourists might describe Cubans as greedy, insatiable, and unrealistic about the spending power of the foreigners with whom they had relations.

Similarly, many gay foreigners recounted times that they had been "cheated" or "ripped off" by Cubans that they trusted. What struck me about the stories was how tourists felt betrayed when hustlers took things that the tourists were willing to give away in another context. Julio, a wealthy forty-year-old Mexican American tourist, who had first vacationed in Havana with Marc and Paul and then returned on his own for six years in a row, told me about his perception that materialism was contaminating Havana:

> There was this one kid who started following me and talking to me. He asked me for my pants. He said he worked hard to support his family, but he still didn't have any pants and asked if I could give him mine. He followed me to Hotel Nacional. I went upstairs, took off my pants and brought them to him. He showed up at the hotel the next day in my pants, shirt, and shoes and came with us to the airport. When I saw him the next year, we hung out a bit and he said he would walk me home because it wouldn't be safe. But he came with me and when he hugged me at the hotel, he stole my camera out of my pocket. A nice Nikon camera too. I couldn't believe it. I haven't seen him to ask him *why the fuck he wouldn't just ask for it*. You have to be straight with these people and just say no and tell them to stop the bullshit.

Julio's role as the generous benefactor had reached its limits. Julio couldn't understand why, after he had been willing literally to give the shirt off his back, the Cuban would betray him during his next visit. Julio failed to connect the commodities that he brought and the wealth he represented to the growing greed he criticized. In contrast, I considered the anger and cynicism that the young hustler may have felt at the injustice of standing on the steps of the Hotel Nacional, forbidden from entering the rooms where his parents might have spent their honeymoon.

Foreigners often commented on Cubans' attachment to commodities and underestimated their need for cash. I saw many designer items sold on the black market for a fraction of the cost the day after tourists left Havana. One time Marc asked me to carry a Dolce and Gabbana jacket, which he purchased in New York City for $300, to his boyfriend. The hustler sold it the same day he received it to another hustler for $10. I gingerly suggested to Marc that he and Paul didn't need to spend so much on designer clothing when that money could support a Cuban and his family for months. "So what are you saying," Marc replied defensively, "that I should downgrade from Prada to Banana Republic? Honey, please!"

How foreigners determined appropriate gifts speaks to the ways in which gay patrons set the terms and limits of the relationships. Whether or not they continued to offer cash and gifts was entirely up to them, often leaving the Cubans they befriended feeling desperate. For instance, Marc and his friends introduced me to Bianca, a white twenty-six-year-old *travesti*, with short platinum blonde hair, skin soft from hormone injections, dark Dolce and Gabbana jeans, and red leather flats. The daughter of a beauty queen, she exuded 1950s sophistication among women and *travestis* in spandex, vying for the attention of tourists. Bianca loved cinema and described meeting Pedro Almodóvar, one of her icons, and Benicio del Toro during Havana's International Film Festival. She recited passages from the *Celluloid Closet* and acted out entire scenes from *What Ever Happened to Baby Jane?* alternating between Joan Crawford and Bette Davis.

Almost immediately, I recognized Bianca's uncanny talent for gauging her audience and inspiring foreign patronage, including my own. Within minutes of meeting her, she grabbed my hand and began telling me a story. "One time, I was dating this prince from Spain," Bianca told me. "He took me to the countryside in this limo. We were sniffing cocaine the entire way. It was fabulous. When we got there, I stumbled out with a long ponytail on and these huge sunglasses, I was so high!" The image that Bianca described—a limousine in the countryside, an expensive wig, and a foreign dignitary—represented a queer fairy tale in which Bianca appeared painstakingly cosmopolitan and shipwrecked on an island that staggered behind her. In her story, Bianca aligned herself with her foreign clients, rather than the provincial Cubans who served as a backdrop for adventures.

Bianca acutely understood that the realities of poverty dampened the party and disrupted Marc and Paul's vacation fantasy. Her private life differed dramatically from the public image of glamour that she so seamlessly projected. Bianca waited until months after Marc and Paul left before she allowed me to visit her home. On the outskirts of Havana, she and Eduardo, a former pimp, shared a tiny, one-room studio that held a fold-up bed, three wooden chairs with the backs broken out, and a ten-inch black and white television set. Bianca's hair was swept up in a rag. She wore a stained tank top, and had allowed a stubbly beard to make its way across her face. Perhaps sensing my surprise at the difference, Bianca quickly turned my attention to a stack of plastic Mickey Mouse photo albums. In the photographs, she smiled into the camera wearing an outrageous pair of zebra print platform boots and a dress made entirely of feathers. "I had caviar for the first and last time," she said, describing the party at which the pictures were taken. "It was so divine!"

When Marc and Paul returned to Havana, Bianca used me as her translator, even though she spoke a fair amount of English. I was given the task of requesting a few dollars on her behalf for cigarettes or beer, and then Bianca would pocket the money for living expenses. Eventually the tourists grew tired of Bianca and began to complain that she was around too much and that her constant requests for cash had become annoying. As they began to refrain from inviting her to clubs and the beach, she became more desperate and, therefore, increasingly aggressive. They eventually ignored her completely.

Gay patrons like Marc and Paul did not rationalize their sexual ties with notions of benevolence or rescue. They associated primarily with lighter-skinned and white Cubans, which mirrored their friendships in the United States and allowed them to feel more "at home," while still offering the exoticism of Latin racial and class differences. In contrast, heterosexual male sex tourists often utilized notions of charity and "help" to justify their visits to the Caribbean for sex, thus masking the inequalities that enabled a sex tourist to perceive himself as benevolent and desirable (Kempadoo 2004: 124). For gay patrons, however, sex with Cuban men was not seen as taboo, but rather was naturalized through notions of promiscuity and sexual adventure popular in mainstream U.S. gay male culture. The gifts and money they "gave" to hustlers were instead symbols of their own affluence and fortified their position as queer gatekeepers when it came to designer panache. If they were saving Cuban hustlers, it was from fashion disaster rather than humanitarian tragedy.

MARKETING CUBA, STRUCTURING SEX TOURIST EXPERIENCE

The sexualized overtones of the marketing of Cuba suggested that gendered, racialized, and sexualized representations crafted the island in visitors' imaginations before they landed. These visions often served as a foundation for contemporary tourist perspectives regarding the island. Just as the circulation of tourists' gifts and cash signaled the changing nature of social relationships in the post-Soviet era, Cuba itself became a commodity on the global market for the first time since the 1950s. Anthropologist Paulla Ebron (2002: 23) describes a similar process in which "African culture," in the form of art objects, clothing, music, and folklore, has been refashioned into a cultural commodity that can hold political resonance for international consumers. In the post-Soviet era, a wide range of Cuban cultural experiences were packaged and sold to tourists, including Afro-Cuban religion, socialist health care, and tropical beaches. Revolutionary kitsch, antique Chevrolets, and eroticized representations of Cuban bodies emerged as iconic selling points. For instance, in volumes compiled by photographers from Europe and the United States that portray life in post-Soviet Cuba, the exposed body of the *mulata* looms large.

The prerevolutionary tourist boom continued to inform contemporary tourist fascinations with the island. During the prerevolutionary era, discourses of personal freedom and liberty to indulge in pleasure constructed Cuba as a place to "flaunt conventions, to indulge unabashedly in fun and frolic in bars and brothels, at the racetrack and the roulette table, to experiment with forbidden alcohol, drugs and sex" (Pérez 1999: 187). By the late 1950s approximately 270 brothels operated in Havana with more than 11,500 women working as prostitutes, prompting *Time* magazine to describe Havana as "one of the world's fabled fleshpots" (Pérez 1999: 193). In particular, the tourist industry trafficked in racialized sexual images, such as the figure of the sexually voracious *mulata*, which appeared in prominent campaigns for transnational consumers (Moore 1997).

Despite the revolutionary rupture, tourists often set out with the hope of discovering a timeless artifact of louche behavior and sexual indulgence. Tourists harkened to a prerevolutionary Havana in which

Figure 5.1. The Hotel Habana Libre (Free Havana Hotel) was an iconic symbol of the Cuban revolution but prohibited Cuban guests during my research.

Cuban entrepreneurs, foreign investors, and the tourist commission linked Cuba to "entertainment, excitement, recreation, romance, and indulgence" (Schwartz 1997: 15). Because capitalist tourism to Cuba was suspended after the revolution, Western tourists assumed that the island had been isolated until the 1990s—ignoring Cuba's ongoing exchange with the Socialist Bloc and intensive involvement with countries in Latin America and Africa. Tourists I spoke to often described how Cubans had been "cut off from the world" or were not prepared for the "real world" that would invade after the death of Fidel Castro. In her analysis of Cuban tourism, anthropologist Florence Babb has observed how multiple forms of nostalgia operated simultaneously in the experiences of tourists on holiday in Havana. Travelers were nostalgic for the days of the early Cuban revolution when socialism was untainted by the reintroduction of a mixed-market economy, and also longed for the prerevolutionary Cuban past, which they associated with a racy and glamorous nightlife (2011: 23). As Babb suggests, Cuba represented a relic of multiple pasts— revolutionary and racy—that could be reenacted through visits to the Museum of the Revolution and nights at the Tropicana.

In the post-Soviet era, the allure of Cuba lay precisely in both its suffering and survival, and the Caribbean warmth and availability, "sexual and otherwise" (Dopico 2002: 461). For instance, during the first few years of the development of Cuba's tourist industry, despite objections from the Federation of Cuban Women, the Cuban tourist board sponsored advertising campaigns featuring dark-skinned women in bikinis to lure foreigners to Cuba. In 1990, the government allowed *Playboy* to photograph topless Cuban women on the beach at Varadero. The three primary tour operators in Cuba—Cubatur, Cubanacan, and Cimex—hosted a *Playboy* trip at the start of the post-Soviet crisis, and the government allowed the magazine to feature an article on the "Girls of Cuba" as long as there was also coverage of the island's tourist facilities (Smith and Padula 1996: 186). As sex tourism erupted in the 1990s, the Ministry of Tourism later recognized this initial entrée into the global market as a mistake and set out to reform the image that Cuba promoted to the world. Yet Cuban efforts did little to tame the erotic imaginings of foreign tourists, who arrived ready to lose their inhibitions and succumb to the sensual pleasures they associated with the brown and black bodies of the Caribbean.

Anachronistic ideas remained especially entrenched within the international gay media following the opening of Cuba to foreigners in the 1990s. Rather than socialism or death, as Castro frequently declared in his speeches about the vital role of government, for many tourists socialism had meant the death of progress. The *Gay Times Travel Guide* entry for Cuba warned of the state-sponsored homophobia on the island but concluded, "The barmy political system and the official homophobia is very wearing. Nonetheless it is a totally different destination and has the feel of going back in time."[13] The gay website Metro G featured an article titled, "Havana Boys: A Country Frozen in Time," written by Lorenzo Gomez, who reported, "It's a country that seems to have been frozen in time. Vintage American cars from the 1950s roam Havana's cobblestone streets. Century old buildings, shamefully neglected, in need of paint and basic maintenance, are literally crumbling to the sidewalks below."[14]

In terms of queer sexual representations, a number of gay pornographic sites emerged that promoted Cuba as a hotbed of masculine, muscle-bound men who were excited to have sex with foreigners. Sites such as *Cruzin for Cubans, Havana Bananas, Cocks of the Caribbean, Cuban Cock Tales*, and *Latin Balls* all suggested that Cuban men were raring to go. The formulaic sexual narratives spun by the sites played up the transnational encounter. For instance, the plot of *Cuba Libre II*, a pornographic film, revolves around gay Hungarians on vacation who befriend a muscular Cuban who wants to leave the island. The site explains, "The Cuban approaches a man about paying for a boat and after sex, the hero is disappointed to find that the boat owner has screwed him over. What will he do for money? Well, he could also do erotic dancing."[15] In a reincarnation of relations between two post-Soviet communist nations, young Cuban men emerge in the role of sexual laborers. On another site, next to a broken-down Chevy, the text reads, "That's a typical vehicle, and these are typical boys in Cuba." In another scenario two young Cubans approach a bald European foreigner with a Mercedes. The absence of go-go bars, strip clubs, massage parlors, or adult movie theaters in Cuba forced pornographers to transform mundane images of daily life into erotic kitsch. The websites included images of Che Guevara, cigars, antique Chevys, rum and coke cocktails, palm trees, and murals that read *Viva Cuba Libre* (Long Live a Free Cuba). One website depoliticized the *balsero* crisis, when Cubans fled the island in dangerous homemade rafts, by showing a blinking image of a truck full of Cubans sailing toward Miami.

The Cuban tourist industry, however, was well aware of foreigners' anachronistic stereotypes and drew on these tropes in the renovation projects that cleaned up rather than redeveloped old sections of Havana, such as the colonial district, which was declared a UNESCO World Heritage site.[16] In addition to the modern tourist taxis, the state began to fix up the iconic antique Chevy cars for tourists. They tellingly called the Chevy business "Rent a Fantasy." Ironically, Cubans used the Chevy cars or *máquinas* (machines) as an informal transportation system, which works like a shuttle and picks up passengers along routes throughout the city. The drivers are licensed by the state and pay taxes on their earnings. The government used some of these cars, however, to serve as taxis for tourists in which foreigners pay up to twice as much as they might in a normal tourist taxi in order to experience a "true" Cuban reality. The government cleverly recognized the symbolic value of the cars and turned an everyday vehicle into a tourist commodity that allows foreigners to "rent their fantasy."

Gay tourists arrived in Cuba with predetermined ideas about traveling into the past to an island where sensuality and socialism combined. Transnational representations of Cuba perpetuated these tropes. The images of Cuba that circulated in the post-Soviet era have been described by Ana Dopico as an "image boom" and similarly by Ruth Behar (2002) as the "Buena Vista Socialization" of Cuba, riffing on the popular documentary by Wim Wenders. These representations bestowed an aura of hipness and exclusivity to the island, especially for tourists from the United States, who viewed Cuba as forbidden fruit. The artistic, literary, and academic representations produced by Cubans in the diaspora often reinforced a fixation with the island's past. In the United States, the accounts of diasporic Cubans came to dominate representations of Cuba because the embargo limited information and intellectual exchange between the two countries. In response, many Cuban American scholars, such as performance artist and theorist Coco Fusco (1995) and anthropologist Ruth Behar (1995), have criticized the tendency of diasporic tourists to "speak for" Cuba. Despite the efforts of self-reflexive Cuban Americans to nuance popular perceptions of the island, many gay tourists upheld outdated fantasies that exoticized Cuba.

RAUNCH AS REALITY TOURISM

Many gay tourists' patronage bonds with Cubans challenged traditional conceptions of sex tourism. While associations may have started as an exchange of cash or gifts for sex acts, they frequently evolved into long-term affinities. Other gay travelers described themselves as solidarity activists, whose support for the Cuban Revolution and homosexuals on the island further complicated the bonds between sex and travel. Yet gays were not the only visitors who mixed passion with politics. In fact, sex between straight tourists and Cubans was more easily subsumed under the cover of "romance" and less prone to accusations of sex tourism. Even for niche tourists—those who focused on cultural, medical, or LGBT experiences—and activists that traveled in solidarity with the Cuban revolution, sex could play an integral role. Gay and straight foreigners alike felt distanced from the daily realities of Cubans and sought to collapse the gap through sex and romance. I discovered this dynamic during my first trip to Cuba as a participant in the nonprofit Global Exchange's Havana tour.

It was the welcoming meeting of Global Exchange's "Language and Culture" month-long educational program, in which Cuban staff guided foreigners through a month of Spanish classes at the University of Havana, museum visits, and lectures on Cuban society, history, and politics. The hot slanting sun was setting over Havana, and from the rooftop lounge of the four star Ambos Mundos hotel in Havana Vieja, you could watch the skyline recede into an endless stretch of sea. Waiters in long sleeves, vests, and bow ties served trays of mojitos as the program coordinator welcomed everyone and introduced a muscular black dance teacher and his voluptuous *mulata* assistant. Flashing a wide smile, the instructor spoke into the microphone, "The most important thing to know is that Cubans love to dance." As visitors took turns performing their new salsa and rumba moves on a makeshift stage, they laughed at the sexual innuendos made by their Cuban hosts and felt more adventurous after only a few hours on the island—their education about Cuba had indeed begun.

Even in the context of Global Exchange's "reality tour," which the company presented as a culturally sensitive and politically oriented program, performances of Cuban sensuality and tourist transgression framed the foreigners' introduction to the realities of the island. The opening mixer implied that Cuba did signify socialism and political history, but more important, Cubans loved to drink rum, grind with foreigners, and share their culture. The program coordinators demanded that foreigners set aside politics and suggested tourists do things the Cuban way—smile, shake their hips, and have a good time. Heterosexual sex was the subtext for an education regarding Cuba, and for tourists to resist this home-grown Caribbean sensuality would be a rude denial of their hosts' invitation to experience the island.

For the course of the month, participants lived in a four star hotel near Parque Central and ate their buffet-style meals with cloth napkins at the restaurant on the seventh floor overlooking a crumbling urban expanse. Global Exchange participants rode a large, luxurious air-conditioned bus to scheduled tours and classes at the university. A Cuban tour guide always accompanied them and affectionately took to calling them her "little chickens," a reference to a famous Cuban song, as she translated what they were seeing out of the oversized bus windows into digestible bits of history and culture. From the perspective of the program's participants, however, Cuba existed outside the bus and seemed to pass them by. Many of them had signed up for the Global Exchange program because it was the only way they could receive a legal travel visa to Cuba, and they expressed frustration that there was no clear path to being a "traveler" as opposed to a "tourist" in Havana. As a group, they were well traveled, and many participants emphasized that they were not the "tour group type." Shut out of Cuban realities, the world beyond the bus remained uncharted, inaccessible, and alien.

Figure 5.2. Tourists wait to board a tour bus on La Rampa.

As the month progressed, many of the participants began to express frustration at being kept within the safe boundaries of tourist hotels and group events. They vied to see whose daily adventures allowed them the most access to the island and its people. A thirty-year-old, heavy-set, Italian American high school teacher from Chicago took to smoking black market cigars and announced that he was determined to see how many Cuban women he could "have sex with without having to pay." A forty-nine-year-old Irish American social worker from Michigan started a long-term romance with a handsome, thirty-one-year-old Afro-Cuban taxi driver. A hip Puerto Rican photographer from Brooklyn connected with "the salsa scene" and had a series of Cuban dance teachers who took her to different music events. A contingent of white, dreadlocked, hippie college students from Amherst bought used Chinese bicycles and rode to the beaches outside Havana, where they turned down Cubans to make out with one another. At the nightly buffet, participants would compare notes: buying food in Cuban pesos, taking Cuban transportation instead of the tour bus, finding socialist kitsch to buy in the black market, and meeting the exiled Black Panther Assata Shakur all received reactions of envy and awe and became stories worth repeating.

Many of the educational tourists found that their best guides to the real "reality tour" of Cuba were Cubans whose friendly attitudes and sexual appetites happened to result in casual romances. The coordinator warned the group about *jineteros* and implied that within the spaces regulated by the program—the bus, the hotel, and the classroom—foreigners could trust the Cubans they met, and encounters were motivated by a genuine interest in cross-cultural exchange. Although the coordinator admitted that she herself was working for tips, participants were taught to recognize appropriate modes to acquire foreigners' hard currency. None of the participants in Global Exchange's Havana program would ever identify as sex tourists: they were leftist political activists, artists involved in cross-cultural exchange, curious open-minded retirees, and sympathizers with the revolution. Yet, transnational sexual encounters, including sex as a vehicle of cultural access, structured their experiences of Cuba from the start. They rarely used the group context to recount stories about being taken advantage of, paying too much for goods and services, or finding out that the Cubans they befriended were only after their money. Being accepted in the "real" Cuba meant knowing that Cubans hustled foreigners, but those foreigners were not you.

Even in a "reality tour," staff members assumed that participants traveled to the Caribbean to experience their first world lifestyles in a better climate and to learn about culture from a safe distance, not to actually live on the island. Tourism is an experience away from the stressful realities that make up modern life, and when these realities do impede upon tourist experiences in the form of shortages, transportation crises, theft, or crime, they are understood as interruptions. The post-Soviet Cuban tourist industry abided by these assumptions and created miniature zones of affluence within a greater landscape of scarcity. Reality tourists with Global Exchange did not travel to Cuba with the singular goal of having sex. Yet the Cuban coordinators of the program suggested the central role of Cuban sexuality in understanding the island, and the tourists came to feel that having sex with Cubans was, in a way, a leftist political act that showed their ability to connect with "the people" beyond the constraints of cultural and linguistic difference. The sexual border crossing, rather than a deviation from the program, determined its success, as reality tourists felt empowered by their ability to "get over" what were seen as superficial racial and cultural differences to access the universal humanity they shared with Cubans.[17] Associating the denial of transnational sexual encounters as a kind of presexual revolution prudish hang-up, they articulated visions of a shared consciousness that consisted of the right to health care and education, rum and rumba, and passionate casual sex.

GETTING OFF THE BUS

While these dynamics existed for the heterosexual participants in the Global Exchange tour, they were exacerbated for gay tourists who traveled to Havana outside the auspices of an organized tour group and whose drive to participate in *el mundo gay* required them to transgress segregation lines. Like most tourists, gay travelers held a partial understanding of how Havana's gay enclaves had become a production staged for foreign audiences and often failed to grasp the type of cultural and social impact they were having on Cuba's transition to late socialism. By insulating tourists from Cubans, the government contributed to the idea that tourists must stray from the beaten path to access the "real" Havana.[18] The Cuban Ministry of Tourism inadvertently colluded with foreign capitalists' fantasies of an authentic experience beyond the segregation line by creating a tourist spectacle that hinted at an authentic Cuba just beyond the tourist bubble. For tourists coming from cultural contexts in which sex represents the ultimate access, sex offered a bridge for tourists to get beyond the air-conditioned buses, overpriced cocktails, and bland buffet style hotel food. What better way to feel as if one is embracing the real Cuba than to participate in Havana's sexual economies that allow foreigners skin to skin contact with the body of the Other?

As one gay tourist proclaimed in celebration of Havana's gay underground, "Girl, you've got to get off the bus! Live the *vida loca,* get down and dirty with life in Havana!" The tourist bus resonated as a key metaphor because tourists rode around in enormous, spacious, air-conditioned buses while Cubans suffered a transportation crisis that forced them into tightly packed, hot, unreliable, and overcrowded broken-down buses. By getting off the bus, many gay tourists sought to position themselves as partial insiders in a landscape that the Cuban government hoped to make impenetrable to foreigners. Ironically, gay travelers were unaware that once they got off the plush tour bus and sat on the Malecón, they were participating in yet another experience in part constructed by the performances and practices of Cuban gays and hustlers on behalf of foreign tourists.

The fact that gay tourists transgressed state-imposed boundaries added a sense of adventure and discovery to their experiences, making their encounters with Cubans all the more taboo. Gay tourists in Havana who engaged in transnational sexual encounters paid for more than unlimited access to Cuban bodies; they bartered for a chance to get off the bus and penetrate the "real" queer Cuba. Moreover, this process encouraged gay tourists to feel above the law. The segregation resulted in a sustained misunderstanding of their role in the Cuban economic and cultural crisis despite their sensitivity to these issues and allowed them to depoliticize their presence. In general, gay tourists had a difficult time imagining the utility of state-imposed restrictions and failed to understand how performances of *pingueros* may be adversely affecting Havana's gay enclaves.[19] Even when tourists discovered the fabricated nature of nightlife on the Malecón, gay visitors did not feel their experiences were any less authentic or exciting. Within the context of *tourist realism*, markers of the staging can add to the intrigue of the site (Bruner and Kirshenblatt-Gimblett 1994: 457).

The multiple meanings of gay tourism, queer patronage, and leftist political solidarity in the Cuban case therefore challenge how anthropologists have understood sex tourism as an exercise in neocolonial control. Sex workers and tourists often held conflicting understandings of the social meaning of the goods, sex, and cash that they traded. This fact suggests how commodities can hold divergent meanings at the same time; their symbolic force is by nature multiple and fragmentary. A hustler might see his role as a simple matter of "dick-work" or *pinguerismo*, which does not involve emotional labor. Yet his client might feel a degree of intimacy that leads him to describe the hustler as a "boyfriend." On the other hand, the gay tourist might offer gifts as a way to mark the encounter as a marketplace transaction, outside the realm of intimacy, while the hustler might see these gifts, as opposed to cash, as initiating ongoing reciprocity similar to kin networks. In post-Soviet Havana, the collision of socialist and capitalist understandings of reciprocity intensified opportunities for creative bargaining and misunderstanding between hustlers and tourists.

Love in Crisis

THE POLITICS OF INTIMACY AND SOLIDARITY

Zombies have overtaken Havana. Cuban leaders insist that they are dissidents funded by the U.S. government, but the lone handful of survivors realize that the national threat is supernatural. The only one who can save Havana is Juan. "I survived Mariel, Angola, the Special Period and that thing that came after, and I will survive this," Juan says. How will he make it through? By starting a business, of course. "Juan of the Dead—we kill your loved ones," he cheerily tells his customers when they call. As Juan exclaims to his trusty sidekick, "What do Cubans do when there is a crisis? We charge people!"

The 2012 science fiction comedy *Juan of the Dead*, directed by Cuban filmmaker Alejandro Burgués, spares no state institution or Cuban stereotype from affectionate social criticism. Zombies provide an especially poignant jab at those hypnotized by revolutionary ideologies because they are bereft of self-awareness, but still react to stimuli and kill. The band of misfit survivors tasked with saving the island includes Juan, a self-proclaimed slacker and conman; his dim-witted best friend Lazaro; Lazaro's grown son "California," who hustles tourists; Juan's daughter, who has left for Spain as a child and despises her deadbeat dad as well as Cuba; "China," a *mulata travesti*, and her mute, muscular, towering black strongman, who sports a facial tattoo and faints at the sight of blood.[1]

The only Cubans immune to zombification are those who have been maligned and forsaken by government leaders for not embracing revolutionary rhetoric. In a twisted way, however, the film promotes a certain embrace of socialist principles. Motivating the arc of the film is the question of whether or not Juan can act out of true altruism. Will Juan always be motivated by money and self-interest? Can he do anything but take advantage of a crisis to make a quick buck? Can the purest aspects of socialism—social solidarity, paternal love, and sacrifice for the common good—override the contemporary hustle to survive? The film invites us to reflect on how we might reconsider the meaning of love, greed, and marginality while facing an apocalypse. This question lingers in *Juan of the Dead* and is what I have explored in a different way in this book.

The rapid loss of state-subsidized food and clothing and the arrival of millions of capitalist foreigners dramatically altered life for people with nonconforming genders and sexualities in Havana. As prosperous black marketeers enjoyed comforts and privileges that many professional gays could not afford, gay men, lesbians, and *travestis* grappled with impossible decisions to trade low-paying professional careers for low-skilled jobs in tourism or risk arrest to work in black markets. Within this topsy-turvy social landscape, new values of possessive individualism gained momentum over what many gays described as a previous focus on social solidarity. Nostalgia blossomed for a bygone era in which one could live comfortably on government rations and meager state salaries, people's earnings were relatively equal, and educational and cultural achievements were prized.

Most surprising was how many urban gay men and women felt that post-Soviet poverty overshadowed the benefits of increasing gay tolerance. Instead of associating the 1990s and 2000s with unprecedented queer visibility, urban gays focused on how post-Soviet economic restructuring had left them vulnerable to new social hierarchies. Political belonging in the traditional sense of membership in the Communist Party and national labor organizations still held symbolic value for some older generations, but for many younger Cubans these forms of acceptance were largely irrelevant in the new mixed-market economy. What mattered was not inclusion in a crumbling national imaginary, but the intimate forms of inequality that threatened to undercut the things one had always taken for granted—sex, love, family, and social bonds. According to many, urban gays had received the hesitant embrace of the revolutionary apparatus when the state was too weak and too anachronistic to grant any kind of satisfying redemption. Although state repression had diminished, many of my gay respondents were far from feeling free.

Among the most hotly debated changes to queer enclaves in the post-Soviet era was the widespread commodification of sex and intimacy. The eruption of commodified sex redefined nonnormative sexuality, and not just for those who bought or sold sex. Urban gays often described the impact of sex work on their personal and public lives, lamenting financially motivated betrayals, lax work ethics, and the violent dispositions of sex workers. Many educated gays born after 1970 believed that they could no longer seek partners solely based on emotional and physical attraction because those intimacies had become infected with financial motives. They sought to erect boundaries between a private realm of emotion and affection and a public arena of market aspirations and performances. Yet, in practice, the boundaries between genuine and strategic affections were constantly blurred and crossed, at times reshaping people's fundamental assumptions about intimacy and equality.

While gay men, lesbians, and *travestis* erected boundaries between themselves and sex workers, these borders proved permeable in practice. Even some of the harshest critics of the sex trade experimented with transactional sex. The prevalence of transactional sex in Havana fostered an environment in which even Cubans opposed to erotic labor could find themselves weighing the benefits and risks of maintaining strategic sexual relationships with foreigners. For instance, Javier, a gay student at a continuation high school, often criticized *pingueros* yet had sex with an older foreign man he found unattractive with the hope of receiving gifts and cash. The ironies of these contradictions were not lost on urban gays, who remained reflexive about the chasm between their ideals and the realities they faced. In this way, the transition to post-Soviet socialism challenged people's most fundamental self-perceptions.

Through criticism of the commodification of sex and affect, people with nonconforming genders and sexualities challenged the explosion of economic inequities endemic in the post-Soviet era. Yet they often drew on preexisting hierarchies of whiteness, urban privilege, and standards of gender conformity to challenge new inequalities of social class and status. Urban gays praised those who held onto their values in the face of great adversity, emphasizing how people living with poverty could still make fundamental choices about the direction of their lives. Many gay men and women accentuated the boldness it took to remain dedicated to their careers, even when hard work and dedication failed to guarantee a comfortable existence. In doing so, many urban gays distinguished their beliefs, values, and practices from those of sex workers in Havana's informal queer nightlife, but without recognizing the forms of privilege that made these differences possible.

Even though urban gays often reinvested in privileges of color, class, and culture, they did not impose traditional standards of respectability common throughout the Caribbean, such as middle-class propriety and sexual decorum. In contrast to heteronormative criticism of the sex trade, which often drew on morality discourses that echoed hygienic campaigns reaching back to colonialism, many of my urban gay respondents embraced promiscuity, bawdy sexuality, and rebellion against sexual social norms. Havana's queer nightlife was therefore different from capitalist contexts in which the privileged distance themselves physically and socially from the disenfranchised. Gay men and women did not shun the sex workers whom they maligned. Participants in queer enclaves criticized one another, but social judgments did not result in segregation. Even the harshest gay critics incorporated sex workers from their neighborhoods and hometowns into tightly knit social circles. In this way, gay criticism was more akin to trash-talking about misfit relatives than forcing a group of people to the back of the bus.

Not all gay men and women sought to distance themselves from the rising tide of commodified sex. Some gay men, like Oscar and Ivan, participated wholeheartedly in sexual transactions with male hustlers. Wanting to craft an authentic boyfriend experience, they often chose lighter-skinned hustlers to keep with endogamous dating trends in Havana. Yet, even for those who purchased sexual services or, more commonly, supported male hustlers for weeks at a time, the personal ramifications of commodified sex and affect were still fraught with ambivalence. Gay men openly acknowledged sex workers' financial motives and harbored no qualms about paying for sex but hoped for an authentic connection. They often felt dehumanized by *pingueros'* slang terms, such as "killing the game," and described how an obsession with commodities and money had left young hustlers in a state of "emptiness."

The post-Soviet era was not the first time that younger men had received housing and food in exchange for sex. Yet, the degree of commodification in the post-Soviet era struck many as more alienating than in the past, as the sex trade came to signify broader structural changes in Cuban society. Gay men, therefore, described their dilemma as an internal battle between their desire for attractive, manly sex workers and their knowledge that the interaction would likely end in betrayal. Gay male clients disparaged the violence, petty theft, and emotional distance that characterized their bonds with young hustlers, but ironically, many adopted the very detached stance that they criticized as a way to protect themselves in the relationships with young *pingueros*. For Oscar, this meant applying market logics of labor and authority to manage his household in a way that influenced his relationship with his live-in *novios* as well as his best friend Ivan. Drawing on gendered notions of submission and domination, some suggested that their acquiescence to male hustlers ultimately positioned them in a desired feminine role.

Like Oscar, many participants in Havana's queer social networks who openly rejected the cultural tenets of neoliberal capitalism nevertheless discovered that their daily lives and domestic intimacies were reordered by the far reach of market logics and aspirations. In particular, market logics often manifested in the domestic sphere and influenced how people negotiated relationships and friendships outside the sex trade. Lauren Berlant (2008) and Eva Illouz (2007), among others, have highlighted how late capitalism brings emotions into the workplace and market logics into intimate realms. Despite common assumptions that a strict divide separates the intimate private sphere and the market-based public arena, Illouz argues, "market-based cultural repertoires shape and inform interpersonal and emotional relationships, while interpersonal relationships are at the epicenter of economic relationships" (2007: 5).

Social and economic changes brought about by the post-Soviet transition affected gay men and lesbians differently. Addressing the particular predicament of lesbians, Cuban feminist and social psychologist Norma Guillard Limonta has argued, "We are fatally oppressed by discriminatory thinking so extreme that it cannot be compared with the understanding gradually attained by gay men; the rejection is more open, harsher, and more violent, leading to greater stigmatization and repression" (2009: 70). Lacking the same historical association with the fine arts, lesbians were often inadvertently excluded from increasing public tolerance campaigns toward gay cultural producers. Lesbian-specific gatherings or "girl parties" were similarly off the tour maps of gay male tourists in Havana, which made them less cosmopolitan in the minds of participants. At the same time, lesbians were more sheltered from the rapid influx of commodity culture and sex work that troubled gay social life. Moreover, women often engaged their invisibility in creative and resourceful ways.

For instance, Amanda used her ability to "pass" as heterosexual to foster a relationship with a young Italian male tourist, who married her and moved her to Milan. Once in Italy, she reestablished a lesbian identity and initiated relationships with women. Being white or lighter-skinned and educated protected many lesbians from identifying their behavior with foreign men as *jineterismo* because the stereotypical vision of a *jinetera* was an uneducated black Cuban woman. Attention to the gendered dynamics of lesbian relationships also reveals increasing trends away from female masculinity and toward notions of "*normal*" same-sex desire and performativity among women. In other words, even as women challenged heteronormative codes of behavior, they often reinforced gendered ideas about appropriate forms of behavior and dress for women.

Similarly, rather than question the fixed nature of gender and sexual categories, many sex workers reinvested in traditional roles as a means to secure their place within gendered hierarchies. For example, urban gays criticized how homoerotic male sex workers reinforced their masculine status by disparaging gay men and emphasizing womanizing appetites. Yet not all sex workers reinforced heterosexual norms; some unabashedly undermined reductive readings of gender and sexuality. Moreover, within Melba's household those involved in the sex trade engaged in interracial dating more than other social networks. These dynamics inspired Melba and Yolanda to define themselves as "*modernas*," more advanced then Cubans stuck in antiquated ways of thinking about sex and sexuality. Similarly, some young men discovered that sexual labor allowed them to defer categorization and simply call themselves "*locos*." In a challenge to urban gay criticism that sex workers were lazy, many emphasized their industriousness and detailed the profound economic divides between rural and urban areas that put them at a disadvantage.

Just as sex workers spoke back to gay criticism, many queer foreign tourists also interpreted sexual encounters in queer enclaves in unexpected ways. Many gay male tourists described their role in Havana's queer nightlife as an empowering form of leftist political solidarity. For gay tourists, participating in Cuban gay enclaves seemed like a type of righteous rebellion that allowed them to connect with gay "brothers and sisters," who were like them enough to inspire confidence but still different enough to qualify as exotic. Sex figured into these relationships as a pleasurable way to bridge cultural distance. Gay male tourists more often hired Cubans for sex, but the notion that gay foreigners could modernize Cuban sexual politics appeared in the narratives of men and women tourists alike.[2]

Representations of Cuba that circulated transnationally encouraged tourists' perspectives that Cuba could be a symbol of socialist resistance and an erotic sexual playground suspended in anachronistic time. Unlike heterosexual white tourists who exoticized a racist image of the voracious black Caribbean woman, tourists were not always white and wealthy, and those who were saw "Latin-ness" rather than blackness as the marker of difference. Likewise, structural factors such as tourist-Cuban segregation contributed to tourists' perspectives because tourists traversed tourist-Cuban segregation lines to participate in same-sex enclaves. Finding the "real" Cuba beyond the state-sanctioned tourist zones encouraged travelers to feel as if they had escaped the superficial, fabricated tourist enclaves for the gritty realities of Cuban daily life. Many failed to recognize that nonsanctioned spaces, such as gay gatherings in Havana, were already thoroughly produced by sex workers and others looking to foster the fantasy of tourist realism (Bruner and Kirshenblatt-Gimblett 1994) for foreigners.

SEXUAL SUBJECTIVITY AND THE POST-SOVIET STATE

Unlike the widespread privatization and embrace of neoliberal policies in Russia and Eastern Europe, the Cuban government maintained a fidelity to socialist principles, but Cubans still experienced many of the same changes that other post-Soviet nations reported, such as a rise in tensions between urban and rural dwellers, a predominance of black markets, diminished state subsidies, and heightened class inequalities. Similar to these other post-Soviet contexts, many Cubans embraced an entrepreneurial spirit of innovation, finding creative ways to utilize informal economies to survive increasing poverty. Yet, while many crafted businesses out of any resource they could find—beauty services, home-made food, stolen goods from state factories, illegal taxi services—they also remained critical of the changing values that this new cultural order imposed. This forceful criticism of market incursions offers an important counterpoint to contexts in which people adopt and internalize neoliberal notions of self-management, for instance in postcommunist transition to market economies (Friedman 2005) or rapidly developing zones in the Caribbean (Freeman 2011). The position of nonconforming gender and sexual populations within the post-Soviet revolutionary nation-state can teach us a great deal about social belonging in the post-Soviet era. Their stories offer an acute understanding of who would be excluded from mainstream ideals of respectability and on what grounds.

Urban gay criticism of the post-Soviet sex trade makes sense when one considers how homosexuality had been linked to criminality and prostitution in the past. In the prerevolutionary era, homosexuality was associated with foreign exploitation and corruption in the Cuban popular imagination. During the late 1970s and 1980s, homosexuality was increasingly distinguished from forms of criminality, but the explosion of sex tourism in Havana's queer enclaves in the late 1990s associated homosexuality with prostitution. In this context of growing gay tolerance, gay citizens faced new opportunities for national belonging but were forced to demonstrate their adherence to mainstream socialist values in order to ward off public accusations of delinquency. In post-Soviet Cuba, homosexual citizens who aligned themselves with socialist principles posed less of a threat than young people who traded socialist egalitarianism for consumerist desires. As *jineterismo* and *pinguerismo* became common in Havana, the "deviancy" of patriotic homosexuals paled in comparison to heterosexual young men and women having sex for cash.[3]

Interestingly, urban gays and sex workers alike drew and creatively appropriated state rhetoric to disparage shifting social values and rising poverty and to characterize sex work. In scholarly and popular accounts of homophobia in Cuba, an embrace of socialist ideologies among gays is often unexplored. Many assume gay citizens would have to be duped into supporting a political system that has violently repressed them. Yet my findings suggest a nuanced understanding of the relationship between urban gays and post-Soviet state ideologies. More than simply parroting official policies and rhetoric, many urban gays demonstrated a genuine belief in socialist notions of hard work and decency. These ideas may have originated with revolutionary rhetoric but had become second nature to many urban gays, even among those who criticized state policies. As Herzfeld's (1978) notion of cultural intimacy between citizens and the state describes, cynicism toward the government paired effortlessly with fervent patriotism.

Although many urban gays appreciated the emergence of official gay tolerance discourse, others did not cite queer visibility as the most substantial symbol of Cuban state policy in quotidian life. These differences often appeared along generational lines, as older gays who had lived through violent eras of state homophobia were moved by the appearance of tolerance rhetoric, while younger gay men and lesbians had higher expectations and less patience for slow-moving progress.[4] For instance, urban gays enjoyed the decriminalization of homosexuality more generally, but those who relied on Havana's nightlife forcefully criticized the government for mounting police persecution. Informal, queer public gatherings suffered from increasing harassment and intervention, often resulting in ongoing sweeps, as Havana's city cops sought to slow the burgeoning sex tourist trade. While gay residents could no longer be arrested for homosexuality, they were, on occasion, mistakenly detained alongside others who qualified as "socially dangerous," including sex workers and gay rural migrants who lacked the proper paperwork to stay in the capital.[5] These crackdowns on queer public space recriminalized queer gatherings in the public eye, associating homosexuality with deviancy. Likewise, these effects were intensified for darker-skinned and Afro-Cubans because the Special Period initiated new forms of racial discrimination. Black and darker-skinned gay Cubans were more likely to be criminalized and harassed by police, who often assumed that they were working in the sex trade.

The inefficacy of state-sponsored gay tolerance campaigns to remedy the struggles of daily life for Cubans with nonconforming genders and sexualities has parallels with the government's approach to racial inequality in the post-Soviet era. For instance, Alejandro De la Fuente and Laurence Glasco (1997) discovered that younger generations of educated and upwardly mobile blacks had come to expect certain forms of educational mobility and standards of living that were no longer available. Afro-Cubans often felt that government leaders had finally addressed racial inequalities and permitted previously prohibited Afro-Cuban religions to flourish, but these new forms of state-sponsored racial tolerance were undermined by the realities of daily survival in the post-Soviet landscape (Pérez Sarduy and Stubbs 2000).[6] Just as state-sponsored gay tolerance campaigns could not remedy the daily struggles of gay Cubans, so too Afro-Cubans often described discourses of racial equality as too little too late.

In Cuba, gay appeals to decency and mainstream socialist values of hard work that I have described could often qualify as normative. Lisa Duggan (2004) describes homonormativity as a process through which queer politics upholds, rather than contests, dominant institutions. In the United States and Europe, homonormativity arose alongside neoliberal cultural politics during the late 1980s and 1990s, as gay rights organizations sought legitimacy within mainstream politics, and many activists abandoned more radical efforts to legitimate all forms of nonnormative sexual practice. For instance, activists emphasized gay "family values," organizing for marriage equality and gay adoption. The demands of monogamous, middle- and upper-class, white gays and lesbians often took precedence over queers of color, transgender people, and working-class queers. As homonormative movements gained precedence, those who failed to conform to gender roles and standards of middle-class respectability were increasingly ostracized. Duggan outlines how neoliberalism presented a cultural outlook that promised "freedom" through consumption and depoliticization.

Yet, the Cuban case offers an important counter to critiques of homonormativity because gay sentiments of decency arose in opposition to, rather than as a handmaiden of, neoliberal capitalism. Urban gay men and lesbians drew on socialist normatives to criticize rising wealth inequalities, rather than augment them. Some may argue that when people living in poverty delineate categories of respectability, they suffer from false consciousness, internalizing upper-class values. Yet, this was not the case in post-Soviet Cuba, where a rampant black market meant that educational achievements, social status, wages, and wealth were often detached. Gay critics suffered through the same shortages and scarcity as the sex workers they criticized. Moreover, sex workers themselves represented their struggles in patently socialist terms of hard work and fairness. Instead of imposing a dominant value system on a minority, socialist normatives in Cuba offered a common language to interpret desires and experiences and to criticize the new inequalities that troubled daily life. Nevertheless, at times, these sentiments of hard work, decency, and mutual respect were simultaneously used to perpetuate people's longstanding associations between whiteness and morality, as well as gender conformity and normalcy. In other words, homonormative values could both accommodate a radical intervention into class injustice and, at the same time, appeal to conservative ideas about race and gender.

Just as I have shown how urban gays responded differently to revolutionary rhetoric and state policies, so too I have emphasized the nuanced contradictions and outright disagreements between various state-sponsored entities around issues of nonnormative gender and sexuality. It is important not to conflate a diversity of government agencies and individual leaders under the umbrella of "the Cuban state." Although Cubans experienced a continuity of presidential leadership, the government changed as the loss of Soviet subsidies widened leaders' approaches to economic and social issues and restricted the capabilities of state agencies. Leaders in Cuban state-run film and cultural agencies enlisted a queer intelligentsia to craft an "authentic" Cuban culture in what they described as a fight against encroaching capitalist globalization. Cuban health specialists depoliticized gay advocacy by utilizing psychological frameworks and implementing AIDS prevention policies. Yet Havana city police sought to eliminate queer gatherings and frequently clashed with the ongoing campaigns within CENESEX to promote gay tolerance. The government's hegemony over a unified message regarding forms of deviancy diminished after the crisis of the Special Period, making conflicts more apparent to outside observers. Concrete structural transformations can account for some of the changes, but it is also possible that previous depictions of a unified Cuban government were a product of Cold War politics that homogenized "the Cuban state" and erased the existence of a civil society on the island.

The post-Soviet context allows queer scholars and activists to rethink our fundamental assumptions regarding homonormativity. Rather than applying critiques of homonormativity to the Cuban context, the notion of a normative queer culture may provide a useful framework to analyze how U.S. and European gay tourism, alongside the birth of a global gay rights movement, remained implicitly linked to neoliberal philosophies that translate social equality as an ability to consume. The inherently depoliticizing nature of neoliberalism promotes consumer empowerment as a remedy for social inequality, and this approach has provided the scaffolding for queer tourists in Cuba to interpret their participation in Havana's queer enclaves as a sign of solidarity.

FUTURE RESEARCH DIRECTIONS

Recognizing the links between post-Soviet socialism and nonnormative desire and practice proves that erotic subjectivities correspond to political economic forces. The incursion of capitalist markets transformed Cuban same-sex sexualities, but these changes were merely the most recent chapter in a much longer saga in which political economic systems shaped desires and norms. An anthropological model that probes the intersections between sexual subjectivities and macroeconomic change will continue to offer insight into the unfolding social and political realities in Cuba. A number of important developments have already occurred since my research, including the continuing privatization of state enterprises and a significant shift away from tourism as a major engine of economic growth. Moreover, the Cuban government relaxed many prominent tourist segregation policies. Hence, it remains to be seen if wealthier Cubans' ability to utilize tourist luxuries will lessen resentment about emergent social hierarchies or simply exacerbate inequalities, encouraging people to blame themselves for their poverty.

In looking ahead, the following themes will become increasingly important to gaining a holistic portrait of gay social life in Cuba:

How rising rates of HIV *affect sexuality and public discourse*. Although HIV/AIDS did not surface in daily conversations about the commodification of sex and intimacy, in part due to Cuba's low transmission rate, the numbers of gay men with HIV have increased significantly since my research. Hence, I suspect that HIV/AIDS will become a bigger part of gay social life on the island because strict quarantine policies were overturned in the late 1990s and HIV/AIDS was just beginning to make its mark on queer enclaves during my research. When I returned in 2007, people commented that more participants in queer enclaves had contracted the disease, but only a handful of people I knew were open with me about being HIV positive. Hence, greater attention to the relationship between economic hardship and treatment and risk patterns among men will become increasingly central.

How rural nonnormative sexualities were transformed by the transition to post-Soviet socialism. My argument that intimate practices of nonnormative gender and sexuality in Cuba have been transformed by the introduction of queer tourism focuses specifically on the experiences of gay men and women in Havana. People in the capital uniquely experienced the majority of foreign investment and tourists. I have discussed how urban and rural divisions fomented hierarchies among participants in queer enclaves, but my findings suggest the need for greater research into the experiences of same-sex desire and practice in rural areas. Focusing on nonnormative sexuality in Havana revealed the immense changes brought about by the introduction of capital, whereas an inquiry into homosexuality in the provinces might demonstrate how little changed in the post-Soviet era. Rural practices of desire might highlight the limits of capitalist inroads rather than the transformative powers of global capitalism. Likewise, a focus on Havana has lent itself to an analysis of the various and shifting forms of Cuban "whiteness," extending what Pedro Pérez Sarduy and Jean Stubbs have identified as a crucial departure from previous studies of race in Cuba.[7] I would expect different issues of race and poverty to arise in rural areas, where the population is of significantly greater Afro-Cuban descent.

The influence of migration on queer subjectivity. The stories that I collected and analyzed often led me outside Cuba because nearly half of my original contacts emigrated before the end of my study. Research that follows their assimilation process is needed to understand how their ideas about decency, class hierarchies, and sexual difference changed when they were confronted with new economic and social contexts. For instance, one collaborator who enjoyed casual sexual encounters in Cuba settled down with a partner in Miami because he disapproved of the rampant drug use and promiscuity he discovered. Moreover, he felt hesitant to develop sexual relationships because of the number of HIV positive gay men whom he met. Similarly, one respondent who most often criticized the lack of social space for gays in Havana migrated to Madrid, but discovered that he had to work two jobs to support himself and never had any time to socialize. These factors all influenced his decision to abandon the single life for a monogamous relationship. While some migrants found themselves at a disadvantage because of the homophobia in their new countries, queer networks also provided informal support systems that offered stability for new arrivals. On a larger scale, analyzing experiences of queer migration in relation to class and social mobility helps in further considering the political economy of sexuality within a transnational frame.[8] In particular, studies that trace the migration trajectories of Cubans in Spain and other parts of Europe and Latin America are needed since much of the existing literature emphasizes Cuban migration to the United States.

REIMAGINING QUEER SOLIDARITY

I was first drawn to this research when I discovered a tremendous gap between popular understandings of Cuban homosexuality and the lived realities of gay Cubans navigating a changing social terrain. It seemed that scholars and activists painted Cuban gays as the victims of ongoing assault on the part of a homophobic Cuban state, while others celebrated gay life under socialism as a panacea for sexual prejudice. Especially in the United States, this type of polarizing rhetoric is routine when it comes to accounts of life on the island. What struck me as particularly troubling was how gay Cuban perspectives were erased from these accounts. By presenting people's daily lives and concerns, I hope to have demonstrated how the diversity of perspectives and dilemmas of contemporary gays cannot be neatly tucked into any simplistic political agenda. As urban gays framed their struggles for sexual belonging with tropes of decency, civilization, hard work, and appropriate bodily practices, shifting post-Soviet notions of class merged with ideas about nonnormative sexuality.

Queer politics, however, have not offered such a straightforward frame-work. While I feel compelled to criticize assimilationist factions of queer movements in my country, radically different power dynamics arise when gay activists in the United States criticize Cubans for promoting confor-mity to state-sanctioned socialist norms. Movements for sexual equality reflect the particular historical and cultural trajectories within which they arise. To project a universal rubric of pride, visibility, and politicization onto the Cuban context ignores both the specificity of Anglo-European rights movements and the progressive potential of Cuban approaches. Scholars and activists should therefore recognize and respect different strategies for gay advocacy, including tolerance and depoliticization, even when such approaches run counter to our own philosophies.

Queer tourists and gay activists should not be credited with ushering in "modern" ideas about sexual equality. If anything, government leaders' efforts to forestall the impact of capitalist foreigners encouraged them to embrace patriotic gay citizens, whose cultural productions were lauded as an antidote to the mass-produced culture of global capital. Resistance to globalization opened new venues for queer visibility in the public arts and health ministries. The beginning of a new era of gay tolerance on Cuban terms should be attributed to forces within Cuba, in particular the work of Mariela Castro and other activists at CENESEX. Gay advocates likewise constructed a unique trajectory of equality that consciously de-parted from international gay activism in late-capitalist nations. Sexual equality in Cuba should not be measured using a yardstick developed in the United States.

Since same-sex practices and identities are not universal, queer soli-darity movements need to acknowledge an array of local and historical realities. Theorist, activist, and queer icon Leslie Feinberg criticizes LGBT movements that defend gay and lesbian Cubans, but "only against their own people, culture, and national liberation struggle" by ignoring how Cubans could maintain socialist principles and fight for sexual equality (2009: 91). According to Feinberg, gay solidarity activists have used universal gay rights rhetoric to oppose the Cuban government. Effective queer transnational solidarity movements are hindered by the U.S. government's ongoing efforts to punish the Cuban government for remaining communist. While it is difficult to define what "Cuban" terms may be, given the great heterogeneity among the perspectives and priorities of gay Cuban men and women, it is crucial to understand the conflicts and dilemmas that Cubans face in their struggles for equality. In this book, I hope to have revealed some of these intimate discussions that suggest how people on the sexual margins imagine themselves in relationship to one another and to the Cuban nation at large. By attending to these daily conflicts and frustrated desires, outsiders can conceive of new ways to support our Cuban collaborators.

Cuban state homophobia has historically disrupted leftist visions of the island as a tropical, socialist promised land. In 1961, Allen Ginsberg, beatnik poet and gay activist, visited Cuba as the guest of a literary competition. Eager to witness the utopian promise of revolutionary communism, Ginsberg quickly became disillusioned when he discovered "a police bureaucracy that persecutes fairies" (Young 1981). After asking if Raúl Castro was gay and proclaiming his attraction to Che Guevara, Ginsberg was deported. Ginsberg suggested that Fidel Castro and his government would eventually outgrow their homophobia. "They'll learn soon enough," Ginsberg said, predicting that Cubans would "see the end of the world" and "end up with pansexualities" (Young 1981).

Like Ginsberg, I had ventured to Cuba armed with naïve optimism about what I would find. After reading the many celebratory articles about openings toward homosexuality in Cuba, I hoped that the revolution had finally made good on its promise of egalitarianism. What I discovered was much more complicated. The perspectives of the gay men and women whom I met could be summarized by the comments of Francisco Rodriguez, a gay communist militant who has become a prominent Cuban blogger: "Things are getting better. Not as fast as some of us would like, but not as slow as some Castrophobes say either."

Most important, to understand homoerotic love and intimacy in contemporary Cuba takes us outside the realm of state politics and demands looking at the intersection of everyday experience and the dramatic structural economic changes brought about by the end of the Cold War. It necessitates attending to how people make sense of a lover's betrayal, the loss of a friendship, or a foreigner's sudden presence in their home. Tracing the "political economy of love" (Padilla et al. 2007), I have examined how ideas about intimacy and love were diagnostic of broader social trends brought about by post-Soviet economic restructuring, especially the introduction of foreign tourism. Four decades after Ginsberg's visit, I arrived in a radically different Cuba—Cubans had indeed witnessed the end of the world and state homophobia had eased. Questions about the status of gays felt misguided and anachronistic in a new world order that was not quite the zombie Armageddon but felt that way to many. In this unending state of crisis, it became impossible to discern who might simply be parroting outdated ideologies and who was crafting a new world out of the ruins of the past.

Notes

Introduction

1. Rather than parse whether or not declarations of love and intimacy were authentic, I join with analysts who are interested in what these performances mean in practice (e.g., Brennan 2004; Faier 2007).

2. An analysis of medical, scientific, and government discourses reveals the shifting production of categories of homosexuality but does not go far enough to explore how these discourses shaped the experiences of ordinary people (Donham 1998; Robertson 2005). While discourses profoundly affect ideas and practices, people think and act at the intersections of discourses (Yanagisako and Delaney 1995: 18).

3. See, for example, Abu-Lughod (1986), Abu-Lughod and Lutz (1990), Boellstorff and Lindquist (2004), Klima (2004), Lutz (1988), Lutz and White (1986), M. Rosaldo (1980, 1984), and R. Rosaldo (1989). In particular, Abu-Lughod and Lutz (1990) have highlighted that sentiments are socially produced during moments of exchange, rather than as emotions waiting to be expressed. In a similar vein, Boellstorff and Lindquist (2004) as well as Klima (2004) point out how the social construction of emotion can offer a useful lens for understanding economic crisis.

4. Feminist scholars have highlighted how discourses of love and intimacy often disguise underlying issues of status along the lines of race and class that inspire partner choice. Similarly, Marxist feminists have argued that heterosexual women may be expected to provide domestic and emotional labor in the name of love, which renders their work invisible. Throughout this scholarship, analysts emphasize how cultural assumptions about love and intimacy have shifted dramatically over time.

5. In some contexts, this move away from social obligation was not always met with praise but rather was suspect in its links to the market. In Ado, Nigeria, Cornwall (2002) identifies a similar dynamic to Cuba in which men and women alike criticized how a "perverse love of money" replaced a bygone era when love stemmed from "dutiful obedience."

6. Lisa Rofel (1999, 2007) studied the intersection of political economy and queer sexuality in postcommunist Beijing. She observed that "global" gay identities did not supplant Chinese categories, but rather gay Chinese men strategically invoked a universal gay identity to define themselves as more Chinese, not as Western (1999: 459). Likewise, Tom Boellstorff (2002) has argued that local Indonesian nonnormative sexualities were not replaced by Anglo-European categories, but rather reformulated in new ways. Boellstorff challenged the premise that people with nonconforming genders and sexualities would be "modernized or contaminated" by the introduction of Western-style gay identities and activism (2007: 22). More generally within anthropology, this shift reflected other arguments that "the global" and "the local" operated as discursive constructions akin to notions of "modernization" within development rhetoric, rather than lived realities (Ong 2006; Trouillot 2003).

7. Likewise, Kevin Floyd has examined how the devaluation of a Fordist model of production and consumption in the 1960s accompanied a dissolution of traditional models of heterosexual masculinity in popular representations (2009: 79). Typically, Marxists have considered sexual inequalities as a secondary effect of capitalist exploitation, but Floyd demonstrates how gender and sexuality are cornerstones of capitalist accumulation, production, and consumption.

8. By connecting love and intimacy to broader social systems that foster inequality, such as colonialism and, more recently, neoliberalism and global capitalism, we can begin to understand how oft-assumed private feelings generate inequalities. In doing so, I contribute to a growing body of scholarship that demonstrates how the erasure of certain forms of intimacy stigmatizes certain groups and excludes them from the imagined national collective (Berlant 1997, 1998; Padilla et al. 2007; Povinelli 2002; Wiegman 2002).

9. For example, Arguelles and Rich (1984, 1985), Leiner (1994), Lumsden (1996), and Young (1981).

10. By emphasizing how the Cuban transition to a mixed-market economy influenced nonnormative sexual desires and practices, I do not mean to imply that contemporary forms of capitalist globalization are confined to the present day. Cuban sexual practices and identities have always been an amalgam of multiple cultures—including Africa, Spain, China, and the United States— during the island's colonial, neocolonial, and diasporic histories. Rather than an "opening" to the world, I understand the reintroduction of foreign tourism as the latest chapter of a centuries-old tale, as Cuba had always been profoundly transnational.

11. Leading up to the disbanding of the Socialist Bloc in 1991, the Cuban economy was already suffering with its hard currency debt more than doubling

between 1985 and 1989 (Eckstein 1997). Due to the loss of income and imports, the gross domestic product (GDP) was cut nearly in half, from $19.3 billion in 1989 to $10 billion in 1993 (Hamilton 2002: 23). Cubans also lost their ability to produce domestic goods because of the lack of oil and machinery, as agriculture rotted in the fields for lack of transport (Ellwood 1998).

12. Reduced from adequate subsistence levels, food rations included only beans, milk for children and pregnant women, rice, and sugar, with other goods such as cooking oil, eggs, matches, pasta, soap, toothpaste, and textured vegetable protein occasionally available. By 2002, the ration system still adequately provided for young children, infants through six-year-olds, but Cubans between the ages of fourteen and sixty-five received about half of the calories and one-third of the protein recommended by the Cuban Institute for Nutrition and Food (Togores and García 2004: 260).

13. The Cuban government implemented intermittent economic restructuring. For instance, officials approved 140 different categories of self-employment, including "doll repairperson" and "pet stylist" (Córdova 1996: 361). Yet, between 2003 and 2007, the government halted the administration of new licenses—reducing the private sector employment from 209,000 to 142,000 in 2009. In a reversal of this trend, however, in 2010 President Raúl Castro announced that the government would lay off more than 500,000 state employees, 10 percent of the workforce, and expand job permissions in the private sector to absorb the unemployed. By the end of 2010, the government had increased the number of self-employment licenses more than 50 percent from 2009. In a similar gesture toward unprecedented privatization, in April 2011 the Communist Party Congress ruled to allow the purchase and sale of private property and crafted credit mechanisms for small business and cooperatives.

14. Government leaders viewed the partial opening toward foreign capitalism and outsiders as a necessary evil (Espino 2000: 362). For instance, the preamble to Cuba's Foreign Investment Act warned that Cuba could benefit from foreign investment only "on the basis of the strictest respect for national independence and sovereignty" (Foreign Investment Act 1995).

15. The 2010 statistics taken from the U.S. State Department website featuring Cuba. These estimates include "medical tourists" from other Latin American countries seeking treatment in Cuban facilities.

16. My research complicates this racial divide, however, because I focus on white, mixed, or lighter-skinned families who had no connection to family abroad and therefore received no financial support.

17. Historically, Havana's population had grown slowly as a result of balanced development policies, low birth rates, high rates of emigration, and an acute housing shortage in the capital. But net domestic migration to Havana spiked in the mid-1990s in response to the economic crisis (Coyula and Hamberg 2003: 4). An estimated 50,000 people moved to Havana in 1996 alone, and in the first four months of 1997, 92,000 people tried to legalize their status in the city (De la Fuente 2001: 328). By the late 1990s, Havana's population reached nearly 2.19

million—around one-fifth of the country—in an urban area of 139 square miles (ONE 2001).

18. While the laws were repealed in 2008, much de facto segregation remained because of the expensive prices of tourist-oriented goods and services.

19. In distinguishing between symbolic capital and financial capital to describe gay Cubans' frustration over shifting configurations of class and sexuality in post-Soviet Havana, I do not intend to reify economic capital as if it were an acultural universal. I recognize that financial capital is in itself also a symbolic system, not one based in concrete, objective values.

20. The absence of establishments geared toward prostitution make accusations that the Cuban government is "pimping" women to foreign tourists seem implausible.

21. For instance, the scholarly and artistic work of Amir Valle (2001), Elizalde (1999), Fernández Robaina (1998), Gutiérrez (2000), and Valdés (1996). As anthropologist Nadine Fernandez highlights, the establishment of tourist zones heightened Cubans' sensitivities to race and class and fostered new systems of inclusion and exclusion (2010: 130).

22. At times, gay Cubans analyzed the commodification of sex and affect more astutely than scholars because they were able to think outside of traditional understandings of sex workers as victims. Often from the same socioeconomic and ethnic backgrounds as sex workers, gay critics provided insight into the motivations for sexual labor while raising questions about how nascent capitalist markets impacted daily life.

23. Among the most prominent studies of prostitution in Cuba since the post-Soviet crisis are Alcázar Campos (2009), Allen (2007, 2011), Fernandez (1999), Fosado (2005), Fusco (2001), Hodge (2001), Kempadoo (1999), La Cabezas (2009), La Fountain Stokes (2002), and Rundle (2001). Dissertations include Céspedes (2007) and Forrest (1999).

24. Taking a unique view on the political potential of these new subjectivities, Jafari Allen has analyzed the intersection of nonnormative desires and blackness to argue that black Cubans crafted "intimate spaces of autonomy," which qualified as forms of resistance that moved "toward freedom" (2011: 14).

25. For important work on heteroerotic sex tourism in the Dominican Republic, see also Brennan (2004) and Gregory (2007).

26. By attending to the complicated intersections of nonnormative desire and the reinvention of respectability in the post-Soviet era, my work extends Bourdieu's concept of symbolic capital because sexuality is largely absent from his studies. Moreover, I am taking some liberties applying Bourdieu to a socialist context devoid of private wealth because Bourdieu emphasized how forms of cultural capital could be converted into wealth—a reflection of the French context where he conducted his sociological studies.

27. Bourdieu recognized the role of social structures, but emphasized how social actors navigated them, a position that Michael Herzfeld has called a "militant middle ground" between structure and agency (Herzfeld 2005: 151). By moving

class distinctions away from economic determinism into the cultural realm, Bourdieu opened up an analysis of how power and difference operated in the most mundane habits of daily life.

28. In describing changes in Havana's queer enclaves after the introduction of foreign tourism, I do not want to suggest that gay tourists alone transformed nonnormative sexualities in Cuba. This would be especially remiss because it plays into the misleading notion that a Western presence brings change or progress to non-Western countries that lag behind culturally. Instead, the presence of foreign tourists embodied economic changes and the policies of state segregation that provided tourists with elite status transformed the opportunities that Cubans faced. Hence, the influx of foreign tourists to Havana provided a context for the tensions and experiences that I present in this book, but the changes to relationships between Cubans were the focus on my interlocutors.

29. Their resistance to new forms of inequality echoes other contexts in which people draw on local lexicons to make sense of and decry the rise of capitalist economies. For instance, Michael Taussig (1980) described black peasants in Colombia who criticized the exploitative forms of wage labor by drawing on folkloric tales of the devil.

30. For example, see the insightful work on blackness and race in Cuba by Jafari Allen (2011), Kaifa Roland (2011), and Mark Sawyer (2006).

31. The First Congress of the Cuban Communist Party in 1975 declared that sincerity and mutual respect should guide partner choice in the new Cuban society.

32. Andaya observes how heterosexual women in the post-Soviet era were influenced by these ideologies, decrying how material interests played a deciding role in forming romantic relationships. Like urban gays, straight women lamented the decline of morality, social solidarity, and familial cohesion because of these new market-oriented dispositions. Andaya, building on Arjun Appadurai, sees this as a type of "imagined nostalgia" for things that never were (Andaya 2012: 15).

33. See Tom Boellstorff for an insightful discussion of the potential of Foucauldian notions of reverse discourse to analyze queer resistance (2007: 23).

34. Bruce Grant (1995) has demonstrated how marginalized subjects can both identify with dominant socialist state projects and maintain a separate cultural identity.

35. In particular, the lawless and the state can use the same language to justify their actions. For example, Herzfeld describes the case of Cretan sheep rustlers and the authorities of the Greek state, all of whom invoke a "formerly perfect social order" to justify their contradictory actions (2005: 109).

36. Most famously, Peter Wilson (1974) framed the social dichotomy that arose from the enduring cultural traces of colonialism in his iconic model of reputation and respectability. Respectability, Wilson claimed, was the domain of women and found its roots in the colonial moral order that emphasized church attendance, domesticity, and formal marriage. Reputation, in contrast, was associated with street masculinity, sexual prowess, and wit, providing a form of resistance to

colonially imposed notions of respectability. While the gendered binary of male respect and female reputation is an oversimplification in a region in which women often use the tools of reputation (e.g., Barrow 1986; Freeman 2007), the tensions associated with reputation and propriety continue to play out in new ways in the social life of the region (Wardle 2000; Freeman 2007).

37. The historical relationship between race, class, and labor in postcrisis Cuba has been well studied (e.g., De la Fuente 1995, De la Fuente and Glasco 1997), but the shifting nature of nonnormative sexual identities and practices tends to be discussed apart from racialized modes of production and transnational flows.

38. During my time in Havana, La Rampa maintained a reputation as the most popular *ambiente* for urban gays. La Rampa was not just any neighborhood; with each era of Cuban history it had offered a symbolic canvas for social reinvention. The heart of Havana's prerevolutionary nightlife in the 1950s, La Rampa was once famous for luxury hotels, casinos, and nightclubs. In the 1960s, the cabarets with scantily clad women dancing for rich tourists were closed. The revolutionary government transformed the area, allowing all Cubans to stay for free in the hotels on subsidized honeymoons and adding affordable movie theaters and cafés.

39. During this time, I also shot and directed a documentary film exploring the lives of sex workers in queer enclaves. The process of collaborative filmmaking with sex workers served as a rich source of ethnographic insight and has profoundly informed my perspective.

40. Over the years, I have also consulted with and fostered ongoing collaborations with Cuban academics, writers, artists, filmmakers, and medical professionals whose work addressed sexuality, tourism, HIV/AIDS, and popular culture. I also attended a wide variety of arts and cultural events, including plays, film festivals, and art exhibits related to gender and sexuality. In order to survey Cuban social scientific and artistic production often difficult to find in the United States, I conducted archival research at the National Library in Havana, the University of Havana's Psychology Library, and the International Film School in San Antonio de los Baños.

41. By the completion of my research, 64 percent no longer sought clients. The high rate of retirement reflected how sex work was most often a short-term endeavor used to supplement diminishing wages and state subsidies rather than a lifelong career. Jafari Allen notes a similar trend (2011: 183).

42. Emilio Bejel (2001) and Lourdes Arguelles and B. Ruby Rich (1985) provide important exceptions to this trend.

43. Following Judith Halberstam (1998), I see female masculinity not merely as a perverse supplement to dominant configurations of gender but believe that masculinity itself cannot be fully understood unless female masculinity is taken into account.

44. As Mark Padilla has pointed out, one of the benefits of analyzing the political economy of sexuality is that it highlights how same-sex exchanges do not exist in a world of homoeroticism but are connected to heterosexual relations largely through the household (2007: 25).

45. Although I conducted interviews with twelve Cuban Americans who were returning to Havana as tourists, I decided to focus on non-Cuban tourists as a way to examine how foreigners with little direct contact with the island imagined their presence in Havana.

46. For instance, Esther Newton, confessing her attraction to an older lesbian she interviewed during field research, encouraged ethnographers to be more upfront about our feelings (1993: 16).

47. My connection to Cuba was less charged than that of many researchers whose families have left Cuba, yet I did have a relationship to the island. Before I was born, my maternal grandparents and great-grandparents worked as live-in domestics for a wealthy Bostonian family who had amassed a fortune through Cuban sugar plantations. After the 1959 revolution, the Cuban government nationalized the sugar industry, and the family lost its fortune and fired my relatives. My grandfather reminded me of this link when we discussed Cuba, and I found it striking how social movements, transnational economic shifts, and the lives of the working poor had always been intertwined.

48. After 1959, Cuba nationalized all industries, and the loss of U.S. political influence on the island, just ninety miles from U.S. shores, became a thorn in the side of the U.S. government. Cuban migrants, supported by the U.S. military, initiated campaigns to oust Fidel Castro and return Cuba to prerevolutionary levels of foreign investment, an effort that continues to the present day. As Cuban studies scholar Jorge Domínguez (1997) puts it, in Cuba, the Cold War did not end, but became colder.

49. Two male sex workers I knew spent the night partying on the Malecón and fell asleep on the wall. After sunrise, they awoke to find themselves surrounded by a mandatory government march against George Bush that snaked along the Malecón. With nowhere else to go, they joined the protest.

50. During shorter visits, I also spent stretches in middle-class Vedado and the slightly wealthier neighborhood of Miramar.

51. During the Cold War, the absence of gay voices reflected broader trends in which Cuban scholarship in the United States was dominated by highly ideological work that focused on the state, the economy, or Fidel Castro (Bengelsdorf 2009: 140). As Cuban historian Abel Sierra Madero (2006: 15) points out, this absence is also compounded by the dearth of attention to nonnormative sexuality within the Cuban academy. More recent representations of homophobic policies in Cuba also reflect how gay tolerance has increasingly become a measure of governmental "civilization." Akin to the ways that governments historically used the oppressed status of women to justify colonial rule, homophobia in "enemy" nations has become a common symbol for the absence of democracy.

52. Postcolonial and feminist scholars have warned us about homogenizing representations of a group of people in need of "rescue," not by their own devices, but by the "charitable" forces of intervention (Abu-Lughod 1986; Mahmood 2001; Mohanty 1991; Ong 1988). Likewise, I have elsewhere argued that studies of prostitution published outside Cuba often suffer interventionist undertones (Stout 2008).

53. A number of scholars have written on this topic including D'Emilio (1998), Foucault (1990 [1978]), Stoler (1995), and Weeks (1977).

54. Sympathetic to the challenges of studying same-sex eroticism in cross-cultural contexts, I agree with Kath Weston's (1993) conceptualization of a "queer" anthropology, rather than a gay/lesbian anthropology, because it takes nonnormative gender and sexual practices as the point of departure rather than a universal.

55. For an important debate regarding the application of the term *homosexual* to same-sex practices, in Cuba see Roger Lancaster's (1986) comment on Lourdes Arguelles and B. Ruby Rich's (1984, 1985) essays on homosexuality in Cuba. Lancaster argues that the use of the term *homosexual* in studies on Cuba imposes an ethnocentric, universalist model of same-sex practice. I agree with Lancaster's call to chart a movement for sexual equality that reflects the socialist and cultural logics of the Cuban context. At the same time, as Arguelles and Rich maintain in their response to Lancaster, categories of sexuality in Cuba such as "gay" or "homosexual" reflect a transnational history of precolonial, colonial, and revolutionary eras that complicate the notion of a "folk" model.

56. Gayle Rubin (2002) challenges Foucault's prominence in the field by pointing out how similar constructionist arguments were being made by sociologists who predated Foucault.

57. Here I am building on the works of Butler (1993), Duggan (1994), Foucault (1990 [1978]), Herdt (1981), Lancaster (1992), Parker (1991), Sedgwick (1990), and Weeks (1977).

58. Whereas the reification of desire would manifest in categories of homosexuality and heterosexuality, as Kevin Floyd (2009) has insightfully argued, the term "queer" offers no such solid ground.

59. I take my cue from Don Kulick (1998), who in his ethnographic study of Brazilian *travestis,* did not translate the term.

60. Kulick (1998) found a similar pattern in Brazil.

61. Infamous for its creative manipulation of the Spanish language, Cuban slang has historically relied on enlargement, reduction, replacement, switching, reduplicative creation, and personification to conceal the meanings of words (Rivas 2000). Cuban slang was particularly prolific when it came to describing sexual practices and body parts. For instance, the penis could be described by thirty-three different words.

62. Similar trends of homoerotic sex work exist within a variety of Latin American contexts, such as the Brazilian *michê* and Mexican *mayate,* and the *sanky panky* in the Dominican Republic (Padilla 2007; Parker 1999; Prieur 1998).

63. In an analysis of gay kinship in San Francisco, Kath Weston highlighted how urban gays used "community" to conflate a unified identity with gay institutions and geographic space (1991: 122).

64. Since my fieldwork, these numbers have grown, especially among gay men, and I discuss this as a possible direction for future research in my conclusion.

65. My focus on the intersections between affective sentiments and economic change also redresses a gap in social scientific literature on the Caribbean, which,

as Carla Freeman (2007) notes, tends to focus on the economy and leave senti-mental attachments and love outside the scope of analysis.

Chapter 1: The Historical Context of Queer Critiques

1. Desperate, gays and hustlers established a makeshift gathering at a bus stop near the capitol building in Centro Habana. They told officers that they were waiting for a city bus that was delayed (a plausible alibi given Havana's chronic transportation crisis).

2. Many gay men and lesbians with whom I spoke attributed the raids to heightened political tensions with the United States. They reminded me that just a few months before the raid, Fidel Castro had relinquished political control to his brother Raúl after holding presidential power for over forty years. This had left the government vulnerable to foreign intervention and necessitated the control of public forms of deviancy.

3. During this era Dr. Benjamín de Céspedes published a study of prostitution that included "pederasts," men who had homoerotic sexual relationships with adolescent boys. Writing during a time when the number of brothels in Havana was estimated to be as high as 1,400 (Pérez 1999: 207), Dr. Céspedes emphasized pederasts' roots in what he described as a social class of career criminals, alcohol-ics, and staff that served prostitutes.

4. The emphasis on heteronormative masculine prowess as fundamental to na-tional defense was typical of postcolonial and nationalist movements. For instance, see Anderson (1983); McClintock (1992); Mosse (1985); and Parker et al. (1992).

5. For a more in-depth history of revolutionary homophobia, see Arguelles and Rich (1984); Bejel (2001); Hamilton (2012); Leiner (1994); Lumsden (1996); Quiroga (2000); Smith and Padula (1996); Sommer (1991); Young (1981).

6. To demonstrate the power of male homoerotic sexual roles, gay Cubans would recount a popular urban legend. During the 1960s, at the height of governmental homophobia, when police caught two men having sex, they would declare the *pasivo* a homosexual and send him to prison, but release the *activo*. Working in Brazil, anthropologist Don Kulick (1997a) aptly describes a similar system based around an opposition between the "fucked and not-fucked," with women, gay men, and *travestis* on one end, and heterosexual men on the other.

7. As Bejel points out, Cuban health specialists were influenced by Freud and blamed male effeminacy on the presence of a weak or absent father and an obses-sive mother.

8. Guevara did not address the issue of homosexuality overtly, but opposed the New Man to the inauthentic intellectual (Guevara 1965: 49)—code for queer art-ists and thinkers who failed to live up to masculinized standards.

9. Attitudes toward homosexuality stemmed from the conception that it was a choice, rather than a biological fact, as advocates would later argue. For instance, in 1967 Castro told a foreign journalist that to punish a person for something over which he had no control would be wrong (Lockwood 1967: 107).

10. While male homosexuality was portrayed as a manifestation of capitalist vice, female prostitution became a primary symbol of the exploitation of Cubans—women in particular—by global capitalist systems. In 1961, the government began a systematic rehabilitation program through which prostitutes attended schools and received pensions to support their dependents while they underwent job training (Lewis, Lewis, and Rigdon 1977: xvii). More than an occupational program, however, the reform movement shifted the blame from the individual sex worker to emphasize the inherent moral danger of market-driven economies.

11. According to these discourses, the metropolis suffered from the greatest amount of capitalist contamination, whereas the countryside represented unadulterated revolutionary spirit and pure Cuban masculinity. Fidel Castro concluded, "one does not find homosexuals in the countryside because the conditions of the rural areas do not permit the emergence of this deviation" (Salas 1979: 166).

12. The degree to which military leaders created UMAP for punitive, as opposed to reformatory, purposes remains unclear given that the government later executed some of the officials responsible for the inhumane treatment of detainees at the camps.

13. Applying Lauren Berlant's notion of the "intimate public" to communist contexts, Iona Luca (2011) argues that intimate publics may provide a space to avoid ideological indoctrination, but may also serve as a site of state penetration.

14. The heavily censored state-run Cuban newspaper *Granma* (March 7, 2007) featured an article titled "When it comes to gay rights, is Cuba inching ahead of USA?" in which Alarcón told the reporter, "We have to abolish any form of discrimination against those persons." Likewise, Remigio Ferro lamented that homophobic thinking had not been entirely eradicated in Cuba.

15. In part, these trends toward growing tolerance reflected the influence of advances for homosexual citizens in other parts of the Socialist Bloc, especially East Germany (Arguelles and Rich 1984: 692). Hence, the book's communist roots gave the treatise more validity in the eyes of Cubans, and the book became a bestseller.

16. In 1980, Cubans occupied the Peruvian Embassy and demanded exit permits to leave the island. The Cuban government agreed to let citizens leave as long as they would migrate to Miami instead of Peru, and negotiated with President Carter, who agreed to accept 125,000 Cubans. Leaders and citizens orchestrated protests that demonized the migrants as *escoria* (scum) and *gusanos* (worms). Ironically, leaders emphasized that homosexuals did not have to leave Cuba because of discrimination, yet insisted that homosexuality was a behavioral disorder, like drug addiction and gambling, rather than a biological reality.

17. For an in-depth textual analysis of the gay-themed works that emerged, see Bejel (2001), Jambrina (2000), and Navarro (2002).

18. A defining symbol of this movement was the inauguration of the Museum of the Battle of Ideas in Cárdenas in July 2001, which exhibited the repatriation campaign of Elián González and memorialized the education and

cultural programs that the government had announced the year before (Tisdel Flikke 2007).

19. Sociologist Sujatha Fernandes (2006) likewise interprets the loosening of censorship as a way to alleviate widespread discontent, the repression of which leaders feared would foment dissident political movements.

20. For an example of how representations of gay tolerance play out on an international stage, see Stout (2011).

21. For a particularly insightful analysis of audience responses to *Strawberry and Chocolate*, see Fernandes's 2006 account of screening sessions in which Cubans watched and commented on the themes of tolerance in the film.

22. State-funded films such as *Lucia* and *Retrato de Teresa* (Portrait of Teresa) reinforced women's emerging independence from their husbands, fathers, and brothers.

23. By supporting artistic works by Cubans on the island, the government helped to fortify divisions between Cuban citizens and expatriates during a moment when diasporic Cubans might be looking to take advantage of governmental weakness. By funding post-Soviet state cultural campaigns on the island, the government helped to equate authentic Cuban culture with the geographic space of the island and undercut the possibility that Cubans in the diaspora could produce and circulate legitimate Cuban culture outside Cuba.

24. For instance, in 1995, Díaz debuted Virgilio Piñera's *La niñita querida* (Darling Little Girl), which had been censored due to its erotic excess and biting social critique, as well as Piñera's homosexuality. A critique of middle-class values and gender norms, the play used sarcasm and neobaroque techniques to criticize daily life (Manzor-Coats and Martiatu Terry 1995: 53).

25. In one scene, a character is asked, "Who is the *jefe* here?" (*jefe* [boss] is slang for Fidel Castro). Without responding, the actress turned to the audience with raised eyebrows and everyone began clapping. "*I* am the boss!" she responded as the crowd applauded.

26. Reflecting on lesbian visibility in the arts, Guillard Limonta (2009) recognizes the significance of these representations, yet also maintains that they perpetuate stereotypical ideas about lesbian relationships as comprising one masculine and one feminine partner.

27. Carrie Hamilton points out that Cubans' emphasis on positive images of homosexuality might seem outdated to outsiders, but the particular role of media in Cuba as a nexus of public debates makes positive representations more important than they might be in capitalist contexts (2012: 134).

28. On weeknights, all programming ended at 11 PM, but on weekends or during summer vacations pirated Hollywood movies would play until 2 or 3 AM. Due to the embargo, Cuban television stations did not have to pay royalties to screen Hollywood movies.

29. Educational programs such as *Cuando una mujer*, which was advised by the FMC, offered brief mentions of homosexuality but did not have the same impact as *The Dark Side of the Moon*.

30. Gay male or lesbian characters would occasionally appear on telenovelas from Latin America, such as a Brazilian series that featured a lesbian couple. But these stories were highly censored by the Cuban government, despite protests from lesbians who organized through CENESEX (Guillard Limonta 2009: 69).

31. A *telenovela* is a limited-run television drama popular in Latin America. Distinct from soap operas, telenovelas end after a long run. The medium has been used throughout Latin America to promote social messages. Ana López describes how, after the revolution, Cuban television became a "laughing-stock" due to the didactic nature of programming and the eradication of the telenovelas (1991: 264). Then in the 1980s, when anti-Castro Cuban Americans began to use broadcasting to traverse the island's borders, the ICRT decided to make television more relevant and started to import telenovelas from Latin America.

32. Here, I build on the work of anthropologists who have applied Benedict Anderson's notion of an "imagined community" to national televisual productions to show how mass media create a vision of belonging and shared experience among spectator-citizens (e.g., Abu-Lughod 2002b; Mankekar 1999, 2004; Rofel 1994, 2007). In a similar vein, Faye Ginsburg recommends that anthropologists utilize ethnography to interject people into the "massness of media," in order to understand how people produce and interpret media in relation to their cultural circumstances (1994: 137).

33. The term *mariposa* plays on the word *butterfly*, which is also slang for a homosexual man.

34. This suggests that Western categories of sexual identity were not colonizing Cuban local categories, but rather heterogeneous sexual practices and identities coexisted, often in tension.

35. The emphasis on gay tolerance as the purview of public health campaigns corresponds to the role of socialist health programs in daily life. By the 1990s, leaders of Cuban government agencies had successfully produced what Sean Brotherton has identified as a "medicalized subjectivity," an educated populace that had mastered biomedical knowledge, enjoyed access to neighborhood doctors, and consented to a high level of state intervention (Brotherton 2008: 262).

36. The law was still under review at the time of publication.

37. This suggests an interesting contrast to the relationship between the weakening of the nuclear family, the rise of individual autonomy, and the emergence of homosexual identities outlined by John D'Emilio (1983).

38. As Foucault emphasizes, modern states govern by the right to manage life at every level, including the family, bodily practice, and medicalization (1990: 141). Sexuality plays a particularly important role in the biopolitical regulation of selfhood and subjectivity.

39. Although there had been brief periods of respite when police allowed gays to congregate at night, most attempts on the part of gays to gather in Havana's public zones had been thwarted by police.

40. Pierre Bourdieu's (1977, 1984) understanding of how the sociospatial order becomes written onto bodily experience through practice frames my understanding

of the link between subject formation and place-making. In addition to Bourdieu, a number of ethnographies of spatialization in postcommunist and Latin American contexts have informed my analysis (e.g., Low 1996; Parker 1999; Zhang 2001).

41. Government leaders expressed anxiety about what the rise of the sex trade would mean in terms of Cuba's international reputation. Speaking at a 1994 tourist convention, at the height of the explosion of the tourist sex trade, Castro remarked, "We don't want the image of a country of gambling, drugs, prostitution. We want the image of a country with a high level of culture and ability to welcome visitors, for the world to have the image of an honorable, moral country" (Azicri 2001: 78).

42. Not all urban gays found representations of homosexuality to be significant. For instance, after watching a Cuban film at our neighborhood cinema, a group of gay male friends focused on the strapping heterosexual protagonists and had nothing to say about the bisexual character who had a love scene with another man.

43. While I agree that tolerance fixes essentialized identities in a social hierarchy, I believe there is also underexplored potential for marginalized people to utilize these discourses for their own purposes.

Chapter 2: The Complicated Desires of Urban Gays

1. During the 1990s, unemployment and underemployment skyrocketed, hitting rates as high as 51 percent, according to the Cuban Association of Independent Economists. For those who still maintained state jobs, the average wage in 1999 was 223 pesos, rising to 282 by 2005, approximately $9 U.S. (Ritter 2005: 351). While this take-home pay was adequate in the 1980s, because of the generous state welfare, in post-Soviet Havana peso earnings no longer sufficed (Eckstein 2003).

2. As Weston (1997) highlights, coming out often put kin relations to the test. As children were rejected or disowned by their parents for being gay, kinship ties based on blood proved to be more fragile than people often suggested.

3. Many young Cubans' attitudes toward sex had become more open; people had become more sexually active and less judgmental about premarital sex since the revolution (Lumsden 1996: 21). Yet, despite a growing openness toward experimentation, I do not mean to perpetuate stereotypes of the Caribbean as a zone of sexual voraciousness.

4. As mentioned in the introduction, there is a rich literature on marriage, partner choice, and respectability in the Caribbean; see, for example, Findlay (1999), Freeman (2007), Martinez-Alier (1989), Putnam (2002), and Wilson (1969, 1973).

5. By using the term *performance* here, I do not mean to insinuate that some gender performances were more natural than others. Rather, I am borrowing from Judith Butler (1990), who maintains that all gender is performative.

6. Historian Carrie Hamilton acknowledges traditional notions of *activo* and *pasivo* but points out that these roles coexisted with other configurations of homoerotic desire at least as early as the 1980s (2012: 160).

7. My translation; the original reads: "Lo ideal en toda relación sexual es la búsqueda de lo opuesto y por eso el mundo homosexual actual es algo siniestro y desolado; porque casi nunca se encuentra lo deseado."

8. Anthropologists have long debated whether or not a heterosexual man's status is enhanced or challenged by same-sex relations (e.g., Allen 2007; Carrillo 2002; Kulick 1997a, 1997b; Lancaster 1992; Lumsden 1996; Parker 1991, 1999). Roger Lancaster has suggested that in Latin America when a man uses another for sex he acquires masculinity, and when one is penetrated he expends it (1995: 150). In response, Stephen Murray argued that the idea that same-sex relations with other men could enhance Latin American masculinities was a "fantasy" of the anthropologist (1995: xi).

9. I italicize *bisexual* to signal the Cuban use of the word, which has a distinct history from the U.S. term bisexual. Here I take my cue from Tom Boellstorff (2002), who similarly italicized *gay* in the Indonesian context, despite its similarities with English terminology.

10. Scholars of Latin American homoerotic practices have explored the practices and identities linked to "male bisexuality," which are often not labeled as such by the men engaging in homoerotic practices (e.g., Alonso and Koreck 1988; Carrier 1995; Lumsden 1991; Prieur 1998). In contrast, I am exploring the actual emergence of the category of bisexual identity.

11. For instance, the internationally renowned National Ballet had offered a safe haven for gays even in the violently homophobic 1960s. As legend had it, when police entered the García Lorca Theater to expel homosexuals, Alicia Alonso, former prima ballerina and director of Cuba's ballet program, stopped the removal. Similarly, the former director of the film industry and Cuba's famous International Film Festival, Alfredo Guevara was, according to many, "the only *pájaro* (fag) that Fidel would put in power."

12. The four hustlers identified as white, and were all light skinned.

13. The requirement of managing the comfort and experiences of tourists keeps with larger trends in the service industry that demand more emotional labor from workers. Deindustrialization and the rise of service industries have therefore prompted a wide-scale trend toward self-management and the emotional management of others.

14. For a more extensive discussion of the racial politics of the Caribbean tourist industry, see, for example, Cabezas (2009), Enloe (1989), Kinnaird and Hall (1994), Sinclair (1997), Stepick and Grenier (1994), and Thompson (2002).

15. This stereotype has also been perpetuated by foreign scholars, who, as Nadine Fernandez (1999) notes, often fail to recognize relationships between lighter-skinned *jineteras* and white foreign tourists.

16. Javier didn't know his father planned to leave and was on his way home from school when he heard that his father's name had been announced on the radio as part of a list of Cubans who had made it to the United States illegally. Picked up by the U.S. Coast Guard, Javier's father spent a year in Guantanamo military base before he entered the United States.

17. Their migration reflects a broader pattern in which those who emigrated after 1990 were primarily motivated by economic concerns, as opposed to Cold War political concerns (Eckstein and Barberia 2002).

Chapter 3: Urban Gay Men Negotiate Commodified Sex

1. During the crisis, as remittances from family abroad and personal networks became the primary means of securing a reasonable living, race and ethnicity began to play a larger role in economic opportunity. Since white Cubans left in greater numbers, especially during the early waves of migration, their family members were more likely to have access to hard currency in the post-Soviet era.

2. John D'Emilio (1983) describes a similar process during industrialization in the United States, in which the rise of urban centers and industries was a necessary precursor of the emergence of gay communities. While similarities exist, I do not want to imply that Cuba was "catching up" to the gay communities in the United States, as if a singular evolutionary narrative exists for the rise of capitalism and the emergence of gay identities.

3. Although it never seemed entirely clear why *pingueros* would not form similar long-term, transactional relationships with women, one possible explanation is that gay men allowed them to openly maintain girlfriends, wives, and families, whereas women refused to condone infidelity.

4. In a similar vein, Katherine Frank (2002) has also observed the premium placed on authenticity at strip clubs where clients desire the authentic and the real.

5. This is a rough translation since there is no English equivalent of *titimania*, which most often describes older men's love for younger women.

6. Few, if any, official histories of gay relationships during these eras exist, so my own knowledge was pieced together from accounts told to me by older generations of gay men.

7. Despite their protests, Oscar and his friends had become dependent on the attention and affection of the young hustlers they criticized. They frequently criticized the Malécon as too *bajo* (low-class) and felt the lack of gay nightlife separated Cuba from more "civilized" countries, meaning cosmopolitan and gay-friendly. I had assumed that they would prefer a "gay scene" in the stricter sense of the term, but during a trip to *El Mejunje*, the only officially sanctioned, state-run club in Cuba that hosted a gay night, they were disappointed by the absence of young, attractive men willing to have sex with them. Oscar met a couple of younger men that he liked, but when they refused his advances, he decided that everyone was "too queer (*pájaro*)" and told Ivan, "There is not one real man in this town." In the end, Oscar and his friends preferred the option of hiring hustlers.

8. In a similar vein, Lieba Faier (2007) analyzes the declarations of love by Filipina entertainers who marry Japanese men. Faier argues that discourses of love counteract the stigma of their work and help to construct important aspects of gender and sexuality among Filipina migrants.

9. Ivan's suspicions were fueled by the fact that Antonio's foray into sex work was curious, given that he had a good life and stable job paying hard currency back at home.

Chapter 4: Sex, Desire, and Labor among Hustlers

1. Sandra rarely mentioned Melba's involvement in black markets, yet once, lying on the couch after marching against George W. Bush, she complained about the delinquency overtaking Cuba. "All that stuff," Sandra said to me, motioning with her head toward Melba's room. "It's just getting worse, and it will continue if President Bush doesn't stop strangling our little country."

2. The tendency to engage in the sex tourist trade, but not label oneself a prostitute, reflected broader trends in the Caribbean. For example, in the Dominican Republic, where women described themselves as good mothers raising funds for their children's educations and not as prostitutes (Brennan 2004).

3. Rap and hip-hop also served as a source of empowerment for *Las Krudas*, a popular group of black lesbian rappers who eventually left Cuba. For more on their music and lives, see Jafari Allen (2011: 150) and Tayna Saunders (2009a).

4. This dynamic suggests parallels with Mark Anderson's (2009) findings regarding young Garifuna men in Honduras who appropriated "Black American" culture to mark their identities as *negro* when they had previously identified as *moreno*.

5. Similar reflections have been collected by Carlos Ulises Decena in his work with Dominican immigrants in the United States, for whom traditional masculine roles suggest an obstacle to social mobility (2011: 181).

6. I would argue that this represents an appropriation of Wilson's (1973) notion of "reputation," a form of power that he associated with men and masculinity.

7. Widespread among sex workers in queer enclaves, slang and gestures hid activities from Spanish-speaking tourists, as sex workers often referred to a tourist as a *yuma* (foreigner), called the hustle *matando la jugada* (killing the game), or warned others that a client was *ponchado* (literally "popped"), meaning HIV positive. These tactics built on decades-old techniques of using slang, gestures, and double-speak to prevent state informants from understanding criticism of the government and discovering black market transactions.

8. Mark Anderson (2005) has reported a similar trend among young Garifuna men in Honduras who appropriated African American urban masculinity to make themselves into bad boys, as a way to contrast their public personas against stereotypes of Garifuna men as peaceful and passive.

9. In her study of race and tourism in Cuba, Kaifa Roland found a similar trend among the *jineteras* she interviewed, who mobilized the sexualized and racialized stereotype of hypersexuality for their own gain (2011: 81).

10. Unpublished study found at the University of Havana Psychology Library, accessed May 5, 2003.

11. While I highlight the prevalence of sexual pride and banter within urban male hustler discourse, I do not wish to reproduce the stereotype of Cuban hypersexuality that has emerged from a history of slavery and colonialism.

12. For more on the use of sex to sell Cuba in the international marketplace, see De la Fuente (2001); Marrero (2003); O'Connell Davidson and Sánchez-Taylor (1999); and Palmié (2002). Hence, discourses of Caribbean hypersexuality, as Kamala Kempadoo (2004) has argued, are not simply a racist European imposition but have become a lived reality for many.

13. In the United States, feminist analysts have questioned Cuban critiques of contemporary prostitution. Both Teresa Marrero (2003) and Jan Strout (1995) challenge the Cuban Women's Federation's (FMC) assessment that *jineteras* are in search of the freedom to go out dining, dancing, and shopping and to visit resorts. Instead, U.S.-based accounts often emphasize that Cuban women are performing sex acts to survive and that they are victimized by global economic inequities.

14. Sweeping generalizations about the victimhood of sex workers should be avoided, especially when these descriptions contrast with sex workers' accounts of their lives. To understand the complex power dynamics that exist between sex workers and their clients, as well as their relationships to the state and regulatory entities, requires careful analysis and observation.

15. One of the most significant cultural changes of the Special Period, anthropologist Susan Eckstein has observed, was Cubans' embrace of the materialistic lifestyles that their overseas relatives personified (2004: 333).

16. Timothy Burke (1996) describes a similar process in Zimbabwe in which colonial commodity culture produced consumers with needs and desires who also appropriated commodities in unexpected ways.

17. Marx famously explained that a commodity might appear to be "trivial and easily understood," but in reality was "a very queer thing."

18. Anderson maintains that the imitation of signs of African American identity may provide a form of resistance, but it also reinforces the dominant position of the United States (2009: 178).

19. Havana's sexual slang historically reflected political economic shifts. During the sixteenth and seventeenth centuries, for instance, when Havana was an important port city, slang terms in the sex trade reflected the maritime culture; this lexicon was later replaced by terms referring to the processing of sugar (Cluster and Hernández 2006: 15).

20. As Lesley Sharp notes, "body fragments may be emotionally charged objects of desire, embodying prized transformative properties that bear the power to harm or heal" (2000: 294).

21. This pattern indicates how state discourse could be both flexible and fragile in practice (Friedman 2005: 318).

22. See Debra Curtis (2004) for a germane discussion of the relationship between commodities and sexual subjectivities under capitalism.

23. When I attempted to research the girl's story, it was impossible to access any official record. Crimes were not reported to the public.

24. One Spanish tourist told me that Melba had become so upset with him when he refused to give her $50 that she stopped speaking to him.

25. Inspired by feminist critiques, anthropologists have written about feeling conflicted over middle-class or ethnic privilege, confused by attraction to informants, or overjoyed by sexual intimacies in the field. Yet as ethnographers become more transparent about relationships in the field, love stories blossom while experiences of failed intimacies and betrayal remain uncommon. Rarely do anthropologists analyze their fear of the people upon whom they base their ethnographies (for an important exception see Moreno 1995).

26. For a key debate on the duplicity of feminist ethnography, see Aihwa Ong (1995), Judith Stacey (1998), and Kamala Visweswaren (1994).

27. As described by Amalia Cabezas (2009), Coco Fusco (1998), Kaifa Roland (2011), and Mette Rundle (2001) in their studies of female sex workers.

28. For an insightful discussion of the unproductive ends of anthropological debates regarding victimhood and agency within sex work, see Nicole Constable (2009).

Chapter 5: Sex Tourism, Patronage, and Queer Commodities

1. These laws would be repealed by Raúl Castro in 2008.

2. The trips of diasporic Cubans further complicated the pleasure/politics and insider/outsider binaries within tourist discourse, especially as many gays who left Cuba during the Mariel exodus of 1980 have returned to visit. Within the context of diasporic return, a type of primordial connection to the Cuban people becomes especially important to one's own ethnic, sexual, and cultural identity (e.g., Behar 2002).

3. See, for instance, Alcázar Campos (2009), Cabezas (1998), Fusco (1998), Marrero (2003), and Roland (2011).

4. In her review of the anthropological literature on bodily commodification, Nicole Constable argues that too little research has explored how people involved in these relationships actually make sense of their experiences (2009: 55).

5. See, for instance, Bernstein (2007), Brennan (2004), Cabezas (2004), Cheng (2007), Cohen (1986), Constable (2009), and Padilla (2007).

6. In one important exception, Lawrence La Fountain-Stokes (2002) writes openly about his frustration while traveling in Cuba, where same-sex encounters were often motivated by money. La Fountain-Stokes maintains that gay and lesbian tourism in Cuba may offer benefits to gays in Havana such as economic assistance, increased contact with models of gay politics, and the informal import of hormones and AIDS medicines.

7. Embedded within notions that prostitution is the "oldest profession in the world" are assumptions that male heterosexual desire is timeless, rooted in biological destiny, and that the capitalist commodification of services, such as sex, is a natural fact rather than a historical and economic trend. When scholars investigating sex tourism acknowledge the presence of same-sex prostitution, they often force the encounters into an a priori formula based on male domination and female submission.

8. Cuban friends instructed me to ask wealthy foreigners for things. For instance, when I mentioned that I wanted to visit a gay couple from Milan who vacationed in Cuba, a hustler who received ongoing financial support from the couple described in great detail how I should ask them to pay for my flight.

9. For a more in-depth analysis of these practices, see Cohen (1986, 1993), Hobson and Heung (1998), Odzer (1994), and Pruitt and LaFont (1995).

10. Anthropologist Arjun Appadurai (1986) has aptly suggested that Maussian and Marxian frameworks are not mutually exclusive because they both emphasize how objects possess a "social life" or symbolic and sociopolitical value that can change over the life of an object. Similarly, Lesley Sharp (2000) highlights how Marxian and Maussian models of commodification can coexist within one context.

11. This trend reflects colonial mimicry as described by Homi Bhabha (1994) as "the desire for a reformed, recognizable Other, as a subject of difference that is almost the same but not quite."

12. Similarly, Coco Fusco (1998) found that *jineteras* would offer themselves as temporary girlfriends or potential wives to secure migration abroad.

13. Accessed March 12, 2009. http://www.gaytimes.co.uk/Hotspots/GayGuide -action-Country-countryid-312.html.

14. Accessed February 10, 2001. http://www.metrog.com/travel/havana_00 .html.

15. Accessed December 2, 2005. http://maleflixxx.tv/pc/DetailWide.asp?Movie =CubaLibre002.

16. For an interesting discussion of this process, see Mathew Hill (2007).

17. In a similar vein, Richard Parker cites cases of gay tourists' long-term investments in Brazil and contends that these ties use sexuality to bridge cultural difference (1999: 201). Parker acknowledges that inequality may seem implicit in these interactions, but optimistically suggests these relationships may draw on sexuality to break down cultural and socioeconomic hierarchies that might otherwise remain impenetrable.

18. Timothy Mitchell describes how tourism itself developed alongside a set of procedures by which Europeans divided the realm of "mere" representations as opposed to an essentialized realm of "the real" (1992: 313).

19. Critics of the segregation policies have highlighted how the nonfraternization rule means that the only Cubans foreign tourists meet are black-marketeers and *jineteras* (Gunn 1993: 10).

Conclusion

1. Keeping with recent trends toward queer visibility in state-sponsored film, homoeroticism and gender bending are present throughout as a form of comic relief.

2. Anthropologists have often focused on one ethnic or social group in their fieldwork, hence my inclusion of foreign tourists alongside Cubans is somewhat unorthodox. Yet to exclude the complex experiences of gay travelers would

implicitly stereotype gay sex tourists as neocolonial or apolitical, both common characterizations of gay tourists in scholarly renditions.

3. In a similar vein, historian John D'Emilio has traced how the loosening of heterosexual norms advanced gay rights in the United States. As heterosexuals abandoned the nuclear family as an ideal model, gays were thereby seen as less threatening. For this reason, D'Emilio (2006) argues against gay marriage, claiming that it will only serve to normalize sex and relationships when gay advocates should work to loosen the hold of traditional values on sexuality.

4. Von Diaz in her master's thesis, "Tapando la letra: Illuminating Lesbians in the Cuban Revolution," focuses on an older generation of Cuban lesbians, who express gratitude for CENESEX and the emergence of tolerance rhetoric, often contrasting this to the eras of repression they experienced.

5. Likewise, urban gays often told me that they felt unsafe participating in the profoundly heteronormative nightlife of the city because police officers would not protect gays from harassment in heterosexual bars and clubs.

6. For instance, Pedro Pérez Sarduy and Jean Stubbs (2000) present the stories of two black women in the medical field who achieved their goal of becoming doctors, only to find new racial, social, and economic problems dominating their daily life.

7. More specifically, they argue that attention to whiteness both during and after slavery indicates an important shift away from previous scholarship on race that represented Cuba as a racial democracy, the embodiment of *mestizaje* (2000: 8).

8. Some important scholarship offers the cornerstone for future research on this topic, including Lazaro Lima (2005) and Susana Peña (2005).

References

Abu-Lughod, Lila. 1986. "The Romance of Resistance: Tracing Transformations of Power through Bedouin Women." *American Ethnologist* 17, no. 1: 41–55.

Abu-Lughod, Lila. 2002a. "Do Muslim Women Really Need Saving? Anthropological Reflections on Cultural Relativism and Its Others." *American Anthropologist* 104, no. 3: 783–90.

Abu-Lughod, Lila. 2002b. "Egyptian Melodrama—Technology of the Modern Subject?" In *Media Worlds: Anthropology on New Terrain*. Edited by Faye D. Ginsburg, Lila Abu-Lughod, and Brian Larkin, 115–33. Berkeley: University of California Press.

Abu-Lughod, Lila, and Catherine Lutz. 1990. "Introduction: Emotion, Discourse, and the Politics of Everyday Life." In *Language and the Politics of Emotion*. Edited by Lila Abu-Lughod and Catherine Lutz, 1–23. New York: Cambridge University Press.

Acosta, Dalia. 1998. "Cuba TV Opens Debate on Taboo Subject—Homosexuality." April. Accessed March 15, 2002. http://www.oneworld.org/ips2/apr98/17_39_070.html.

Agamben, Giorgio. 1998. *Homo Sacer: Sovereign Power and Bare Life*. Palo Alto, CA: Stanford University Press.

Aggleton, Peter, ed. 1999. *Men Who Sell Sex: International Perspectives on Male Prostitution and HIV/AIDS*. London: University College London Press.

Ahearn, Laura M. 2001. *Invitations to Love: Literacy, Love Letters, and Social Change in Nepal*. Ann Arbor: University of Michigan Press.

Alcázar Campos, Ana. 2009. "Turismo sexual, jineterismo, turismo de romance: Fronteras difusas en la interacción con el otro en Cuba." *Gazeta de Antropología* N 25/1, Artículo 16.

Alexander, M. Jacqui. 2005. *Pedagogies of Crossing: Meditations on Feminism, Sexual Politics, Memory, and the Sacred*. Durham, NC: Duke University Press.

Allen, Jafari Sinclaire. 2007. "Means of Desire's Production: Male Sex Labor in Cuba." *Identities: Global Studies in Culture and Power* 14, no. 1: 183–202.

Allen, Jafari Sinclaire. 2011. *¡Venceremos? The Erotics of Black Self-Making in Cuba*. Durham, NC: Duke University Press.

Allison, Anne. 1994. *Sexuality, Pleasure, and Corporate Masculinity in a Tokyo Hostess Club*. Chicago: University of Chicago Press.

Alonso, Ana María, and María Teresa Koreck. 1988. "Silences: 'Hispanics,' AIDS, and Sexual Practices." *Differences* 1, no. 1: 101–24.

Altman, Dennis. 1997. "Global Gaze/Global Gays." *GLQ* 3: 417–36.

Altman, Dennis. 2001. *Global Sex*. Chicago: University of Chicago Press.

Andaya, Elise. Forthcoming. "'Relationships and Money, Money and Relationships': Family Gender and Changing Economies in Post-Soviet Cuba." *Feminist Studies*.

Anderson, Benedict. 1983. *Imagined Communities: Reflections on the Origin and Spread of Nationalism*. London: Verso.

Anderson, Mark. 2005. "'Bad Boys' and Peaceful Garifuna: Transnational Encounters between Racial Stereotypes of Honduras and the United States." In *Neither Enemies nor Friends: Latinos, Blacks, Afro Latinos*. Edited by Anani Dzidzienyo and Suzanne Oboler. New York: Palgrave Macmillan.

Anderson, Mark. 2009. *Black and Indigenous: Garifuna Activism and Consumer Culture in Honduras*. Minneapolis: University of Minnesota Press.

Appadurai, Arjun, ed. 1986. "Introduction." *The Social Life of Things: Commodities in Cultural Perspective*. Cambridge: Cambridge University Press.

Arenas, Reinaldo. 1992. *Before Night Falls*. New York: Viking.

Arguelles, Lourdes, and B. Ruby Rich. 1984. "Homosexuality, Homophobia, and Revolution: Notes toward an Understanding of the Cuban Lesbian and Gay Male Experience, Part I." *Signs* 9, no. 4 (summer): 683–99.

Arguelles, Lourdes, and B. Ruby Rich. 1985. "Homosexuality, Homophobia, and Revolution: Notes toward an Understanding of the Cuban Lesbian and Gay Male Experience, Part II." *Signs* 11, no. 1 (autumn): 120–36.

Ayorinde, Christine. 2008. "'A Space within the Revolution': Religious Cubans and the Secular State." In *The Changing Dynamic of Cuban Civil Society*. Edited by Alexander I. Gray and Antoni Kapcia. Gainesville: University Press of Florida.

Azicri, Max. 2001. *Cuba Today and Tomorrow: Reinventing Socialism*. Gainesville: University Press of Florida.

Babb, Florence. 2003. "Out in Nicaragua: Local and Transnational Desires after the Revolution." *Cultural Anthropology* 18, no. 3: 304–28.

Babb, Florence. 2006. "Queering Love and Globalization." *GLQ* 13, no. 1: 111–23.

Babb, Florence. 2011. *The Tourism Encounter: Fashioning Latin American Nations and Histories*. Palo Alto, CA: Stanford University Press.

Behar, Ruth. 1995. *Bridges to Cuba—Puentes a Cuba*. Ann Arbor: University of Michigan Press.

Behar, Ruth. 1996. *Vulnerable Observer: Anthropology That Breaks Your Heart*. Boston: Beacon Press.

Behar, Ruth. 2000. "Post-Utopia: The Erotics of Power and Cuba's Revolutionary Children." In *Cuba, the Elusive Nation*. Edited by Damian J. Fernandez and Madeline Camara Betancourt, 134–54. Gainesville: University Press of Florida.

Behar, Ruth. 2002. "While Waiting for the Ferry to Cuba: Afterthoughts about Adio Kerida." *Michigan Quarterly Review* 41, no. 4: 651–69.

Bejel, Emilio. 2000. "Cuban CondemNation of Queer Bodies." In *Cuba, the Elusive Nation*. Edited by Damian J. Fernandez and Madeline Camara Betancourt. Gainesville: University Press of Florida.

Bejel, Emilio. 2001. *Gay Cuban Nation*. Chicago: University of Chicago Press.

Bengelsdorf, Carollee. 2009. "Reading the State and Civil Society: Recent Books about Cuba." *Latin American Perspectives* 36, no. 2 (March): 140–44.

Bengelsdorf, Carollee, and Jean Stubbs. 1992. "Introduction to Part 3." In *Cuba in Transition: Crisis and Transformation*. Edited by Sandor Halebsky and John M. Kirk, 155–59. Boulder, CO: Westview Press.

Berlant, Lauren. 1997. *The Queen of America Goes to Washington City: Essays on Sex and Citizenship*. Durham, NC: Duke University Press.

Berlant, Lauren. 1998. "Intimacy: A Special Issue." *Critical Inquiry* 24, no. 2: 281–88.

Berlant, Lauren. 2008. *The Female Compliant: The Unfinished Business of Sentimentality in American Culture*. Durham, NC: Duke University Press.

Bernstein, Elizabeth. 2007. *Temporarily Yours: Sexual Commerce in Post-Industrial Culture*. Chicago: University of Chicago Press.

Bhabha, Homi. 1994. *The Location of Culture*. New York: Routledge.

Binnie, Jon. 2004. *The Globalization of Sexuality*. Thousand Oaks, CA: Sage.

Blackwood, Evelyn, and Saskia Wieringa, eds. 1999. *Female Desires: Same-Sex Relations and Transgender Practices across Cultures*. New York: Columbia University Press.

Bloch, Alexia. 2003. *Red Ties and Residential Schools: Indigenous Siberians in a Post-Soviet State*. Philadelphia: University of Pennsylvania Press.

Boellstorff, Tom. 2003. "Dubbing Culture: Indonesian *Gay* and *Lesbi* Subjectivities and Ethnography in an Already Globalized World." *American Ethnologist* 30, no. 2: 225–42.

Boellstorff, Tom. 2007. *A Coincidence of Desires: Anthropology, Queer Studies, Indonesia*. Durham, NC: Duke University Press.

Boellstorff, Tom, and Johan Lindquist. 2004. "Bodies of Emotion: Rethinking Culture and Emotion through Southeast Asia." *Ethnos* 69, no. 4: 437–44.

Bourdieu, Pierre. 1977. *Outline of a Theory of Practice*. Cambridge: Cambridge University Press.

Bourdieu, Pierre. 1984. *Distinction: Critique of the Judgment of Taste*. Translated by Richard Nice. Cambridge, MA: Harvard University Press.

Bourgois, Philippe. 2002. *In Search of Respect: Selling Crack in El Barrio*. Cambridge: Cambridge University Press.

Brennan, Denise. 2004. *What's Love Got to Do with It? Transnational Desires and Sex Tourism in the Dominican Republic*. Durham, NC: Duke University Press.

Brennan, Denise. 2007. "Love Work in a Tourist Town: Dominican Sex Workers and Resort Workers Perform at Love." In *Love and Globalization: Transformations of Intimacy in the Contemporary World*. Edited by Mark Padilla, Jennifer Hirsch, Robert Sember, Miguel Muñoz-Laboy, and Richard Parker, 203–25. Nashville: Vanderbilt University Press.

Briggs, Laura. 2002. *Reproducing Empire: Race, Sex, Science and U.S. Imperialism in Puerto Rico*. Berkeley: University of California Press.

Brinkley, Sidney. 2000. "Gay Cuba Then and Now: A Talk with Gisela Arandia Covarrubia." Accessed February 5, 2001. Blacklightonline.com.

Brito López, Marlon. 2006. "Arte y Amor vs. SIDA." Accessed January 15, 2007. http://www.cenesexualidad.sld.cu/.

Brotherton, P. Sean. 2008. "'We have to think like capitalists but continue being socialists': Medicalized Subjectivities, Emergent Capital and Socialist Entrepreneurs in Post-Soviet Cuba." *American Ethnologist* 35, no. 2: 259–74.

Brown, Jacqueline Nassy. 1998. "Black Liverpool, Black America, and the Gendering of Diasporic Space." *Cultural Anthropology* 13, no. 3: 291–325.

Brown, Wendy. 2008. *Regulating Aversion: Tolerance in the Age of Identity and Empire*. Princeton, NJ: Princeton University Press.

Brundenius, Claes. 2002. "Whither the Cuban Economy After Recovery? The Reform Process, Upgrading Strategies and the Question of Transition." *Journal of Latin American Studies* 34, no. 2: 365–97.

Bruner, Edward, and Barbara Kirshenblatt-Gimblett. 1994. "Maasai on the Lawn: Tourist Realism in East Africa." *Cultural Anthropology* 9, no. 4: 435–70.

Burchardt, Hans-Jürgen. 2002. "Contours of the Future: The New Social Dynamics in Cuba." *Latin American Perspectives* 29, no. 3: 57–74.

Burke, Timothy. 1996. *Lifebuoy Men, Lux Women: Commodification, Consumption, and Cleanliness in Modern Zimbabwe*. Durham, NC: Duke University Press.

Butler, Judith. 1990. *Gender Trouble: Feminism and the Subversion of Identity*. New York: Routledge.

Butler, Judith. 1993. *Bodies that Matter: On the Discursive Limits of "Sex."* New York: Routledge.

Buyandelgeriyn, Manduhai. 2008. "Post-Post Transition Theories: Walking Multiple Paths." *Annual Review of Anthropology* 37: 235–50.

Cabezas, Amalia L. 1998. "Discourses of Prostitution: The Case of Cuba." In *Global Sex Workers: Rights, Resistance, and Redefinition*. Edited by Kamala Kempadoo and Jo Doezema, 79–86. New York: Routledge.

Cabezas, Amalia L. 2004. "Between Love and Money: Sex Tourism and Citizenship in Cuba and the Dominican Republic." *Signs* 29, no. 4: 987–1015.

Cabezas, Amalia L. 2009. *Economies of Desire: Sex and Tourism in Cuba and the Dominican Republic*. Philadelphia: Temple University Press.

Carrier, Joseph. 1995. *De los otros: Intimacy and Homosexuality among Mexican Men*. New York: Columbia University Press.

Carrillo, Hector. 2002. *The Night Is Young: Sexuality in Mexico in the Time of AIDS*. Chicago: University of Chicago Press.

Casteneda, Xochitl, Victor Ortiz, Betania Allen, Cecilia Garcia, and Mauricio Hernandez-Avila. 1996. "Sex Masks: The Double Life of Female Commercial Sex Workers in Mexico City." *Culture, Medicine, and Psychiatry* 20: 229–47.

Castro Espín, Mariela. 2004. "Gay Rights in Cuba: How Much Has Changed? Interview with Mariela Castro Espín by Eduardo Jimanez." *Havana Journal*, February 29.

Castro Ruz, Fidel. 1961. "Palabras a los intelectuales." http://www.min.cult.cu/historia/palabras.doc.

Castro Ruz, Fidel. 1998. Excerpts of Cuban President's Address at Cariforum Summit. Accessed March 12, 2004. http://www.hartford-hwp.com/archives/43/101.html.

Céspedes, Benjamin. 1888. *La Prostitución en la Ciudad de la Habana*. Havana: Establecimiento Tipografico.

Céspedes, Karina L. 2007. "¡Ay Mama Ines!: A Decolonial Feminist Critique of Cuban Nationalism, Tourism, and Sex Work." PhD diss., University of California, Berkeley.

Cheng, Sealing. 2007. "Romancing the Club: Love Dynamics between Filipina Entertainers and GIs in US Military Camp Towns in South Korea." In *Love and Globalization: Transformations of Intimacy in the Contemporary World*. Edited by Mark Padilla, Jennifer Hirsch, Robert Sember, Miguel Muñoz-Laboy, and Richard Parker, 226–51. Nashville: Vanderbilt University Press.

Choy, Catherine. 2003. *Empire of Care: Nursing and Migration in Filipino American History*. Durham, NC: Duke University Press.

Cluster, Dick, and Rafael Hernández. 2006. *The History of Havana*. New York: Palgrave Macmillan.

Cohen, Erik. 1986. "Lovelorn Farangs: The Correspondence between Foreign Men and Thai Girls." *Anthropological Quarterly* 59: 115–28.

Cohen, Erik. 1993. "Open-ended Prostitution as a Skillful Game of Luck: Opportunity, Risk and Security among Tourist-oriented Prostitutes in a Bangkok Soi." In *Tourism in Southeast Asia*. Edited by Michael Hitchcock, Victor T. King, and Michael J. G. Parnwell, 155–78. New York: Routledge.

Collier, Jane. 1997. *From Duty to Desire: Remaking Families in a Spanish Village*. Princeton, NJ: Princeton University Press.

Constable, Nicole. 1997. *Maid to Order: Stories of Filipina Workers*. Ithaca, NY: Cornell University Press.

Constable, Nicole. 2003. *Romance of a Global Stage: Pen Pals, Virtual Ethnography, and "Mail Order" Marriages*. Berkeley: University of California Press.

Constable, Nicole, ed. 2005. *Cross-Border Marriages: Gender and Mobility in Transnational Asia*. Philadelphia: University of Pennsylvania Press.

Constable, Nicole. 2009. "The Commodification of Intimacy: Marriage, Sex, and Reproductive Labor." *Annual Review of Anthropology* 38: 49–64.

Córdova, Efrén. 1996. "The Situation of Cuban Workers during the 'Special Period in Peacetime.'" *ASCE: Cuba in Transition*, 358–68. Accessed February 5, 2004. http://cubasindical.org/docs/45Cordova.fm.pdf.

Coyula, Mario, and Jill Hamberg. 2003. *Understanding Slums: Case Studies for the Global Report on Human Settlement*. United Nations Human Settlements Programme. Accessed March 15, 2007. http://www.ucl.ac.uk/dpu-projects/Global_Report/home.htm.

Cruz-Malavé, Arnaldo, and Martin F. Manalansan IV. 2002. *Queer Globalizations: Citizenship and the Afterlife of Colonialism*. New York: New York University Press.

Curtis, Debra. 2004. "Commodities and Sexual Subjectivities: A Look at Capitalism and Its Desires." *Cultural Anthropology* 19, no. 1: 95–121.

Davies, Catherine. 1997. *A Place in the Sun? Women Writers in Twentieth-Century Cuba*. London: Zed Books.

Decena, Carlos Ulises. 2011. *Tacit Subjects: Belonging and Same-Sex Desire among Dominican Immigrant Men*. Durham, NC: Duke University Press.

De Certeau, Michel. 1984. *The Practices of Everyday Life: Volume 2, Living and Cooking*. Translated by Timothy J. Tomasik. Minneapolis: University of Minnesota Press.

De la Fuente, Alejandro. 1995. "Race and Inequality in Cuba, 1899–1981." *Journal of Contemporary History* 30, no. 1: 131–67.

De la Fuente, Alejandro. 2001. *A Nation for All: Race, Inequality, and Politics in Twentieth-Century Cuba*. Chapel Hill: University of North Carolina Press.

De la Fuente, Alejandro, and Laurence Glasco. 1997. "Are Blacks 'Getting Out of Control'? Racial Attitudes, Revolution, and Political Transition in Cuba." In *Toward a New Cuba? Legacies of a Revolution*. Edited by Miguel A. Centeno and Mauricio Font, 53–71. Boulder, CO: Lynn Rienner.

D'Emilio, John. 1983. "Capitalism and Gay Identity." In *The Lesbian and Gay Studies Reader*. Edited by Henry Abelove, Michélle Aina Barale, and David M. Halperin. New York: Routledge.

D'Emilio, John. 1998. *Sexual Politics, Sexual Communities*. Chicago: University of Chicago Press.

D'Emilio, John. 2006. "The Marriage Fight Is Setting Us Back." *Gay and Lesbian Review Worldwide*. Accessed November 20, 2009. http://www.glreview.com/issues/13.6/13.6-demilio.php.

De Moya, E. A., and R. García. 1998. "Three Decades of Male Sex Work in Santo Domingo." In *Men Who Sell Sex: International Perspectives on Male Prostitution and AIDS*. Edited by Peter Aggleton, 127–40. London: Taylor and Francis.

Diaz, Von. 2012. "Tapando la letra: Illuminating Lesbians in the Cuban Revolution." MA thesis, New York University.

Domínguez, Jorge. 1993. "The Political Impact on Cuba of the Reform and Collapse of Communist Regimes." In *Cuba: After the Cold War*. Edited by Carmelo Mesa-Lago, 99–132. Pittsburgh: University of Pittsburgh Press.

Domínguez, Jorge. 1997. "U.S.-Cuban Relations: From the Cold War to the Colder War." *Journal of Interamerican Studies and World Affairs* 39, no. 3: 49–75.

Domínguez, Jorge. 2001. "Cuban Foreign Policy and the International System." In *Latin America in the New International System*. Edited by Joseph S. Tulchin and Ralph H. Espach. Boulder, CO: Lynne Rienner.

Donham, Donald. 1998. "Freeing South Africa: The 'Modernization' of Male-Male Sexuality in Soweto." *Cultural Anthropology* 13, no. 1: 3–21.

Dopico, Ana Maria. 2002. "Picturing Havana: History, Vision, and the Scramble for Cuba." In *Nepantla: Views from the South* 3, no. 3: 451–93.

Dreyfus, Hubert L., and Paul Rabinow. 1983. *Michel Foucault: Beyond Structuralism and Hermeneutics*. Chicago: University of Chicago Press.

Drucker, Peter, ed. 2000. "Introduction: Remapping Sexualities." *Different Rainbows*. London: GMP.

Duggan, Lisa. 1994. "Queering the State." *Social Text* 39: 1–14.

Duggan, Lisa. 2004. *The Twilight of Equality? Neoliberalism, Cultural Politics, and the Attack on Democracy*. Boston: Beacon Press.

Ebron, Paulla A. 2002. *Performing Africa*. Princeton, NJ: Princeton University Press.

Eckstein, Susan. 1997. "The Limits of Socialism in a Capitalist World Economy: Cuba since the Collapse of the Soviet Bloc." In *Toward a New Cuba? Legacies of a Revolution*. Edited by Miguel Angel Centeno and Mauricio Font. London: Lynne Rienner.

Eckstein, Susan. 2003. "Diasporas and Dollars: Transnational Ties and the Transformation of Cuba." Working Paper 16. Massachusetts Institute of Technology Center for International Studies. Accessed November 4, 2010. http://web.mit .edu/cis/www/migration/pubs/rrwp/16_diasporas.pdf.

Eckstein, Susan. 2004. "On Deconstructing Immigrant Generations: Cohorts and the Cuban Émigré Experience." Working Paper #97. Center for Comparative International Studies, University of California, San Diego. Accessed November 4, 2009. http://www.ccis-ucsd.org/publications/working_papers.htm.

Eckstein, Susan, and Lorena Barberia. 2002. "Grounding Immigrant Generations in History: Cuban Americans and Their Transnational Ties." *International Migration Review* 36, no. 3: 799–837.

Ehrenreich, Barbara, and Arlie Russell Hochschild. 2002. *Global Woman: Nannies, Maids, and Sex Workers in the New Economy*. New York: Holt Paperback.

Elizalde, Miriam. 1999. *Flores desechables: Prostitución en Cuba?* Havana: Ediciones Abril.

Ellis, Jo. 1999. "Homosexuality in Cuba: Revolution within the Revolution." *Greenleft News*. Accessed February 2, 2005. http://www.greenleft.org.au/ node/19250.

Elliston, Deborah. 1999. "Negotiating Transnational Sexual Economies: Female Mahu and Same-Sex Sexuality in Tahiti and Its Islands." In *Female Desires: Same-Sex Relations and Transgender Practices across Cultures*. Edited by Evelyn Blackwood and Saskia Wieringa, 230–50. New York: Columbia University Press.

Ellwood, Wayne. 1998. "Facing the Music: Cuba's Revolution 40 Years On." *New Internationalist* no. 301.

English, T. J. 2007. *Havana Nocturne: How the Mob Owned Cuba and Then Lost It to the Revolution*. New York: William Morrow.

Enloe, Cynthia. 1989. *Bananas, Beaches, and Bases: Making Feminist Sense of International Politics*. Berkeley: University of California Press.

Epps, Brad. 1995. "Proper Conduct: Reinaldo Arenas, Fidel Castro, and the Politics of Homosexuality." *Journal of the History of Sexuality* 6 (October): 231–83.

Espín, Vilma. 1991. *Cuban Women Confront the Future: Three Decades after the Revolution*. Melbourne, Australia: Ocean Press.

Espina Prieto, Myra Paula. 2001. "The Effects of the Reform on Cuba's Social Structure: An Overview." *Socialism and Democracy* 15, no. 1: 23–39.

Espino, Maria Dolores. 2000. "Cuban Tourism during the Special Period." In *Cuba in Transition*, vol 8. Washington, DC: Association for the Study of the Cuban Economy.

Fabian, Johannes. 1983. *Time and the Other: How Anthropology Makes Its Object*. New York: Columbia University Press.

Faier, Lieba. 2007. "Filipina Migrants in Rural Japan and Their Professions of Love." *American Ethnologist* 34, no. 1: 148–62.

Feinberg, Leslie. 2009. *Rainbow Solidarity: In Defense of Cuba*. New York: World View Forum.

Ferguson, James, and Akhil Gupta. 2002. "Spatializing States: Toward an Ethnography of Neoliberal Governmentality." *American Ethnologist* 29, no. 4: 981–1002.

Fernandes, Sujatha. 2003. "Fear of a Black Nation: Local Rappers, Transnational Crossings, and State Power in Contemporary Cuba." *Anthropological Quarterly* 76, no. 4: 575–608.

Fernandes, Sujatha. 2006. *Cuba Represent! Cuban Arts, State Power, and the Making of New Revolutionary Cultures*. Durham, NC: Duke University Press.

Fernández, Damián, ed. 2000. *Cuba and the Politics of Passion*. Austin: University of Texas Press.

Fernández, Damián, ed. 2005. "Introduction." *Cuba Transnational*. Gainesville: University Press of Florida.

Fernandez, Nadine. 1999. "Back to the Future? Women, Race, and Tourism in Cuba." In *Sun, Sex, and Gold: Tourism and Sex Work in the Caribbean*. Edited by Kamala Kempadoo, 81–89. New York: Rowman and Littlefield.

Fernandez, Nadine. 2010. *Revolutionizing Romance: Interracial Couples in Contemporary Cuba*. New Brunswick, NJ: Rutgers University Press.

Fernandez Lopez, Amaury. 2001. "Havana in the 1990s: No Longer Choosing Between Thieves or Faggots." Translated by Laura Arce Perez. Accessed April 18, 2005. Afrocubaweb.com.

Fernández Robaina, Tomás. 1998. *Historias de mujeres públicas*. Havana: Editorial Letras Cubanas.

Ferriol Muruaga, Angela. 2003. "Acercamientos al estudio de la pobreza en Cuba." Centro de Información Científico-Técnica of Instituto Nacional de Investigaciones Económicas, Havana.

Floyd, Kevin. 2009. *The Reification of Desire: Toward a Queer Marxism*. Minneapolis: University of Minnesota Press.

Forrest, David Peter. 1999. "Bichos, maricones and pingueros: An Ethnographic Study of Maleness and Scarcity in Contemporary Socialist Cuba." PhD diss., University of London.

Fosado, Gisela. 2004. "The Exchange of Sex for Money in Contemporary Cuba: Masculinity, Ambiguity and Love." PhD diss., University of Michigan.

Fosado, Gisela. 2005. "Gay Sex Tourism, Ambiguity, and Transnational Love in Havana." In *Cuba Transnational.* Edited by Damián Fernández, 201–40. Gainesville: University Press of Florida.

Foucault, Michel. 1983. "On the Genealogy of Ethics." In *Michel Foucault: Beyond Structuralism and Hermeneutics.* Edited by Hubert L. Dreyfus and Paul Rabinow, 2nd ed. Chicago: University of Chicago Press.

Foucault, Michel. 1988. *Technologies of the Self: A Seminar with Michel Foucault.* Amherst: University of Massachusetts Press.

Foucault, Michel. 1990 [1978]. *The History of Sexuality, Volume I: An Introduction.* New York: Vintage.

Foucault, Michel. 1997. *"Society Must Be Defended": Lectures at the Collége de France 1975–1976.* Translated by David Macey. New York: Picador.

Fowler, Victor. 1998. *La Maladición: Una historia del placer como conquista.* Havana: Ediciones Unión.

Frank, Katherine. 2002. *G-Strings and Sympathy: Strip Club Regulars and Male Desire.* Durham, NC: Duke University Press.

Frederik Meer, Laurie. 2005. "Cuba's National Characters: Setting the Stage for the Hombre Novísimo." *Journal of Latin American Anthropology* 10, no. 2: 401–36.

Freeman, Carla. 2007. "Neoliberalism and the Marriage of Reputation and Respectability: Entrepreneurship and the Barbadian Middle Class." In *Love and Globalization: Transformation of Intimacy in the Contemporary World.* Edited by Mark Padilla, Richard Parker, Jennifer Hirsch, Miguel Munoz-Laboy, and Robert E. Sember. Nashville: Vanderbilt University Press.

Freeman, Carla. 2011. "Embodying and Affecting Neoliberalism." In *A Companion to the Anthropology of the Body and Embodiment.* Edited by Frances E. Mascia-Lees. Malden, MA: Wiley-Blackwell.

Friedman, Sarah. 2005. "The Intimacy of State Power: Marriage, Liberation, and Socialist Subjects in Southeastern China." *American Ethnologist* 32, no. 2: 312–27.

Fusco, Coco. 1995. "Miranda's Diary." In *Bridges to Cuba—Puentes a Cuba.* Edited by Ruth Behar, 198–216. Ann Arbor: University of Michigan Press.

Fusco, Coco. 1998. "Hustling for Dollars: Jineterismo in Cuba." In *Global Sex Workers: Rights, Resistance, and Redefinition.* Edited by Kamala Kempadoo and Jo Doezema, 155–66. New York: Routledge.

Fusco, Coco. 2001. *The Bodies That Were Not Ours and Other Writings.* London: Routledge.

Gal, Susan, and Gail Kligman. 2000. *The Politics of Gender after Socialism: A Comparative-Historical Essay.* Princeton, NJ: Princeton University Press.

Giddens, Anthony. 1992. *The Transformation of Intimacy: Sexuality, Love, and Eroticism in Modern Societies.* Palo Alto, CA: Stanford University Press.

Ginsburg, Faye. 1994. "Some Thoughts on Culture and Media." *Visual Anthropology Review* 10, no. 1: 136–41.

Gopinath, Gayatri. 2005. *Impossible Dreams: Queer Diasporas and South Asian Public Cultures*. Durham, NC: Duke University Press.

Grant, Bruce. 1995. *In the Soviet House of Culture: A Century of Perestroikas*. Princeton, NJ: Princeton University Press.

Green, James Naylor. 1997. *Beyond Carnival: Male Homosexuality in Twentieth-Century Brazil*. Chicago: University of Chicago Press.

Gregory, Steven. 2007. *The Devil behind the Mirror: Globalization and Politics in the Dominican Republic*. Berkeley: University of California Press.

Guerra, Lillian. 2010. "Gender Policing, Homosexuality and the New Patriarchy of the Cuban Revolution, 1965–70." *Social History* 35, no. 3: 268–89.

Guevara, Che. 1965. *El socialism y el hombre nuevo en Cuba*. Minneapolis: Ocean Sur Che Guevara Publishing Project.

Guillard Limonta, Norma R. 2009. "Cuba and the Revolutionary Struggle to Transform a Sexist Consciousness: Lesbians on the Cuban Screen." *Latin American Perspectives* 36: 63.

Gunn, Gillian. 1993. "The Sociological Impact of Rising Foreign Investment." In *Cuba Briefing Paper Series* 1 (January). Washington, DC: Georgetown University.

Gutiérrez, Pedro Juan. 2000. *El Rey de La Habana*. Madrid: Anagrama.

Gutiérrez Alea, Tomas. 2002. "We Are All Losing Our Values; Interview with Tomas Gutiérrez Alea," by Michael Chanan. *boundary 2* 29, no. 3 (fall): 47–53.

Halberstam, Judith. 1998. *Female Masculinity*. Durham, NC: Duke University Press.

Halperin, David. 2007. *What Do Gay Men Want?* Ann Arbor: University of Michigan Press.

Hamilton, Carrie. 2012. *Sexual Revolutions in Cuba: Passion, Politics, and Memory*. Chapel Hill: University of North Carolina Press.

Hamilton, Douglass. 2002. "Whither Cuban Socialism? The Changing Political Economy of the Cuban Revolution." *Latin American Perspectives* 29, no. 3: 18–39.

Herdt, Gilbert. 1981. *Guardian of the Flutes: Idioms of Masculinity*. New York: McGraw-Hill.

Hernandez-Reguant, Ariana, ed. 2009. "Writing the Special Period: An Introduction." *Cuba in the Special Period: Culture and Ideology in the 1990s*. New York: Palgrave Macmillan.

Herzfeld, Michael. 2005. *Cultural Intimacy: Social Poetics in the Nation-State*. 2nd ed. New York: Routledge.

Hill, Matthew. 2007. "Reimagining Old Havana: World Heritage and the Production of Scale in Late Socialist Cuba." In *Deciphering the Global: Its Scales, Spaces and Subjects*. Edited by Saskia Sassen, 59–77. New York: Routledge.

Hirsch, Jennifer, and Holly Wardlow. 2006. *The Anthropology of Romantic Courtship and Companionship Marriage*. Ann Arbor: University of Michigan Press.

Hobson, Perry J. S., and Vincent Heung. 1998. "Business Travel and the Modern Chinese Concubine." In *Sex Tourism and Prostitution*. Edited by Martin Oppermann, 132–43. New York: CCC.

Hodge, G. Derrick. 2001. "Colonization of the Cuban Body: The Growth of Male Sex Work in Havana." *NACLA Report on the Americas* 34, no. 5: 20–28.

Humphrey, Caroline. 1998. *Marx Went Away, but Karl Stayed Behind*. Ann Arbor: University of Michigan Press.

Hurston, Zora Neale. 1943. "The 'Pet Negro' System." *American Mercury* 56: 593–600.

Hurston, Zora Neale. 1990. *Mules and Men*. New York: Harper Perennial.

Illouz, Eva. 2007. *Cold Intimacies: The Making of Emotional Capitalism*. Cambridge: Polity Press.

Inda, Jonathan Xavier. 2005. *Anthropology of Modernity: Foucault, Governmentality, and Life Politics*. Malden, MA: Wiley-Blackwell.

Íñiguez, Luisa, et al. 2001. "La exploración de las desigualdades espacio-familias en la ciudad de La Habana." Informe de investigación, CESBH (unpublished paper), Universidad de la Habana.

Jambrina, Jesús. 2000. "Sujetos queers en la literatura cubana: Hacia una posible genealogía homoerótica." *La Habana Elegante* (fall).

Jankowiak, William. 1995. *Romantic Passion*. New York: Columbia University Press.

Kane, Stephanie C. 1993. "Prostitution and the Military: Planning AIDS Intervention in Belize." *Social Science and Medicine* 36, no. 7: 965–79.

Kempadoo, Kamala. 1999. *Sun, Sex, and Gold: Tourism and Sex Work in the Caribbean*. New York: Rowman and Littlefield.

Kempadoo, Kamala. 2004. *Sexing the Caribbean: Gender, Race, and Sexual Labor*. New York: Routledge.

Kempadoo, Kamala, and Jo Doezema. 1998. *Global Sex Workers: Rights, Resistance, and Redefinition*. New York: Routledge.

Kennedy, Elizabeth, and Madeline Davis. 1994. *Boots of Leather, Slippers of Gold: The History of a Lesbian Community*. New York: Routledge.

Kinnaird, Vivian, and Derek Hall, eds. 1994. *Tourism: A Gender Analysis*. London: John Wiley.

Klima, Alan. 2004. "Thai Love Thai: Financing Emotion in Post-crash Thailand." *Ethnos* 69, no. 4: 445–64.

Kopytoff, Igor. 1986. "The Cultural Biography of Things: Commoditization as a Process." In *The Social Life of Things: Commodities in Cultural Perspective*. Edited by Arjun Appadurai. Cambridge: Cambridge University Press.

Kulick, Don. 1997a. "The Gender of Brazilian Transgendered Prostitutes." *American Anthropologist* 99, no. 3: 574–85.

Kulick, Don. 1997b. "A Man in the House: The Boyfriends of Brazilian Travesti Prostitutes." *Social Text* 52/53, 15, no. 3–4: 135–62.

Kulick, Don. 1998. *Travesti: Sex, Gender and Culture among Brazilian Transgendered Prostitutes*. Chicago: University of Chicago Press.

Kulick, Don. 1999. "Transgender and Language: A Review of the Literature and Suggestions for the Future." *GLQ* 5, no. 4: 605–22.

Kulick, Don, and Margaret Willson. 1995. *Taboo: Sex, Identity, and Erotic Subjectivity in Anthropological Fieldwork*. New York: Routledge.

Kutzinski, Vera. 1993. *Sugar's Secrets: Race and the Erotics of Cuban Nationalism.* Charlottesville: University of Virginia Press.

Lacey, Marc. 2007. "A Castro Strives to Open Cuban's Opinions on Sex." Saturday Profile. *New York Times*, June 9.

La Fountain-Stokes, Lawrence. 2002. "De un pájaro las dos alas: Travel Notes of a Queer Puerto Rican in Havana." *GLQ* 8, no. 1–2: 7–33.

Lancaster, N. Roger. 1986. Comment on Arguelles and Rich's "Homosexuality, Homophobia, and Revolution: Notes toward an Understanding of the Cuban Lesbian and Gay Male Experience: Part II." *Signs* 12, no. 1 (autumn): 188.

Lancaster, N. Roger. 1992. *Life Is Hard: Machismo, Danger, and the Intimacy of Power in Nicaragua.* Berkeley: University of California Press.

Lancaster, N. Roger. 1995. "'That We Should All Turn Queer?' Homosexual Stigma in the Making of Manhood and the Breaking of a Revolution in Nicaragua." *Conceiving Sexuality: Approaches to Sex Research in a Postmodern World.* Edited by Richard Parker and John Gagnon. New York: Routledge.

Leiner, Marvin. 1994. *Sexual Politics in Cuba: Machismo, Homosexuality, and AIDS.* Boulder, CO: Westview Press.

Lewin, Ellen. 1996. *Inventing Lesbian Cultures in America.* Boston: Beacon Press.

Lewis, Oscar, Ruth Lewis, and Susan Rigdon. 1977. *Living the Revolution: An Oral History of Contemporary Cuba.* Urbana: University of Illinois Press.

Lima, Lazaro. 2005. "Locas al Rescate: The Transnational Hauntings of Queer Latinidad." In *Cuba Transnational.* Edited by Damián Fernández, 79–103. Gainesville: University Press of Florida.

Lipset, David. 2004. "Modernity without Romance?" *American Ethnologist* 31, no. 2: 205–24.

Lockwood, Lee. 1967. *Castro's Cuba, Cuba's Fidel.* New York: Macmillan.

López, Ana. 1991. "The Melodrama in Latin America: Films, Telenovelas, and the Currency of a Popular Form." In *Imitations of Life: A Reader on Film and Television Melodrama.* Edited by Marc Landy, 596–606. Detroit: Wayne State University Press.

Low, Setha M. 2000. *On the Plaza: The Politics of Public Space and Culture.* Austin: University of Texas Press.

Luca, Iona. 2011. "Communism: Intimate Publics." *Biography* 34, no. 1 (winter): 70–82.

Lumsden, Ian. 1996. *Machos, Maricones, and Gays: Cuba and Homosexuality.* Philadelphia: Temple University Press.

Lumsden, Ian. 1999. *Homosexuality, Society, and the State in Mexico.* Mexico City: Solediciones.

Lutz, Catherine. 1988. *Unnatural Emotions: Everyday Sentiments on a Micronesian Atoll and Their Challenge to Western Theory.* Chicago: University of Chicago Press.

Lutz, Catherine, and Geoffrey M. White. 1986. "The Anthropology of Emotions." *Annual Review of Anthropology* 15: 405–36.

Mahmood, Saba. 2001. "Feminist Theory, Embodiment, and the Docile Agent: Some Reflections on the Egyptian Islamic Revival." *Cultural Anthropology* 6, no. 2: 202–36.

Mahmood, Saba. 2004. *Politics of Piety: The Islamic Revival and the Feminist Subject.* Princeton, NJ: Princeton University Press.

Manalansan, Martin F., IV. 2003. *Global Divas: Filipino Gay Men in the Diaspora.* Durham, NC: Duke University Press.

Mankekar, Purnima. 1999. *Screening Culture, Viewing Politics: An Ethnography of Television, Womanhood, and Nation in Postcolonial India.* Durham, NC: Duke University Press.

Mankekar, Purnima. 2004. "Dangerous Desires: Television and Erotics in Late Twentieth-Century India." *Journal of Asian Studies* 63: 403–31.

Manzor-Coats, Lillian, and Inés Martiatu Terry. 1995. "VI Festival Internacional de Teatro de La Habana: A Festival against All Odds." *TDR* 39, no. 2: 39–70.

Marrero, Teresa. 2003. "Scripting Sexual Tourism: Fusco and Bustamante's STUFF, Prostitution and Cuba's Special Period." *Theatre Journal* 55: 235–50.

Martínez, Milagros, Magaly Martín, Blanca Morejón, Guillermo Milán, and Lourdes Invalis Rodríguez. 1996. *Los balseros cubanos.* Havana: Piños Nuevos.

Martinez-Alier, Verena. 1989. *Marriage, Class, and Colour in Nineteenth-Century Cuba: A Study of Racial Attitudes and Sexual Values in a Slave Society.* Ann Arbor: University of Michigan Press.

Marx, Karl. 1978. *Capital: A Critique of Political Economy, Volume III.* New York: Penguin.

Matory, J. Lorand. 1999. "The English Professors of Brazil: On the Diasporic Roots of the Yorùbá Nation." *Society for Comparative Study of Society and History* 41, no. 1: 72–103.

Mauss, Marcel. 1967 [1923]. *The Gift: Forms and Functions of Exchange in Archaic Societies.* London: W. W. Norton.

McClintock, Anne. 1991. "'No Longer in a Future Heaven': Women and Nationalism in South Africa." *Transition* 15: 104–23.

McClintock, Anne. 1992. "Angel of Progress: Pitfalls of the Term 'Post-colonial,'" Third World and Post-Colonial Issues. *Social Text* no. 31/32: 84–98.

Mesa-Lago, Carmelo, and Jorge Pérez-López. 2000. *Market, Socialist, and Mixed Economies: Comparative Policy and Performance—Chile, Cuba, and Costa Rica.* Baltimore: Johns Hopkins University Press.

Mesa-Lago, Carmelo, and Jorge Pérez-López. 2005. *Cuba's Aborted Reform: Socioeconomic Effects, International Comparisons, and Transition Policies.* Gainesville: University Press of Florida.

Mintz, Sidney W. 1966. "The Caribbean as a Socio-Cultural Area." *Cahiers d'Histoire Mondiale* 9: 912–37.

Mintz, Sidney W. 1971. "Men, Women and Trade." *Comparative Studies in Society and History* 13, no. 3: 247–69.

Mintz, Sidney W. 1978. "Was the Plantation Slave a Proletarian?" *Review* 2, no. 1: 81–98.

Mintz, Sidney W. 1998. "The Localization of Anthropological Practice: From Area Studies to Transnationalism." *Critique of Anthropology* 18, no. 2: 117–33.

Mitchell, Timothy. 1992. "Orientalism and the Exhibitionary Order." In *Colonialism and Culture*. Edited by Nicholas B. Dirks, 289–317. Ann Arbor: University of Michigan Press.

Mohanty, Chandra Talpade. 1991. *Third World Women and the Politics of Feminism*. Indianapolis: Indiana University Press.

Moore, Robin. 1997. *Nationalizing Blackness: Afrocubanismo and Artistic Revolution in Havana, 1920–1940*. Pittsburgh: University of Pittsburgh Press.

Moreno, Eva. 1995. "Rape in the Field: Reflections from a Survivor." In *Taboo: Sex, Identity, and Erotic Subjectivity in Anthropological Fieldwork*. Edited by Don Kulick and Margaret Willson, 219–50. New York: Routledge.

Mosse, George L. 1985. *Nationalism and Sexuality: Middle-Class Morality and Sexual Norms in Modern Europe*. Madison: University of Wisconsin Press.

Murray, Stephen O. 1995. *Latin American Male Homosexualities*. Albuquerque: University of New Mexico Press.

Navarro, Desiderio. 2002. "In Medias Res Publicas: On Intellectuals and Social Criticism in the Cuban Public Sphere." Translated by Alessandro Fornazzari and Desiderio Navarro. *boundary 2* 29, no. 3: 197–203.

Negrón-Muntaner, Frances. 2008. "'Mariconerías' de estado: Mariela Castro, los homosexuals y la política cubana." *Nueva Sociedad* no. 218.

Newton, Esther. 1993. "My Best Informant's Dress: The Erotic Equation in Fieldwork." *Cultural Anthropology* 8, no. 1 (February): 3–23.

O'Connell Davidson, Julia. 1995. "Sexploitation? Sex Tourism in Cuba." *WRI Women* 1995/03. Accessed January 10, 2004. www.gn.apc.org/warresisters/news/1994-97.

O'Connell Davidson, Julia, and Jacqueline Sánchez Taylor. 1999. "Fantasy Islands: Exploring the Demand for Sex Tourism." In *Sun, Sex, and Gold: Tourism and Sex Work in the Caribbean*. Edited by Kamala Kempadoo, 37–54. New York: Rowman and Littlefield.

Odzer, Cleo. 1994. *Patpong Sisters: An American Woman's View of the Bangkok Sex World*. New York: Arcade Publishing and Blue Moon Books.

ONE (Oficina Nacional de Estadísticas). 2001. *Anuario Estadístico de Cuba 2000*. Havana: ONE.

Ong, Aihwa. 1988. "Colonialism and Modernity: Feminist Re-Presentations of Women in Non-Western Societies." Feminism and the Critique of Colonial Discourse. *Inscriptions* 3–4.

Ong, Aihwa. 1995. "Women Out of China: Traveling Tales and Traveling Theories in Postcolonial Feminism." In *Women Writing Culture*. Edited by Ruth Behar and Deborah A. Gordon, 350–72. Berkeley: University of California Press.

Ong, Aihwa. 2006. *Neoliberalism as Exception: Mutations in Citizenship and Sovereignty*. Durham, NC: Duke University Press.

Ortner, Sherry. 1984. "Theory in Anthropology since the Sixties." *Comparative Studies in Society and History* 26, no. 1: 126–66.

Ortner, Sherry. 1991. "Reading America: Preliminary Notes on Class and Culture." In *Recapturing Anthropology: Working in the Present*. Edited by Richard Fox, 163–89. Santa Fe, NM: School of American Research.

Ortner, Sherry. 1995. "Ethnography among the Newark: The Class of '58 Weequahic High School." In *Naturalizing Power: Essays in Feminist Cultural Analysis*. Edited by Sylvia Yanagisako and Carol Delaney, 257–73. New York: Routledge.

Padilla, Mark. 2007. *Caribbean Pleasure Industry: Tourism, Sexuality, and AIDS in the Dominican Republic*. Chicago: University of Chicago Press.

Padilla, Mark, Jennifer Hirsch, Robert Sember, Miguel Muñoz-Laboy, and Richard Parker, eds. 2007. "Introduction." *Love and Globalization: Transformations of Intimacy in the Contemporary World*. Nashville: Vanderbilt University Press.

Palmié, Stephan. 2002. *Wizards and Scientists: Explorations in Afro-Cuban Modernity and Tradition*. Durham, NC: Duke University Press.

Parker, Andrew, Mary Russo, Doris Sommer, and Patricia Yaeger, eds. 1992. "Introduction." *Nationalisms and Sexualities*. New York: Routledge.

Parker, Richard. 1991. *Bodies, Pleasures, and Passions: Sexual Culture in Contemporary Brazil*. Boston: Beacon.

Parker, Richard. 1999. *Beneath the Equator: Cultures of Desire, Male Homosexuality, and Emerging Gay Communities in Brazil*. New York: Routledge.

Parker, Richard, and John H. Gagnon. 1995. *Conceiving Sexuality: Approaches to Sex Research in a Postmodern World*. New York: Routledge.

Parreñas, Rhacel Salazar. 2001. *Servants of Globalization: Women, Migration, and Domestic Work*. Palo Alto, CA: Stanford University Press.

Paz, Senal. 1991. *El lobo, el bosque y el hombre nuevo*. Mexico City: Ediciones Era.

Paz Pérez, Carlos. 1998. *De lo popular y lo vulgar en el habla cubana*. Havana: Editorial Ciencias Sociales.

Peña, Susana. 2005. "Visibility and Silence: Mariel and the Cuban American Gay Male Experience and Representation." In *Queer Migrations: Sexuality, U.S. Citizenship, and Border Crossings*. Edited by Eithne Luibhéid and Lionel Cantú Jr. Minneapolis: University of Minnesota Press.

Pérez, Louis A. 1988. *Cuba: Between Reform and Revolution*. Oxford: Oxford University Press.

Pérez, Louis A. 1999. *On Becoming Cuban: Identity, Nationality and Culture*. New York: Ecco.

Pérez Sarduy, Pedro, and Jean Stubbs. 2000. *Afro-Cuban Voices: On Race and Identity in Contemporary Cuba*. Gainesville: University Press of Florida.

Povinelli, Elizabeth. 2002. *The Cunning of Recognition: Indigenous Alterities and the Making of Australian Multiculturalism*. Durham, NC: Duke University Press.

Povinelli, Elizabeth. 2006. *The Empire of Love: Toward a Theory of Intimacy, Genealogy, and Carnality*. Durham, NC: Duke University Press.

Povinelli, Elizabeth, and George Chauncey. 1999. "Thinking Sexually Transnationally: An Introduction." *GLQ* 5, no. 4: 439–50.

Prieto, Abel. 2004. "The Cuban Revolution Reminds Him of Many Who Were Intellectuals and Who Are Not Now." Interview by Alejandro Massia and Julio Otero Tiempo. *CubaNews*, November 7.

Prieur, Annick. 1998. *Mema's House, Mexico City: On Transvestites, Queens, and Machos*. Chicago: University of Chicago Press.

Pruitt, Deborah, and Suzanne LaFont. 1995. "For Love and Money: Romance Tourism in Jamaica." *Annals of Tourism Research* 22, no. 2: 422–40

Puar, Jasbir K. 2002. "Circuits of Queer Mobility." *GLQ* 8, no. 1–2: 101–37.

Puar, Jasbir K. 2007. *Terrorist Assemblages: Homonationalism in Queer Times*. Durham, NC: Duke University Press.

Putnam, Lara. 2002. *The Company They Kept: Migrants and the Politics of Gender in Caribbean Costa Rica, 1870–1960*. Chapel Hill: University of North Carolina Press.

Quiroga, José. 2000. *Tropics of Desire: Interventions from Queer Latino America*. New York: New York University Press.

Quiroga, José. 2005. *Cuban Palimpsests*. Minneapolis: University of Minnesota Press.

Rebhun, L. A. 1999. *The Heart Is Unknown Country: Love in the Changing Economy of Northeast Brazil*. Palo Alto, CA: Stanford University Press.

Ritter, Archibald. 2005. "Survival Strategies and Economic Illegalities in Cuba." *Association for the Study of the Cuban Economy: Cuba in Transition*, 342–59.

Rivas, Anthony T. 2000. "Enigmas of Cuban Spanish." *Newsletter of the National Association of Judiciary Interpreters and Translators* 9, no. 3 (summer).

Robertson, Jennifer. 2005. *Same-Sex Cultures and Sexualities: An Anthropological Reader*. Malden, MA: Blackwell.

Robledo Diaz, Luis. 2001. "El regreso." *Sexología y Sociedad* 7, no. 17: 12–16.

Rodríguez García, José Luis. 2002. "Globalization and Equity: A Brief Critical Analysis." In *Cuba Socialista: Revista Teórica y Política*. Edited by Central Committee of the Communist Party of Cuba. Accessed May 20, 2006. http://www .cubasocialista.cu/TEXTO/csi0003.htm,

Rodríguez Ruiz, Pablo. 2008. "Espacios y contextos del debate racial actual en Cuba." *Temas* 53: 86–96.

Rofel, Lisa. 1994. "'Yearnings': Televisual Love and Melodramatic Politics in Contemporary China." *American Ethnologist* 21, no. 4: 700–722.

Rofel, Lisa. 1999. "Qualities of Desire: Imagining Gay Identities in China." *GLQ* 5, no. 4: 451–74.

Rofel, Lisa. 2007. *Desiring China: Experiments in Neoliberalism, Sexuality, and Public Culture*. Durham, NC: Duke University Press.

Roland, Kaifa. 2010. *Cuban Color in Tourism and La Lucha*. Oxford: Oxford University Press.

Roque Guerra, Alberto. 2009. "Sexual Diversity in Cuba: Smokescreen or Academic Myopia?" *CubaNews*, December 8. Accessed January 5, 2010. http:// www.walterlippman.com/docs2569.html.

Rosaldo, Michelle. 1980. "The Use and Abuse of Anthropology: Reflections on Feminism and Cross-Cultural Understanding." *Signs* 5, no. 3: 389–417.

Rosaldo, Michelle. 1984. "Toward an Anthropology of Self and Feeling." In *Culture Theory: Essays on Mind, Self, and Emotion*. Edited by Richard A. Sweder and Robert A. LeVine, 137–57. Cambridge: Cambridge University Press.

Rosaldo, Renato. 1989. *Culture and Truth: The Remaking of Social Analysis*. Boston: Beacon.

Rubin, Gayle. 2002. "Studying Sexual Subcultures: Excavating the Ethnography of Gay Communities in Urban North America." *Out in Theory: The Emergence of Gay and Lesbian Anthropology*. Edited by Ellen Lewin and William Leap. Urbana: University of Illinois Press.

Rundle, Mette L. B. 2001. "Tourism, Social Change and Jineterismo in Contemporary Cuba." *The Society for Caribbean Studies (UK) Annual Conference Papers*, vol. 2. Accessed March 10, 2005. http://www.caribbeanstudies.org.uk/papers/2001/olv2p3.pdf.

Safa, Helen. 2009. "Hierarchies and Household Change in Postrevolutionary Cuba." *Latin American Perspectives* 164, no. 36.1: 42–52.

Sahlins, Marshall. 1985. *Islands of History*. Chicago: University of Chicago Press.

Salas, Luis. 1979. *Social Control and Deviance in Cuba*. New York: Praeger.

Sanchez Taylor, Jacqueline. 2001. "Dollars Are a Girls' Best Friend? Female Tourists' Sexual Behaviour in the Caribbean." *Sociology* 3, no. 3: 749–64.

Sansone, Livio. 2003. *Blackness without Ethnicity: Constructing Race in Brazil*. New York: Palgrave Macmillan.

Sarduy, Celia, and Ada C. Alfonso. 2000. *Genero: Salud y Cotidianidad*. Havana: Editoral Cientifico-Tecnica.

Saunders, Tayna. 2009. "La Lucha Mujerista: Krudas CUBENSI and Black Feminist Sexual Politics in Cuba." *Caribbean Review of Gender Studies*. November.

Saunders, Tayna. 2010a. "Black Lesbians and Racial Identity in Contemporary Cuba." *Black Women, Gender, and Families* 4, no. 1 (spring).

Saunders, Tayna. 2010b. "Grupo OREMI: Black Lesbians and the Struggle for Safe Social Space in Havana." *Souls: A Critical Journal of Black Politics, Culture, and Society* 11, no. 2: 167–85.

Sawyer, Mark Q. 2006. *Racial Politics in Post-Revolutionary Cuba*. Pittsburgh: University of Pittsburgh Press.

Scarpaci, Joseph L., Roberto Segre, and Mario Coyula. 2002. *Havana: Two Faces of the Antillean Metropolis*. Chapel Hill: University of North Carolina Press.

Schein, Louisa. 1999. "Of Cargo and Satellites: Imagined Cosmopolitanism." *Postcolonial Studies* 2, no. 3: 345–75.

Schwartz, Rosalie. 1997. *Pleasure Island: Tourism and Temptation in Cuba*. Lincoln: University of Nebraska Press.

Sedgwick, Eve. 1990. *Epistemology of the Closet*. Berkeley: University of California Press.

Sharma, Aradhana, and Akhil Gupta. 2005. "Introduction: Rethinking Theories of the State in an Age of Globalization." In *The Anthropology of the State: A Reader*. Edited by Aradhana Sharma and Akhil Gupta, 1–42. Malden, MA: Blackwell Publishing.

Sharp, Joanne P. 1996. "Gendering Nationhood: A Feminist Engagement with National Identity." In *BodySpace: Destabilizing Geographies of Gender and Sexuality*. Edited by Nancy Duncan. London: Routledge.

Sharp, Lesley. 2000. "The Commodification of the Body and Its Parts." *Annual Review of Anthropology* 29: 287–328.

Sibley, David. 1995. *Geographies of Exclusion: Society and Difference in the West.* London: Routledge.

Sierra Madero, Abel. 2001. "La Habana de carmín." *Revista Temas* 47: 93–104.

Sierra Madero, Abel. 2006. *Del otro lado del espejo: La sexualidad en la construcción de la nación cubana.* Havana: Casa de las Americas.

Sierra Madero, Abel. 2013. "Cuerpos en venta: Pinguerismo y masculinidad en la Cuba post-socialista." *Nómadas* 38 (April): 167–83.

Sinclair, Thea M., ed. 1997. *Gender, Work, and Tourism.* New York: Routledge.

Smith, Lois M., and Alfred Padula. 1996. *Sex and Revolution: Women in Socialist Cuba.* New York: Oxford University Press.

Sommer, Doris. 1991. *Foundational Fictions: The National Romances of Latin America.* Berkeley: University of California Press.

Stacey, Judith. 1988. "Can There Be a Feminist Ethnography?" *Women's Studies International Forum* 11: 21–27.

Stepick, Alex, and Guillermo Grenier. 1994. "The View from the Back of the House: Restaurant Sand Holes in Miami." In *Newcomers in the Workplace: Immigrants and the Restructuring of the U.S. Economy.* Edited by Louise Lamphere, Alex Stepick, and Guillermo Grenier, 181–98. Philadelphia: Temple University Press.

Stoler, Ann Laura. 1995. *Race and the Education of Desire: Foucault's* History of Sexuality *and the Colonial Order of Things.* Durham, NC: Duke University Press.

Stout, Noelle. 2008. "Feminists, Queers, and Critics: Debating the Cuban Sex Trade." *Journal of Latin American Studies* 40, no. 4: 721–42.

Stout, Noelle. 2011. "The Rise of Gay Tolerance in Cuba: The Case of the UN Vote." NACLA *Report on the Americas* 44, no. 4: 34–38.

Strathern, Marilyn. 1992. *After Nature: English Kinship in the Late Twentieth Century.* Cambridge: Cambridge University Press.

Strout, Jan. 1995. "Women, the Politics of Sexuality and Cuba's Economic Crisis." *Socialist Review* 25, no. 1: 5–15.

Suárez Findlay, Eileen J. 1999. *Imposing Decency: The Politics of Sexuality and Race in Puerto Rico, 1870–1920.* Durham, NC: Duke University Press.

Taussig, Michael T. 1980. *The Devil and Commodity Fetishism in South America.* Chapel Hill: University of North Carolina Press.

Thomas, Deborah. 2004. *Modern Blackness: Nationalism, Globalization, and the Politics of Culture in Jamaica.* Durham, NC: Duke University Press.

Thompson, Eric. 2002. "Engineered Corporate Culture on a Cruise Ship." *Sociological Focus* 35: 331–44.

Tisdel Flikke, Michelle. 2007. "The Museum of the Battle of Ideas, Cardenas, Cuba." *Museum of Anthropology Review Weblog.* Accessed May 3, 2007. http://museumanthropology.net/2007/04/16/mar2007-1-15/.

Togores, Viviana, and Anicia García. 2004. "Consumption, Markets and Monetary Duality in Cuba." In *The Cuban Economy at the Start of the Twenty-First Century.* Edited by Jorge I. Domínguez, Omar Everleny Pérez, and Lorena Barberia, 245–96. Cambridge, MA: Harvard University Press.

Trinh, T. Minh-Ha. 1989. *Woman, Native, Other: Writing Postcoloniality and Feminism*. Bloomington: Indiana University Press.

Trouillot, Michel-Rolph. 1992. "The Caribbean Region: An Open Frontier in Anthropological Theory." *Annual Review of Anthropology* 21: 19–42.

Trouillot, Michel-Rolph. 2003. *Global Transformations: Anthropology and the Modern World*. New York: Palgrave Macmillan.

True, Jacqui. 2003. *Gender, Globalization, and Postsocialism: The Czech Republic after Communism*. New York: Columbia University Press.

Tsing, Anna. 2000a. "Inside the Economy of Appearances." *Public Culture* 12, no. 1: 115–44.

Tsing, Anna. 2000b. "The Global Situation." *Cultural Anthropology* 15, no. 3: 327–60.

Urrutia, Consuelo Martín, Antonio Aja, and Marta Díaz. 1996. *Los balseros cubanos*. Havana: Piños Nuevos.

Urrutia, Lourdes. 1997. "Aproximación a un análisis del proceso migratorio cubano." *Papers* 52: 49–56.

Valdés, Zoé. 1996. *Te di la vida entera*. Barcelona: Planeta.

Valentine, David. 2007. *Imagining Transgender: An Ethnography of a Category*. Durham, NC: Duke University Press.

Valle, Amir. 2001. *Las puertas de la noche*. Madrid: Malamba.

Valle, Amir. 2006. *Habana Babilonia: Prostitutas en La Habana*. Madrid: Planeta.

Vance, Carol. 1991. "Anthropology Rediscovers Sexuality: A Theoretical Comment." *Social Science and Medicine* 33, no. 8: 875–84.

Visweswaren, Kamala. 1994. *Fictions of Feminist Ethnography*. Minneapolis: University of Minnesota Press.

Wardle, Huon. 2000. "Subjectivity and Aesthetics in the Jamaican Nine Night." *Social Anthropology* 8, no. 3: 247–62.

Weeks, Jeffrey. 1977. *Coming Out: Homosexual Politics in Britain from the Nineteenth Century to the Present*. San Francisco: Quartet Books.

Wekker, Gloria. 2006. *The Politics of Passion: Women's Sexual Culture in the Afro-Surinamese Diaspora*. New York: Columbia University Press.

Werbner, Prina. 1999. "Global Pathways: Working Class Cosmopolitans and the Creation of Transnational Ethnic Worlds." *European Association of Social Anthropologists* 7, no. 1: 17–35.

Weston, Kath. 1991. *Families We Choose: Lesbians, Gays, Kinship*. New York: Columbia University Press.

Weston, Kath. 1993. "Lesbian/gay Studies in the House of Anthropology." *Annual Review of Anthropology* 22: 339–67.

Whitfield, Esther. 2009. "Truths and Fictions: The Economics of Writing, 1994–1999." In *Cuba in the Special Period: Culture and Ideology in the 1990s*. Edited by Ariana Hernandez-Reguant. New York: Palgrave Macmillan.

Wiegman, Robyn. 2002. "Intimate Publics: Race, Property, and Personhood." *American Literature* 74, no. 4: 859–85.

Wilson, Ara. 2004. *The Intimate Economies of Bangkok: Tomboys, Tycoons, and Avon Ladies in the Global City*. Berkeley: University of California Press.

Wilson, Peter. 1969. "Reputation and Respectability: A Suggestion for Caribbean Ethnology." *Man* 4, no. 1: 37–53.

Wilson, Peter. 1973. *Crab Antics: A Caribbean Study of the Conflict between Reputation and Respectability*. New Haven, CT: Yale University Press.

Yanagisako, Sylvia. 2002. *Producing Culture and Capital: Family Firms in Italy*. Princeton, NJ: Princeton University Press.

Yanagisako, Sylvia, and Jane Collier. 1987. *Gender and Kinship: Essays toward a Unified Analysis*. Palo Alto, CA: Stanford University Press.

Yanagisako, Sylvia, and Carol Delaney. 1995. *Naturalizing Power: Essays in Feminist Cultural Analysis*. New York: Routledge.

Yang, Jie. 2010. "The Crisis of Masculinity: Class, Gender, and Kindly Power in Post-Mao China." *American Ethnologist* 37: 550–62.

Young, Allen. 1981. *Gays under the Cuban Revolution*. San Francisco: Grey Fox Press.

Yurchak, Alexi. 2006. *Everything Was Forever, Until It Was No More: The Last Soviet Generation*. Princeton, NJ: Princeton University Press.

Zhang, Li. 2001. *Strangers in the City: Reconfigurations of Space, Power, and Social Networks within China's Floating Population*. Palo Alto, CA: Stanford University Press.

Index

Bejel, Emilio, 35
Berlant, Lauren, 175, 196n13
Bernstein, Elizabeth, 5, 96
bestiality, 64, 79
Bhabha, Homi, 205n11
Bianca (*travesti*), 159–60
Binnie, Jon, 146
bisexual, bisexuality (*bisexualidad*):
    distrust of, 66–67; identities of, 24,
    65–67, 114; *moderna* vs., 121; normalcy
    of, 49; as term, 1, 200n9
black market, 4; consumerism and, 131;
    criminality and, 138; jobs in, 89, 91, 172;
    rise of, 93, 115, 119; as source of hard
    currency, 12, 158–59; tourists and, 167
blacks, blackness: appropriated by
    Cubans, 116, 132–33; associations
    with, 70; criminality associated with,
    13–14; in Cuba, 27, 117–19; desire and,
    190n24; in leisure industry, 78
Boellstorff, Tom, 188n6, 200n9
boundaries, 98, 104, 105, 143, 169, 173; blur-
    ring of, 3, 14, 72, 83, 107, 121; crossing, 4,
    22, 23, 67, 75, 148; erection of, 13, 98, 99
Bourdieu, Pierre, 190n26, 190–91n27,
    198–99n40
Boyd, 145–46
brand names, Cuban obsession with,
    131–32, 135, 146–47, 159
Brazil, 45, 194nn59–60, 194n62, 195n6,
    198n30, 205n17
Brennan, Denise, 100
Britain, British, 145, 150
Brothers Saiz Organization, 42
Brotherton, P. Sean, 34–35, 198n35
Brown, Wendy, 54
bugarrónes: in Dominican Republic, 107; as
    gay, 65; as identity, 47–48; as term, 27
Burgués, Alejandro, 171
Burke, Timothy, 203n16
Bush, George W., 23, 193n49, 202n1
Butler, Judith, 199n5

Cabezas, Amalia, 10, 11
La Cage aux Folles (The Birdcage), 91
Camagüey labor camps, 37
capitalism: brand names and, 132; in
    communist context, 42; in Cuba, 30,

40, 134; desire and, 4; gender and, 104;
globalization of, 181; global markets
of, 5; hip-hop and, 117; homonormativity and, 180; hustlers as emblematic
of, 10, 96; industrialization and, 6;
intimacy and, 4, 188n8; late, 175;
marriage under, 14; queer nightlife
and, 174; rejection of, 175; self-interest
and, 3; sexual desire under, 135; social
bonds and, 153; socialism vs., 119–20,
153, 170
Caribbean, 4, 11, 38, 143, 162, 168; Cuba
as brothel of, 9, 20; HIV/AIDS in, 28;
leisure industry in, 78; neoliberalism
in, 177; respectability in, 15, 16, 38,
60, 174; sensuality of, 166, 203n12;
transactional sex in, 108, 114, 123, 160,
202n2
Carter, Jimmy, 196n16
Castro, Fidel: apologizes for labor camps,
39; attitudes toward, 140; art policy of,
36; "Battle of Ideas" and, 41; Decree 232
signed by, 52; energy crisis and, 85, 93;
on homosexuality, 196n11; political control relinquished by, 195n2; on sex tourism, 199n41; speeches of, 163; as state,
34, 74, 145; United States and, 193n48
Castro, Raúl: attitudes toward, 145, 185;
daughter of, 49; political power given
to, 195n2; tourist apartheid overturned by, 23
censorship, 37, 40, 45, 50, 196n14, 197n19,
197n24
Centro Habana, 23, 69, 111, 135
Centro Nacional de Educación Sexual
    (National Center for Sexual Education,
    CENESEX), 79, 198n30; gay tolerance
    initiatives by, 49–51, 181, 184, 206n4
Chevy cars, as iconic, 164
China, Chinese, 27, 188n6
choteo (informal teasing), 44, 128
Christianity, 42, 112
Ciego de Ávila, 2
class: bias and, 63; consumerism and, 131;
    culture and, 12; exoticism and, 160;
    inequalities of, 16, 173; mobility of,
    136; nonnormative sexuality and, 184;
    status and, 187n4

Cold War, 18, 181, 193n48, 193n51
Cole, 148–49
Collier, Jane, 5
Colombia, 191n29
colonialism, 11, 188n8, 192n36
Committees to Defend the Revolution
  (CDRs), 36, 40, 124
commodification, commodities, 96–100,
  170; of affect, 5, 12, 34, 88; bodies
  as, 135–36, 204n4; of Cuba, 161–65;
  culture and, 13, 161; desires for, 108,
  159; fashion and, 156–57; of love and
  intimacy, 5, 6, 39, 72, 104; materialism
  and, 158; selfhood and, 136; of sex,
  10–13, 29, 34, 66, 88, 103, 157–58; of
  U.S. street culture, 132–33
communism, communists: capitalism
  and, 42; Cuba punished for, 185;
  egalitarianism under, 77; homophobia
  under, 35–36; intimacy under, 196n13;
  older generation and, 12; religion
  banned under, 90, 112; Soviet-style, 4,
  36; tourism vs., 8
Communist Party, 36, 172
condoms, 28, 105
Constable, Nicole, 204n4
consumerism: among sex workers,
  130–36; socialism vs., 178
Costa Rica, 16
criminality: blackness and, 13; homosexuality and, 51, 53, 59, 178; sex trade
  and, 53, 138
Cuando una mujer (educational program),
  197n29
Cuba, Cubans: as "brothel of the Caribbean," 9, 161; commodification of, 13,
  161; culture of, 71, 90, 181, 188n10,
  197n23; depictions of, 163–64; fashions
  of, 156–57; as greedy, 158; HIV in, 47;
  human rights abuses by, 24; marketing of, 161–65; media representations
  of, 147, 177; nationalism of, 130; in
  popular lyrics, 1; shortages in, 8; slang
  of, 194n61, 203n19; Soviet Union and,
  2, 3, 9, 41, 181; socialism in, 3, 166, 169;
  threats to independence of, 35–36;
  United States and, 23, 145–46, 184–85,
  193n48

Cuba Libre II, 163
cubanidad (Cuban culture), 71
Cuban Institute of Radio and Television
  (ICRT), 45
Cuban National Assembly, 8
Cuban Revolution: female desire and, 19;
  gay tolerance and, 50; homophobia
  and, 34; maturation of, 42; nostalgia
  for, 162; racial integration and, 12;
  respectability and, 16; tourist support
  for, 165
Cuban Union of Writers and Artists, 37, 40
currency, hard, 23, 188n11; access to,
  8–10, 12, 91, 140, 151; black market
  and, 80, 89, 90, 93, 108; from foreign
  tourists, 2, 12, 23, 168; materialism
  and, 130; race and, 8; from remittances, 201n1; sex for, 73; sex workers
  and, 62, 76, 136

Dalia, 57, 60, 62, 66, 70–74, 80
dance, 43, 91, 166; ballet, 18, 69, 70, 81,
  200n11. See also music, musicians
The Dark Side of the Moon (La cara oculta
  de la luna), 45–48, 47, 197n24
Decena, Carlos Ulises, 202n5
decolonization movements, 35
Decree 232, 52
De hortensias y de violetas (Of Hydrangeas
  and Violets), 44–45
De la Fuente, Alejandro, 179
del Toro, Benicio, 159
D'Emilio, John, 6, 198n37, 201n2, 206n3
Department of Revolutionary Orientation (DOR), 45
depoliticization of gay rights, 184
Díaz, Carlos, 44; La niñita querida, 197n24
Diaz, Von, 206n4
discourse, reverse, used by gays, 61
discrimination, 38, 50
Domingo (Melba's roommate), 112,
  116–18, 117, 122, 125–30, 133–40
Domínguez, Jorge, 193n48
Dominican Republic, 81, 100, 107,
  202n2, 202n5; homoerotic labor in, 11,
  194n62
Dopico, Ana, 156, 164
drag shows, 52, 67

176, 178–81; strategies for, 184; on television, 45–48; in theater, 43–45

gender, 7; conformity, 173; discrimination by, 38; in leisure industry, 78; in marketing of Cuba, 161; nonconformity of, 63, 67, 121–25; norms of, 104, 180; as performative, 199n5; power dynamics and, 5; regulation of, 34; sex tourism and, 148; sex work, 123; submission and, 175; systems of, 103

Germany, Germans, 22, 40, 58, 196n15

Ginsberg, Allen, 185–86

Ginsburg, Faye, 198n32

Glasco, Laurence, 179

Global Exchange, Havana tour of, 165–69

globalization: capitalist, 181; gay, 6; queering of, 7; neoliberalism and, 5; resistance to, 184

Gomez, Lorenzo, 163

González, Elián, 197n18

González, Rafael, 46

Gramma (state-run newspaper), 196n14

guajiros (country folk), 79

Guerra, Alberto Roque, 51

Guerra, Lillian, 37

Guevara, Alfredo, 200n11

Guevara, Che, 50, 185; *Hombre Nuevo* and, 37, 195n8

Guillard Limonta, Norma R., 25, 175, 197n26

Hamilton, Carrie, 19, 63, 197n27, 199n6

Havana: affection in, 39; anonymity in, 93, 122; Central, 23; Colon neighborhood of, 36; as escape from homophobia, 146; gay tourists in, 2, 36; International Film Festival of, 159, 200n11; materialism of, 131, 158; migration to, 2, 79; population of, 189n17; prerevolutionary, 161; prostitution in, 3, 161; queer enclaves of, 13, 75, 157, 169, 175; queer gatherings in, 17; queer nightlife of, 4, 29, 34, 51, 67, 174, 176, 179; racial privilege and, 12; race in, 19, 122; sex work in, 7; sexual margins of, 4; theater in, 44; tourism and, 8–9, 155, 172; 23rd Street in, 1;

as UNESCO World Heritage site, 164; violence in, 67–68

The Havana Company, 156

health care, 15, 115, 140, 161, 169

Hernandez-Regaunt, Ariana, 10

Herzfeld, Michael, 15, 178, 190n27

heteronormativity: challenges to, 176; government policies of, 37–38; nationalism and, 195n4; privilege of, 65; sex trade criticisms and, 174

heterosexuality, heterosexuals, 5, 6; cultural regime of, 37; desired by gays, 64, 88, 95, 97, 107; marriage and, 15; norms of, 206n3; of *pingueros*, 65, 100, 103, 129; same-sex relations and, 200n8; sex tourism and, 157, 160, 165; sex workers, 176; as tourists, 177

HIV/AIDS, 192n40; discussion of, 28; drugs for, 204n6; prevention of, 181; in telenovelas, 45–48; transmission rates of, 47, 46, 48, 182

Hodge, G. Derrick, 11

Hombre Nuevo (New Man), 37, 195n8

hombres (masculine women), 68

El hombre y la mujer en la intimidad (Men and Women in Intimacy), 40

homoeroticism, 5, 6, 11, 103, 124–25

homonormativity, 179–81

homophobia: Cuba as escape from, 146; Cuban history of, 51, 178; institutionalized, 7, 63, 82; masculinity and, 129; police and, 53; in small towns, 93, 95; of sex workers, 114, 128; state sponsored, 15, 24, 34–39, 40, 163, 178, 185–86; in television, 48

homosexuality: Anglo-European ideas of, 24, 107; attitudes toward, 195; criminalization of, 36, 51, 53, 196n10; decriminalization of, 40, 179; discourses of, 187n2; HIV/AIDS and, 28; identity of, 6, 24, 62, 124; national contamination associated with, 35; normalcy of, 49; prostitution and, 29, 38, 51, 54, 178; suppression of, 35–39; visibility of, 48–49

homosexuals: as negative, 15, 33; as term, 25, 194n55. *See also* gays; queerness, queers

by, 15; strategic relationships and, 75–77; as term, 25; theatrical representations of, 44; urban, 3; visibility of, 197n26; vulnerability of, 68–76

liberalization: queer social life and, 10

Lisette, 57–59, 60–62, 63, 66–67, 82–83; breakup of, 80–82; sexual identity of, 62–63

Lista de Espera (2000), 44

loca, las locas: as term, 102–4

loco, los locos: as identity, 176; as term, 102–4

López, Ana, 198n31

López, Marlon Brito, 46

love: capitalism and, 188n8; framing of, 4–7; heterosexuality and, 6; illusion of, 96; intimacy and, 12, 55, 106, 185–86, 187n4, 188n8; market logics and, 99; marriage and, 14; queering of, 7; social power and, 5; status and, 187n4; strategic intimacy and, 14, 100

Luca, Iona, 196n13

Lucia, 197n22

Lumsden, Ian, 66

Madero, Abel Sierra, 27, 193n51; on CENESEX, 51; on Havana's homoerotic scene, 17; on masculinity, 11; on national hygienic campaigns, 35

Malecón, 1, 10, 17, *103*; billboards on, 23; fabricated nightlife of, 170; as pickup place, 2, 4, 31, 69, 71, 73, 90, 118, 124; police raids on, 33, 53; as queer gathering spot, 52, 67, 68

Marc (tourist), 153–60

market economy, 13, 153; global, 115, 188n10; inequality and, 12; intimacy and, 96; new mixed, 12, 79, 92–93, 98, 134, 162, 172; physical attraction and, 65; rules of, 108

marketing of Cuba, 161–65

marriage: alternate systems of, 152; anthropologists on, 5; equality, 180; historical emphasis on, 14–16; as reserved for elites, 35; respectability and, 60

Mariel exodus, 133–34; gay emigration during, 40, 204n2

Martí, José, 35

Martínez-Alier, Verena, 35

Marx, Karl, 132, 153, 203n17

masculinity: in commodified sex, 114; desired by gays, 64; feminine, 192n43; forms of, 11; privilege of, 104, 106, 129; same-sex relations and, 200n8; of sex workers, 128, 176

materialism: criticism of, 15, 158; rising, 4, 12; sex trade and, 11; of sex workers, 130; tourism and, 147

Mauss, Marcel, 153, 204n10

media: Cuba in international, 147; gay, 6, 163–64; homosexuality in, 28, 197n27; mass, 198n32; queer visibility in, 34; state-run, 7

medio pájaro (half fag), 87

Melba, 111–14, 132–34, 140–43: black market and, 115–20, 202n1; sexuality of, 120–25, 176; state and, 136–40

mestizaje (racial mixing), 35

mestizo, 27

Metro G (website), 163

Mexico, Mexicans, 139, 141, 158, 194n62; gay and lesbian tourists from, 20, 73; homoerotic sex work in, 194n62; smuggling through, 118; telenovelas from, 45

Mi Cayito, 70

migration, 7–9; control of, 93; financial security through, 82; as goal of *jineteras*, 205n12; to Havana, 2, 79, 138, 189n17; motivations of, 201n17; of queers, 183

military: homosexuality in, 64, 89; U.S., 24, 145, 193n48, 200n16. *See also* Military Units to Increase Production

Military Units to Increase Production (UMAP), 37, 196n12

Ministry of Culture, 42, 44, 147

Ministry of National Commerce, 52

Ministry of the Interior, 52

Ministry of Tourism, 163, 169

Mitchell, Timothy, 205n18

moderna, as sexuality, 114, 120–21, 123, 176

mujeres fuertes (strong women), prejudice against, 63

P. M., censorship of, 37

police: black market and, 115; gays unprotected by, 206n5; migrants targeted by, 93; queers vs., 51, 124, 181, 198n39; raids by, 33, 36, 52, 195n2; sensitivity training for, 49; sex workers targeted by, 10, 52, 68–69, 75, 118, 138–40, 178; *travestis* harassed by, 79–80

political economy: of love, 6, 186; queer sexuality and, 188n6; of sexuality, 183, 192n44

por interés (motivated by status or money), 3, 13, 14, 94, 96, 108

pornography, 44; Cuba depicted in, 163–64

postcommunist transition, 4, 177

poverty: cultural advances undermined by, 54, 172; rising, 3, 7, 82, 177–78; sex work and, 130, 133, 143, 160, 173; vulnerability to, 140

Povinelli, Elizabeth, 6

Prieto, Abel, 41

Prieto, Ileana, *El último bolero*, 44

Prieto, Myra Espina, 9

privatization, 8, 61, 189n13; neoliberalism and, 12, 177; relationships and, 106; tourism and, 182

prostitutes, 12, 26, 36, 51, 54, 195n3, 202n2; as *jineteras*, 10; female, 9; in Havana, 161; as label, 202n2; rehabilitation of, 196n10

prostitution: changes in, 96; critiques of, 203n13; eradication of, 3; as exploitation, 196n10; homosexuality and, 29, 38, 51, 54, 178; pederasts and, 195n3; prerevolutionary, 161; respectability impacted by, 16; sex tourism vs., 152, 204n7; as target of police, 52; *travestis* and, 79

provincialism of sex workers, 79

Puar, Jasbir, 42

public health, 46, 115; gay tolerance and, 49–51, 198n35; same-sex practice and, 47–48, 54

public space: absence of gay, 19; fragility of queer, 51–53, 179; homosexual access to, 53

Puerto Rico, Puerto Ricans, 16, 51, 118, 167

queer enclaves, 13, 75, 173; police in, 139; sex tourism and, 52, 157; sex workers in, 114, 118–19, 122–23, 174, 202n7; tourists and, 176–78, 191n28; violence in, 128

queerness, queers, 6; contested love and intimacy of, 7; feminized, 103; identities of, 21; as term, 25–26, 194n58; visibility of, 48, 178, 184, 206n1. *See also* gays; homosexuals

queer studies, 6

Quintero, Héctor, *Te sigo esperando*, 44

race, racism: bias and, 63; in Cuba, 183; culture and, 12; desire and, 97, 122; discrimination of, 38, 78, 179; elimination of, 48; exoticism and, 160; in Havana, 19; in marketing of Cuba, 161; mixing of, 35; privilege of, 20, 148; racialization and, 7; status and, 187n4; terminology of, 27; tourism and, 8

La Rampa (The Ramp; Havana), as queer gathering spot, 17, 51–52, 167, 192n38

Rebull, Cristina, *El último bolero*, 44

"Rectification of Errors and Negative Tendencies," 40

relationships: capitalism and, 175; as endogamous, 97, 122–23; *por interés*, 14, 96, 108; real, 98, 105; self-interest in, 123; tactical, 72–78, 88, 173

religious organizations: Afro-Cuban, 179; ban lifted, 42, 112; elimination of, 16, 90

remittances: from foreign patrons, 151–52; racial inequalities of, 8, 201n1

Resolution Number Three, repeal of, 40

respectability: marriage and, 60, 192n36; transformations of, 16; urban gays and, 174

Retrato de Teresa (Portrait of Teresa), 197n22

Rodríguez, Carlos Rafael, 40

Rodriguez, Francisco, 185

Rofel, Lisa, 188n6